Mental Illness Is an Asshole

And Other Observations

Mental Illness Is an Asshole

And Other Observations

Gabe Howard

DGC PRESS • SACRAMENTO

ISBN 978-0-9741337-1-3

First DGC Press printing, December, 2018
Printed on acid-free paper

Acknowledgements

Kendall Howard
Most wives wouldn't like being referred to as "Three." For that reason, and more, you're special.

Granny Knight
Thank you for always believing in me. (P.S. – We both know I'm the favorite.)

My Family
My work often features stories that include all of you. Thank you for encouraging me to share, rather than being embarrassed by it.

Lisa Kiner
Some people say that "so and so saved my life" and they mean it *figuratively*. When I tell people you saved my life, I mean it *literally*.

Dr. John Grohol
Thank you for giving me a chance and for answering all my emails.

Juliet Dorris-Williams
You helped restore my confidence and continue to encourage, inspire, and educate me to this day. I would not have taken a chance on me if I had been in your shoes. Thank you.

All My Fans, Readers, Listeners, and Supporters
Without all of you, I'm just a guy in a room talking to myself. Thank you.

Special thanks to everyone who donated to help with my book project, especially those at the $150 level:
Aunt Chris & Uncle Tom, Angie Merriam, Christine Anderson, Chris Ward, Jeff Brown, Jennifer Jacquet-Murray, Julie A. Fast, and Lisa Kiner. This is *not* the memoir book, but it *is* a step closer!

Dedication

To Vincent M. Wales...

The only person who has read everything I have ever written professionally about mental illness.

I'm unlikely to ever learn to use commas correctly, so please don't die.

Table of Contents

Foreword

Like most people, I have a number of individuals in my life whom I admire and respect. Some are family, some are teachers, some are friends, and some are colleagues. Gabe Howard falls into those last two categories.

It's one thing to live well in spite of a devastating mental illness. It's entirely another to then become a prominent advocate for others with mental illnesses. Gabe has made advocacy a large part of his life, and I can't help but admire him for it. Especially because he's really good at it.

Me, I'm an introvert. I'm able to speak in front of crowds, and will do so when asked, but it's not something I seek to do. Gabe, though, is a born extrovert. He thrives in such environments, which is one thing that makes him so good at advocacy. If you've never had the opportunity to see him speak to a crowd, I hope you can find a chance to do so.

If you can't see him speak, you can still listen to him. He has two weekly podcasts, both hosted on PsychCentral.com. One is with his co-host, Michelle Hammer, called *A Bipolar, a Schizophrenic, and a Podcast.* The other is with his other co-host, me, and is called *The Psych Central Show*. One is fun and a bit irreverent and the other is fun and educational. I'll let you listen and then decide which is which.

If you're not into podcasts, you might have seen his writings here and there online. They're in a lot of places and, unless you're a stalker, they can be hard to track down. That's why he's gathered up his favorite pieces and slapped them together between these covers.

Now you don't have to scour the internet looking for them. You don't have to be a stalker.

Unless that's your thing.

As for Gabe's writings, sure, they're informational and occasionally inspirational. But what makes them so good, to me, is that they're filled with passion and understanding. Gabe, himself, is full of passion and understanding (and a bunch of smarts, too). It's this passion that drives him to write, to speak, to do podcasts, and all the other things he does that I don't have space to mention.

Read on, and I think you'll agree.

Vincent M. Wales

Preface

One of the most frequent questions I'm asked is, "What does your logo mean?"

To answer this question, I need to take you back to the 1980s when I was a kid who loved computers. Long before the internet was a thing, if nerds wanted to connect to other nerds we had to use a service called a Bulletin Board Service – or BBS.

One of the primary features of a BBS was the message board. As the name would suggest, this was a place to have open discussions about a variety of subjects. And it was purely text – no pictures, colors, or graphics of any kind.

Obviously, that meant that we didn't have emojis, but we did have text-based emoticons. Not surprisingly, the three most popular and widely used were:

:) for "happy"   :(for "sad"   ;) for "wink"

But there were a few others that people like me used and one of them was called "the bipolar symbol" and it meant, very simply, "crazy."

:):

It was a simple design. It was made to be both :) and :(smooshed together so that the symbol was showing someone happy and sad at the same time. Or, depending on how you looked at it, the symbol could be *just* happy or *just* sad. The point, of course, is that it didn't make sense.

Because it was *crazy*.

Even though I regularly used the "bipolar symbol" for years, I had no idea what bipolar was until after I was diagnosed. Using the symbol without ever considering its meaning is something I regret to this day.

Years later, when I became a speaker and wanted a logo, I remembered that symbol. I honestly don't know if I picked it so that I could "take back" some of the negative power that I unknowingly spread or if I wanted a permanent reminder for myself that *anyone* can be ignorant and unintentionally hurt someone else.

Most likely, I picked it because it was cheap and easy to create and, when I started, I couldn't afford a graphic artist. However it started, it encompasses all three of those reasons now. It's a permanent reminder of who I once was and of who I want to be.

Moreover, for the people who support me, it has come to represent something more. It's not just "the bipolar symbol" anymore. It's *our* symbol.

And it can mean whatever *you* want it to.

NOTE:

All of these articles were published between 2014 and 2018, mostly online. Because of this, some articles that originally included links may seem to be lacking information. Also, titles that work well for blogs and on social media tend to feel odd in print. For the most part, I opted to leave these articles as-is, rather than risk compromising my original point of view. The majority of these articles are still available online and, whenever possible, I put the website and publishing date at the end, so you are welcome to find the original for more information.

Please keep in mind my opinions and feelings may have changed over time. This is most apparent when you read my birthday blogs published for my 38th to 42nd birthdays. There are some contradictions in there, and that's okay. I left these articles intact to illustrate that the way I see my life and illness changes from year to year.

Also, nothing in this book should be considered a medical recommendation or substitute for medical advice, because I'm not a doctor. I do suggest that you use these articles as a starting point with your medical team, but please remember no guarantee of accuracy is expressed or implied. All information here is accurate to the best of my knowledge at the time of publication.

Finally, if you are considering suicide, please get help immediately. Talk to a friend, loved one, or go to the local hospital and ask for help. I am living proof that it gets better. You are important, and the world *needs* you in it. You can also call the National Suicide Prevention Lifeline at 1-800-273-8255. Please do not make a permanent decision based on a temporary issue. Help is available.

Advice, Tips & Tricks

Mental Illness Is an Asshole

Living with mental illness is a difficult thing.

Despite television's desire to cast us all as creative geniuses, the simple fact is: living with any chronic and persistent health condition is a *burden.*

While I am proud that I regularly "win" my battle with bipolar and anxiety disorders, I would much rather not have to deal with these issues. I have accepted my lot in life and it is my cross to bear, but it in no way means I have to like it.

In a world where friends are assholes, parents are assholes, and even adorable, little three-year-olds are assholes, there is no reason that psychological disorders get a pass. Internet trends, memes, and themes being what they are, I'm going to throw it straight under the bus: Mental illness is an asshole. A big, angry, twisted asshole. It's a self-righteous, inconsiderate jerk. If it were a person, it would be Hitler.

For as much fuss as bloggers and activists make about fighting mental illness, we often forget to mention that this isn't a *fair* fight. Not even a little bit. The disease doesn't respect us at all and uses sneak attacks and old-fashioned bullying to torment us.

Take my anxiety disorder as an example. It takes a great deal of pride in being completely unpredictable. Anxiety will almost always wait until a big event I have been planning for months arrives, before it begins screwing with me.

Anxiety stays away during the preparation stages to ensure I've already spent the money on tickets and invited all my friends, guaranteeing that the ensuing panic attack will be witnessed by as many people as possible. What else can you call that but an asshole move?

Bipolar disorder, clinical depression, schizophrenia and the like have no respect for the people whose lives they impact. But, if those people want to have any chance at wellness, they'd better show their opponent a great deal of respect. It would be counterproductive not to. While mental illness is a complete asshole, it is a formidable foe and pretending it isn't will only give it more power.

I look at this asshole like a house fire. I don't want my house to catch on fire and I don't want to be harmed or injured. Smoke detectors, fire escapes, fire extinguishers and so on all help keep me safe in the event a fire breaks out. Even though I have never been in a burning house, I'm ready. I am prepared.

If we start thinking about mental illness like a fire, we can start thinking about reasonable ways to prepare. Just as not all fire safety tips are good ones, the same holds true here. We need to look for reasonable and successful ways to ready ourselves. While this won't eliminate all the pain and suffering, it will take away some.

My strategy is not to ignore what I cannot control, but to prepare for it. Assholes don't like to be confronted and a lot of their power comes from surprise attacks. As annoying as it is, every day when I wake up, I think to myself, *"Mental illness is an asshole."*

Because I'm always on guard for assholes and love putting them in their place.

Elephant Journal, 10/14/14

What I Wish the World Knew About Bipolar Disorder

The Internet is filled with blog posts titled, "What I wish the world knew about..." and then filled in with something that, while seemingly common, like "being on food stamps," is actually quite misunderstood. I love reading these articles because what I thought I knew to be true isn't true at all. I've found that I only knew half the story or believed a stereotype or wasn't aware of a key fact and that changed my perspective. Since these types of articles were able to enlighten me, I thought it a good idea to write one about bipolar disorder. So, without further ado, what I wish the world knew about bipolar disorder.

When it comes to bipolar disorder, what people don't understand greatly outweighs what people do understand. This isn't to insult the average person; it really isn't their fault. Mental illness, including bipolar disorder, isn't discussed openly. It isn't taught in most schools and, since most people don't understand it, they either aren't educating their children at all or are passing on stereotypes and misinformation.

If I wanted to be a smart aleck, and I have been known to be one, I'd write a 25-word blog that simply said: *I wish the world knew any actual fact about bipolar disorder that wasn't based on something they saw on TV or read in a book.* I do understand that wouldn't be very helpful, although it would be very satisfying to me and to many misunderstood people living with bipolar. In the interest of enlightening the general public, I narrowed the list to three main things I wished everyone knew.

Bipolar disorder symptoms aren't equally split

The basic definition of bipolar disorder is alternating between extreme highs (mania) and extreme lows (depression). This incorrectly leads a person to believe that the depression and mania comes in equal parts. In other words, if a person is depressed for two weeks, then they get two weeks of mania.

That isn't true at all. It is possible to be depressed for months and then manic for two days and then right back to depressed for two months. There is no biological meter that ensures the depression and manias get equal time.

While we are talking about the symptoms of bipolar disorder, I'd like to say that mania isn't a good thing, overall. I will admit to having some pretty incredible stories to tell about times I was manic, but I could have been hurt or hurt someone else, and those times are still affecting my life and the lives of others. Just because it was "fun while doing it" doesn't make it okay. Mania can be dangerous and life threatening. There is a reason the stories of people who are manic are so engaging. They are filled with bad decisions, drama, and danger.

Treatments for bipolar disorder take time to work

Treatments for bipolar disorder don't just take time to work, they take *a lot* of time to work. From the day I was diagnosed to the day I really felt like I had a handle on my disorder was every bit of four years.

This isn't television. It takes a lot more than a few days or few weeks to find the correct treatment regimen. The medications don't work quickly, like aspirin, but need to be taken on a schedule over the long term so they can begin to do their job. They are maintenance drugs, not "take as needed" drugs.

As an example, on *Homeland* this season, one of the characters has bipolar. She starts having symptoms, so she goes to the medicine cabinet, takes some pills, and a few hours later is better. She seems to be taking them on an as-needed basis. Two pills make her symptoms better, but not gone, so later in the day she goes back and takes two more. This is not a correct portrayal of being on medication. It is barely the correct portrayal of having a headache.

Medication aside, this says nothing about the time it takes in therapy to master coping skills, learn any limitations we might have, and just learn how to go about living with a chronic illness day in and day out.

Bipolar disorder is a serious illness with a 15% death rate. It isn't a colorful personality trait. It only makes sense that something this serious would take a significant amount of time to recover from.

Not everyone with bipolar disorder is the same

There is a lot of talk in the mental health community about how we aren't our labels. Just because both Julie A. Fast and I have bipolar disorder doesn't mean we are the same. Our disorders share commonalities, such as having both experienced depression and mania, but as people, we are quite different. Even though we both have bipolar disorder, my personality is nothing like hers. Her mania took her to different places than mine did, and even side-by-side, we don't act "the same." The way our moods cycle in and out, and even the way we personally feel about what is happening is very different, just as two people watching the same movie can feel very differently about the experience. All we actually have in common is bipolar disorder; our symptoms, and the way we react to them, are different.

Once you decide that an illness, any illness, defines a person, you have taken a piece of their humanity away. Their lives, in your mind, become more about their illness and less about them. You can see where that would be a devastating blow to anyone, and why the world should know that isn't true.

Bipolar Magazine, 6/16/2015

How Do I Know if I Am Crazy?

In the world of mental illness activism, there are questions that have a way of coming up more often than others. The most common question, by a landslide, is, "How do I know if I am crazy?" I know what they're asking is how to tell if they're experiencing the symptoms of a mental illness. I do take a quick second to correct the word choice. After all, I don't like to be called crazy and I don't like it when other people are called crazy, even if it's self-referential. Although poorly worded, the question is valid: "How does a person know if they are in need of psychiatric intervention?"

Crazy (Mental Illness) Exists on a Spectrum

First, we need to discuss that mental illness – or "crazy" – exists on a spectrum, just as physical illness does. A person with stage four cancer and a person with a headache can both be described as physically ill, but there is a world of difference between the two.

As advocacy groups continue to throw out the statistic that one in four will experience mental illness in a given year, the truth is that everyone has mental health, just as everyone has physical health. So it is certainly possible to experience a mental health issue without having a chronic life-long illness such as schizophrenia, major depression, bipolar and anxiety, etc.

Am I Crazy (Mentally Ill)?

As a mental illness activist, I look forward to the day when, if someone believes they might be experiencing symptoms of mental illness, they just call their local doctor and make an appointment. We are currently pretty far removed from that reality for a number of reasons, not least of which is because many people don't know that a general practitioner or family doctor is a good place to start.

The standard rule of thumb is that, if you are experiencing symptoms that interfere with the activities of daily living for more than two weeks, you *might* have a mental health issue. So if you have been unusually sad for two weeks and it has prevented you from going to work or enjoying your hobbies, you might need some help.

If you are experiencing any suicidal thoughts, or otherwise thinking of harming yourself or others, please call 9-1-1 or go to a local emergency room and seek medical care immediately. Mental illness, even if you call it "crazy," is an illness and illnesses are treated by medical professionals. Don't be afraid to seek help — it'll make a world of difference.

Psych Central, 4/15/2015

It's Not My Fault; I'm Bipolar

Living with bipolar disorder is a difficult thing. I often start articles this way because I know the general public believes people like me have more control than we actually do. There is this notion that persists that if we just do what the doctors tell us to we'll be just fine.

But then something goes "wrong." A person living with bipolar experiences depression, mania, rage, or some other undesirable outcome and those around us are quick to blame the *person* instead of the *illness*.

As an example, depression is a symptom of a bipolar. Not being able to maintain employment is a common result of depression. Sadly, more often than not, people with bipolar disorder are considered to be "not trying" or "not following their doctor's instructions" when the very reasonable consequence of employment difficulties occurs.

As a result, we are left sick, suffering, and now accused of wrongdoing all because of a cruel illness we never asked for. People are *blaming* us for something that is difficult to control and we feel isolated and misunderstood. People keep judging what they don't understand as our lives continue to deteriorate. All the while, the people around us are telling us to work harder and get our lives together.

And the solution to many of our problems is as counterintuitive as bipolar disorder is unpredictable: accept that they are *correct*.

Bipolar disorder is our responsibility

Assuming you are still reading, I'll clarify a bit. The fact remains that bipolar disorder, like any illness, isn't the *fault* of the one diagnosed. However, every illness is the *responsibility* of the person who has it. So, while the people in the above example reached the right conclusion for the wrong reasons, the idea that we need to work harder is, I'm sad to say, perfectly accurate.

When I was at my sickest points, I spent so much energy hating my life. I hated the people around me, too. They were insensitive, but they also kept insisting I could be better and I vehemently disagreed with them. Then, one day, it dawned on me that if I stripped away all the emotions and insensitivity, what they were saying is that they believed in me.

And, besides all that, what other choice do we have? *Not* fighting back against bipolar and choosing, by way of indecision, to stay sick seems foolish. More than foolish, it's a waste of our lives. It's a waste of what we can become *after* we learn to manage bipolar disorder through some combination of therapy, medication, lifestyle changes, and experience.

It took me a long time to reach recovery and most people I've talked to have had similar experiences. The first step for all of us was to acknowledge we were sick, take responsibility for everything that has happened to us, and then start to build a better life.

Bipolar Magazine, 11/8/2016

Accomplishing Goals with Bipolar Disorder

The other day, I received a Facebook question from a follower. She asked, "Due to my bipolar and depression and all that, I have a horrible habit of not being able to finish or follow through with things. Jobs, school etc. There is something I really want to do (complete a college degree) and the classes are supposed to be very rough. How do you do it?"

After I read her question, I stared at the screen for a long while because I was struck by the fact she thought I was "doing it" at all. In truth, procrastinating and talking myself out of things has pretty much become a lifestyle choice.

The mere fact that someone, somewhere, thinks I'm accomplishing anything at all made me feel fantastic, but confused. Intellectually, I do recognize that I am accomplishing many things. My blogs are written, published, and promoted on a regular basis. I do hold down a job, as well as do speaking engagements.

However, I *feel* like I'm failing, because I know the number of things I set out to do versus the number of things I actually accomplish. I also know how long it took to achieve some of my goals and it seems ridiculous that I could add them to the achieved column given the sheer amount of time I wasted before getting my butt in gear to complete the task.

She went on to admit that she has started and quit a number of things and, like so many of us living with bipolar disorder, has wasted a lot of time and money in the process. She ended her message with "...I lack confidence, I guess."

How to Achieve Goals with Bipolar Disorder

First, as I'm sure you know, there is no magic solution. I wish there was. It is so hard some days just to take a shower, let alone complete a more formidable task. But here's the thing: My wife has *zero* mental illness. She is the most stable person I know. And she has been working on her CPA for over two years. She was supposed to complete everything in less than nine months. But she hasn't finished because she worries, makes excuses, and so forth. Sound familiar?

We all have a tendency to run from things outside our comfort zones. Are people living with bipolar disorder more afraid to take a risk? Maybe, but the fear of risking failure is universal. It is irrelevant why someone is afraid; the important thing to focus on is that success lies on the other side of that fear. Refusing to leave our comfort zone holds us back.

The method I use is to take things slowly and build momentum. As an example, instead of taking three classes all at once, take one at a time and see how it goes. Make a schedule with clear, attainable goals and create a practical plan. Leave yourself lots of time to complete tasks, but also have clear deadlines. Be realistic, but be brave, too.

When you have a setback – I said "when" because *everyone* has setbacks — don't judge yourself. Pick yourself up, dust yourself off, and keep moving forward. Don't let yourself fall into the trap of, "My friend did it in two weeks and it has taken me a year." To that, I always say, "So what?" People achieve things others can't all the time. Am I a failure because I haven't won a Super Bowl? Of course not. Not everything is a competition and we would all be much better off if we didn't constantly compare ourselves to others.

Finally, no one truly fails until they quit. Don't give up. It simply does not matter how long it takes to accomplish most goals. Just keep inching forward and success will come.

No matter how long it takes.

Bipolar Magazine, 3/22/2016

Are Bipolar Disorder and Sleep Related?

Living in recovery with bipolar disorder isn't a matter of mastering one skill. There is no single activity a person can do to be well. Rather, in order to keep the symptoms of bipolar disorder from taking over our lives, we have to learn to master multiple skills.

Most people are aware that medication and coping skills help alleviate the symptoms brought on by bipolar disorder. And many are even aware that diet and exercise play important roles in our ability to minimize the highs and lows. Yet most people are still unaware that sleep, too, is crucial in helping us manage the symptoms of bipolar disorder.

Why don't people with bipolar pay attention to their sleep?

Before we get into how vital sleep is in the management of bipolar disorder, let's first discuss our lack of respect for sleeping. According to the Centers for Disease Control and Prevention (CDC), one-third of Americans aren't getting enough sleep. Assuming that you know two other people beside yourself, one of you isn't getting the amount of sleep you need for your body to function properly.

Whether you're managing a health issue or not, far too many Americans aren't getting enough sleep. For reasons unknown, sleep is seen as laziness or a hobby. If we need extra time in a day, we tend to take that time from our sleep schedule, often with unintended consequences. And this is just the average person who isn't also suffering the symptoms of bipolar disorder.

In short, the answer to why people with bipolar disorder don't respect sleep is because *most* people don't respect sleep. People living with bipolar have many of the same misconceptions as everyone else.

How sleep plays a role in the proper management of bipolar disorder

The importance of sleep — for everyone — has long been understood by the medical community. But certain situations make the need for sleep all the more important. If you're fighting off an infection, for example, or if you recently had surgery, then sleeping is vital to getting healthy faster.

If you're living with bipolar disorder, the same principle applies. Getting the proper amount of sleep and maintaining a consistent sleep schedule can keep you from slipping into depression or mania. It also contributes to the rest of your overall health goals, like being alert and maintaining proper cognitive functioning.

Finally, consider tracking your sleep to help in heading off potential issues. If you notice that you're sleeping more or less than usual, you may have come across an indicator of potential bipolar symptoms. Reporting sleep irregularities to your doctor before full-blown symptoms appear could reduce them — or even prevent them altogether.

And who among us living with bipolar disorder doesn't want to prevent those symptoms from ruining our day — *or worse?*

8 Great Ways to Boost Your Self-Esteem

Low self-esteem is a growing problem, especially in young people. There is so much pressure today to be successful, to have a great job, to look a certain way, to have a perfect life, and to be happy about it. These pressures often lead to low self-esteem and self-confidence, which in turn can lead to depression, anxiety, and other mental health issues. With the number of people suffering from depression growing year on year, it's more important than ever that we find ways to boost our self-esteem. Here are some easy ways you can do just that.

Take a Social Media Break

Social media is wonderful. It is a great way to keep in touch with your friends and family and have fun. However, it can also lead to jealousy and damage your self-confidence. If you find you are always comparing your own life to what others share, perhaps it's time to take a break.

Take a Vacation

Life can be stressful. If you're working, studying, or raising a family, sometimes it can all get too much. Book some time off and get away if you can. If not, just spend some time relaxing at home. This can help you to energize and gain some fresh perspective on your problems.

Cut Negativity

We all know negative people. Those that are always making negative comments or bringing you down. Cut them out. You don't need that kind of friendship. Instead, surround yourself with positive people that make you feel good.

Learn

Learning something new, or updating your existing knowledge can be a great way to boost your self-esteem. Learning is a wonderful way to keep your mind alert, cut negativity, and boost your mood. With online courses available in everything from crafts and hobbies to a health law degree there is no excuse not to.

Focus on One Thing at a Time

There will be times in your life when everything seems too much. You get overwhelmed by everything going on and nothing seems right. In these cases, it's important to focus on one problem at a time. If you're having trouble at home, speak to your family and try to spend quality time with them.

Exercise

Getting some exercise is a brilliant way of boosting your self-esteem. Cardio exercise releases endorphins, serotonin, and adrenaline, all of which will help you to feel great. If you are new to exercise start with a brisk walk or a "couch to 5k program."

Eat Well

Eating a healthy diet will not only help you to maintain a healthy weight, it will also help you to sleep better, feel more energetic and cut your risk of illnesses. Making a few simple changes to your diet can be all it takes.

Reduce Alcohol Intake

Alcohol directly affects the chemistry of your brain. Drinking more than the recommended amount can have a negative effect on your mood. Reducing your intake can improve your mood and the way you feel about yourself.

If you are struggling and these tips don't help consider speaking to a doctor or counselor who can help you find the root of your problems.

Psych Central, 4/25/17

3 Things People with Bipolar Disorder Shouldn't Do

Living with bipolar disorder is a delicate balance of managing symptoms, managing expectations, and – perhaps most importantly – maintaining a hopeful outlook that things can be better or life will stay good. Managing bipolar isn't a weekly or even daily obligation; every moment is, in some way, dedicated to managing the illness. And just as there are plenty of things a person should do to manage bipolar; there are things a person should *not* do. Here are three of them.

People with Bipolar Disorder Shouldn't Drink Alcohol

Let's go ahead and get the big one out of the way, first. There are too many reasons to list why people with bipolar disorder shouldn't drink alcohol. That said, the main reasons are:

1. If the person is on medication, alcohol will most likely interfere with the efficacy of the treatment making it much less effective.

2. Alcohol is also known to lower inhibitions, and by removing your last bit of restraint, you may find the "courage" to do something you'll regret. The effects could remove the final barriers between stability and depression or stability and mania. Either outcome is, frankly, not good.

3. Alcohol is addictive. People with bipolar disorder are particularly susceptible to becoming addicted to many things. In general, people with bipolar disorder are often known to be inflexible or "slaves to their routine." Alcohol is a common choice when it comes to self-medicating because it slows thinking. While slowing thinking may sound like a good thing during episodes of mania and/or racing thoughts, trust me, this cure is worse than the disease.

Consuming alcohol, in general, carries some risk. The effects on "normal" people are well understood and the person imbibing needs to drink responsibly. This advice holds particularly true for people managing bipolar disorder.

People with Bipolar Disorder Shouldn't Rush Into Anything

I've experienced "love at first sight" no less than 100 times. I've started, without exaggeration, thousands of projects over the years. Every single one of them felt amazing.

Until that feeling wore off. Sometimes this was in a couple days, sometimes in a couple minutes. If I acted on them as though they were the only things that mattered in my life, I would have ended up over-promising, spending lots of money, or hurting people I loved. Over the years, chasing the new and shiny bauble has cost me tens of thousands of dollars and multiple friendships and relationships.

One of the most difficult things I had to learn in order to properly manage bipolar disorder was to simply slow down. Just because it feels like a great idea doesn't mean it is. And, more importantly, if it is a good idea, it'll still be one in a week.

People with Bipolar Disorder Shouldn't Stay Up All Night

People with bipolar disorder need to practice exceptional sleep hygiene. Going to bed and getting up at the same time every day is the key to maintaining good physical and mental health for *everyone*. But it's even more important when it comes to managing the highs and lows of bipolar disorder.

Being overly tired can lead to depression or mania and that alone should be reason enough to make proper rest a priority. However, routine has been proven to make symptoms of bipolar more manageable – and even prevent them all together. No routine can be complete without a bed time.

Also, and maybe this is just me, but at 3 a.m. when the house is quiet, I'm all alone, and when I'm overly tired, my mind never ends up in a positive place. I start to dwell on my failures, my regrets, and I often binge eat, which makes me feel physically ill. With rare exceptions, I've never been better off because I stayed up past my bedtime.

In Conclusion...

I've said many times that there is not one magic "thing" a person can do to live well in spite of bipolar. There are, realistically, dozens of little things that a person needs to do every second of every day to live well. Working hard to figure out all of those things and mastering them is the best advice I can give a person to leading a productive, happy, and long life.

After all, I'm not just a bipolar writer and speaker – I'm also a patient.

Bipolar Magazine, 1/12/2016

3 Ways to Stop Blaming Yourself for Bipolar Disorder

There are, of course, more than three ways to stop blaming yourself for bipolar disorder. This list is in no way exhaustive and I am in no position to say that any of these methods will work for you. That said, they are really good ideas and have helped many people, myself included. If you are looking for the easy way out, I'd suggest you just quit reading right now. I've read many lists on the Internet and I work very hard to make my readers think. While eating ice cream on the couch might make you stop blaming yourself for a moment, these methods have a significantly greater potential to work for a lifetime.

1. Stop Feeling Guilty for Having Bipolar Disorder

There is a common theme that I hear a lot from people with bipolar disorder. It is obvious that, on some level, we feel the need to be "forgiven" for having bipolar disorder.

I reject the entire premise outright. Forgiveness implies guilt. If you're not guilty of something, there's nothing to forgive. We no more need forgiveness for an illness than we do for our hair color. Don't buy into the lie that bipolar disorder is a character or personality flaw. It isn't. It's an illness that some people have and has no further moral or ethical implications.

Now, if you made a mistake, hurt someone, or caused a problem and bipolar was the primary cause of that issue, that is different. Which leads us to...

2. Take Responsibility for Your Actions During a Bipolar Episode

For years, I felt a great deal of guilt about the people I hurt when I was at my sickest points. I didn't think there was anything I could do about it, because, after all, it wasn't my fault they were hurt.

I was correct. It wasn't my fault what happened, but it wasn't their fault either. Since it wasn't their fault and my illness caused the issue, this made it my responsibility. This is unfair, yes, but that is just the way it is and accepting it made a world of difference.

There is a lot of power in owning up to our actions, especially the ones we aren't entirely responsible for. Reaching out to people and explaining why I did what I did, apologizing, and making amends felt very good. Remember, bipolar disorder is an explanation for what happened, not an excuse. Taking responsibility helps shift the balance of power away from the disease and back to you.

But what about the things we can't make amends for or the people we've hurt who won't forgive us? This is where it is important to...

3. Focus on Living with Bipolar Disorder in the Present

Above all else, you need to focus on living with bipolar disorder in the present. The truth is that the past is over and we have the most control right now. Focusing on today will help us shape the future we want. Time spent dwelling on what you did wrong years ago won't change anything except today's outlook – negatively.

Blaming yourself for past mistakes is not productive, doesn't make amends for anything, and doesn't make you feel better. If, instead, you used that same amount of time to focus on the present — things you are doing well, accomplishments, and working toward a better future — it makes it much easier to let go of the regrets of yesterday.

The best you can do is to acknowledge what happened, apologize and make things right, and do everything in your power to ensure it doesn't happen again. Blaming yourself is foolish. Treat yourself with the same respect you would expect from others. After all, if you are blaming yourself for having bipolar disorder, why shouldn't others do the same?

Bipolar Magazine, 7/28/2015

3 Ways to be Physically Healthy While Fighting Depression

These days, people have a hard time managing their physical health. From weight issues and lack of exercise to proper sleep and diet, maintaining proper physical wellness is a challenge for many people.

When individuals are fighting depression, simply getting out of bed can be a difficult task. But just because they are dealing with depression doesn't mean that their physical health needs don't need to be addressed. However, if people have an issue simply moving from the bedroom to the living room, suggesting that they go for a run isn't practical advice.

So, how does a person fighting depression maintain proper physical health? Here are three suggestions:

Tip #1: All Movement is Good

I'm the first person to admit that exercise is difficult even when I'm feeling fantastic. I'm not the physical type at all. I enjoy sitting on my butt staring at the television. But, when it comes to maintaining our health, movement is important.

It can be unreasonable to expect a depressed person to "go for a walk" or "get some fresh air." It's that kind of ill-advised suggestion that makes a person feel isolated and alone in the first place. So, rather than setting your sights on the treadmill, set them on the shower.

Often, when depressed, personal hygiene in the first to suffer. Why shower, shave, and get dressed if you are not planning on leaving the house? Because it'll make you feel better, that's why.

Don't get bogged down in how long it takes, either. It once took me an entire day to shower, shave, and get dressed. Write a list on the mirror (look, more movement!) and cross items off as you go. Consider things like brushing your teeth, combing your hair, etc. As you start to feel better, add household chores and errands.

Celebrate the goal and move forward. Trust me. All movement is good, even in small amounts. Add that to the mental burst of energy you'll receive from completing a goal and it's a win-win.

Tip #2: Watch What You Eat

Watching what you eat is the most common advice there is when it comes to maintaining your physical health. It's so common that you already know it, but you're probably not doing it because you think it is too difficult. Especially when you are depressed.

Here's the thing: many people believe the only eating options are healthy and unhealthy. That is simply nonsense. We would all feel better if we ate only fresh fruits and vegetables, lean proteins, and healthy grains. Conversely, we would all feel horrible if we ate only ice cream, cake, and potato chips.

But, there is a middle ground. Drink water, as an example. Before you panic, I'm not suggesting to stop drinking soda or coffee; I'm merely suggesting adding some water.

Many people complain that they can't eat healthy because they are too depressed to cook. I certainly understand that. But there are plenty of *healthier* options than some of the standard junk food you may be consuming. And, I'll point out that cooking will help you get in more of the movement I suggested above.

For starters, "diet" microwave meals, pretzels, and plain bagels are all healthier options than, say, canned pastas, chips, and pop tarts. Eating better and eating perfect isn't the same thing. When I'm depressed, I often eat the worst-of-the-worst types of foods.

Drinking more water and adding foods that are middle-of-the-road will make a huge difference.

Tip #3: Maintain a Stable Sleep Schedule

Like the above, maintaining a proper sleep schedule also has both physical and mental health benefits. Sleeping too little or too much can cause not only adverse physical effects, but mental ones, as well.

Sleep schedules are often set by external factors, such as when we need to get up for work or school. The National Sleep Foundation recommends 7-9 hours of sleep for the average adult between the ages of 26-64, but everyone is a little different.

Once you have determined the proper amount, choose your bedtime accordingly. Then it is lights out at that time every night. Literally, lights out. Not lie in bed on your tablet or phone, not read a book, and absolutely not watch TV. Turn off the lights, crawl under the covers, and shut your eyes. Then lie there until you fall asleep.

No matter when you fall asleep, wake up at the same time every day – or at least as close to it as is reasonable. It's okay to sleep past your normal wake time if necessary, but avoid getting your entire eight hours, or you may not be in a position to be able to fall asleep at your normal bedtime that evening.

The bottom line is this: Respect sleep. Don't abuse it by sleeping too little or too much. Don't force yourself to stay awake watching Netflix when you should be resting. Being physically exhausted will not improve your depression and, in fact, will absolutely make it worse.

Conclusion

A journey of a thousand miles begins with a single step. Maintaining our physical and mental health is no different. We tend to psych ourselves out and decide that if we can't run a marathon or eat perfectly, then there is no need to try at all. Nothing could be further from the truth.

Every day, depressed or not, make *any* small positive step forward and you will be better off. Small changes absolutely lead to gigantic victories.

Psych Central, 3/4/16

Have Social Anxiety? Four Sure-Fire Conversation Starters

In our daily lives, we are required to interact with other people for many different reasons. Even ordering a hamburger at a fast food place requires social interaction – ideally, a positive one.

Having social anxiety, however, makes many interactions very stressful. Here are four suggestions to ensure that your next person-to-person interaction is positive. And hey, you might just make a new friend.

1. Body language matters. A lot.

I can't overstate this. Body language is arguably the most important part of communication. If you approach someone with a positive demeanor (by smiling, for example), people are much more likely to react better toward you. A person's internal defenses are lower when a stranger approaches who appears happy, upbeat, and non-threatening.

2. Knowing what not to say matters

Knowing what *not* to say is almost as important as knowing what *to* say. We understand that being rude or insulting is not the way to make friends, but some topics of conversation should be handled very delicately. These include money, politics, and religion.

These types of conversations have their place. But when you first meet someone, it's best not to start with something as emotionally charged as a person's belief system or world view. There are, of course, exceptions to every rule, but generally we should try to build a rapport on lighter topics.

3. Make it about them and not about you

Social anxiety is often rooted in the idea that people won't like us. My own anxiety grabs hold of my self-esteem and won't let go. It makes me feel worthless.

Most people enjoy talking about themselves, so ask questions that keep the conversation off *you* and about *them*. Ask about their hobbies, children, and what entertainment they enjoy (TV shows, music, sporting events, etc.). If you start a conversation this way and ask appropriate follow-up questions, you'll have an opportunity to get comfortable before you need to begin sharing details about your own life.

4. In the real world, it's okay to, "lead the witness"

I always engage people with a light subject that I'm comfortable with. If there was a local sporting event or a popular television show that I watched, I'll open with that. Popular culture has a wealth of things to discuss that aren't very deep and are unlikely to raise emotions (sports rivalries notwithstanding).

By starting the conversation and leading it somewhere unobtrusive and within my comfort zone, I can ensure that things stay light. Holding a conversation about my latest Netflix binge is much easier that explaining that I live with bipolar disorder. It allows me to get a feel for a person and have a positive interaction without risking much.

That positive interaction becomes a building block for deeper conversations down the road. While these conversations may seem meaningless, they aren't. Establishing rapport takes time and building relationships with people isn't something we need to rush.

Bringing it all together

In my opinion, Maya Angelou explained human interactions best:

"I've learned that people will forget what you said, people will forget what you did, but people will never forget how you made them feel."

If you make someone feel good by having a simple conversation about seemingly nothing, you've accomplished a lot. Take *that,* social anxiety!

MailBag: Social Anxiety Causes Me To Miss Family Events

Hi, Gabe.

I need some advice. I have bipolar depression and high anxiety. I say yes to doing things and back out at the last minute. I just let my goddaughter down last night, backing out of her singing concert. She is 12. Her mom and I have a rocky friendship. But she messaged me this morning on how I let her little girl down again. I know I did, many times. But I don't know how to get over this last-minute panic feeling. And I also don't know how to explain how I feel when this happens. I try very hard not to make it about my illness, but she also doesn't even try to understand me, either. Her child gets hurt by me and nothing else matters to her, and I understand that. One thing is her mom makes me a nervous wreck when I am around her. What do I do?

Thank you,
A Fan

Dear Fan,

There are hundreds of ways to manage anxiety and different methods work for different people. You can easily find such resources online.

However, what I want to focus on in your letter is not how to manage your anxiety, but how to manage the expectations of those around you. And for that matter, how to manage your own expectations.

You have a basic understanding that your actions are hurting that little girl's feelings. You even indicate that you understand your friend's anger about this. First, if you haven't already, apologize. Typically, people give the half-hearted, "I'm sorry, but my anxiety…" apology. Make sure your apology is in absolute terms – no excuses. While it may not be exactly your fault that you let them down, it's by no means *their* fault. Let them know you are truly sorry. Don't be afraid to express it.

Second, you need to have more realistic expectations of what you can and cannot accomplish. As someone who also lives with an anxiety disorder, I only commit 100% to things that I'm reasonably certain I can do. Otherwise, I ask if it is okay to make a "game time decision." If they need an answer immediately, I politely decline, knowing that I might not be able to make it. If they say yes, then I do my best to make it, knowing that if I am unable to do so, I prepared them for the possibility in advance.

Third, you need to talk about how anxiety affects your life *before* it affects someone else's. I have a tendency to believe that my issues won't affect people, so I don't talk to them about it until after it does. But this is the worst time to clue them in. By this point, the person is already upset, or at least confused. You've also implied that you don't trust them with this information, since you were hiding it. Finally, you didn't give them an opportunity to assist you.

So, in addition to explaining your anxiety issues, you also have to repair the relationship. Separately, each of those conversations can be challenging, and now you've put yourself in the position of having to do both at the same time – and probably while emotions are already high.

Simply put, anxiety is going to cause issues and those issues are ours to manage. We must do our best to educate those around us on what we need in order to have the best odds of success. If we aren't willing to be honest with ourselves and our loved ones, then we can't very well expect things to improve.

It's not too late to have a conversation. Don't let anxiety prevent you from building the best relationships you can with people. It's going to be difficult, but it often will pay huge dividends in terms of both managing anxiety and in building stronger and more fulfilling connections with those around you.

Psych Central, 11/3/16

Three Big Mistakes for Someone with Social Anxiety

Human interactions are filled with potential pitfalls for everyone. A person doesn't need to have social anxiety or depression to find it difficult to connect with others.

We can't read each other's minds, we fear rejection, or we are worried that we will be seen as annoying. The phrase "coming on too strong" applies to friendships and romantic relationships equally.

Living with socially anxiety means a person fears social interaction. It doesn't mean a person doesn't want friends, but finds it more difficult than the typical human.

However, there some key mistakes that someone with social anxiety can make, especially at the beginning of a friendship. Here are the top three, and how to avoid them.

1. Don't assume the worst; You're not a mind reader.

I get it. You sent a text message or left a voicemail message an hour ago and you haven't heard back. It *must* mean the other person hates you. *What other possible explanation could there be?*

Here are just some of the reasons you haven't heard back that have nothing to do with you: sleeping, at the movies, phone battery has died, working, spending time with another friend or family member, binge watching on Netflix, swimming, or writing an article on social anxiety for HealthCentral.com.

There are millions of reasons people don't answer their phones, and they have absolutely nothing to do with negative feelings toward you.

Having friends means having trust in those people. It means having faith that they find value in your presence in their lives. Even if the friendship is brand new, there is still a base amount of trust you should have. After all, there is a reason you're pursuing the friendship in the first place.

The worst thing you can do is stalk them, whether by phone, text, or in person. It makes people uncomfortable and it sends a clear message that you don't trust them. And who wants to be friends with someone who thinks so little of them?

2. Anger kills relationships.

To piggyback on mistake number one, assuming the worst often leads us to become angry. It's an understandable progression: if you feel someone has treated you poorly, then it only makes sense that this would anger you. Pointing that anger at another person, however, probably isn't going to turn out well, especially if what you're mad about is the result of your own paranoia or misunderstanding.

Solid friendships carry an unspoken, but extremely valuable, social contract. Both parties need to agree not to jump to conclusions. Even if you are positive the other person is wrong, you need to proceed with caution. Be direct, but polite. You aren't waging war, here; you are attempting to clear up a misunderstanding.

Move forward with the goal of getting both parties on the same page and making amends. It isn't about blame. It isn't about retribution. A solid friendship is built largely on understanding and forgiveness.

Passive-aggression, hostility, and anger will destroy any relationship. Value your friendship more than your anger at what the friend may or may not have done. Keep an open mind and give your friend the benefit of the doubt.

3. It isn't about you; it's about the both of you.

Arguably the most important mistake a person can make is forgetting that a friendship involves two people, not just one. Looking at every situation from the viewpoint of how it impacts only you is a sure way to ruin any relationship.

Imagine that your friend only cared about his or her own feelings and never considered yours. Many of us with social anxiety, myself included, often feel that people aren't taking into account our emotions. We feel abused, mistreated, or even just misunderstood, and it makes us feel terrible.

It is imperative that we don't make others feel that way. Not only is that the right thing to do, but it pays big dividends when it comes to maintaining friendships. By putting yourself in other people's shoes, you can make sure that you are meeting their emotional needs.

When you do this, they'll be inspired, encouraged, and have the emotional reserves to help meet *your* needs. This is the natural give-and-take that exists in healthy and stable friendships.

It may seem cliché, but the best way to *keep* a good friend is to *be* a good friend.

3 Tips to Avoid Panic Attacks and Anxiety when Moving

My wife and I just bought a new house and are in the process of packing up our old one and moving to the new one. As a person who lives with bipolar and anxiety disorders, any interruption in my routine can spell trouble. Moving is difficult for even the most well-adjusted, so I don't need to convince you of the potential pitfalls for those of us living with mental illness.

Here are three tips to avoid having a panic attack, reduce anxiety, and help to make your move as mentally healthy as possible. Please keep in mind this list is in no way exhaustive and, in this case, it assumes the move is a desirable one (i.e., moving to someplace you want to move and for positive reasons).

Tip #1: Preparation is Key

The number one tip I can offer to reduce the potential for anxiety and panic attacks is to be prepared. Make a plan well ahead of time. If my middle school science teacher taught me anything, it is that most people don't plan to fail, they fail to plan. Cheesy? Yes. But 100% true.

When making your plan, it is important to set reasonable expectations. Don't fall into the trap of getting behind schedule because you only gave yourself 30 minutes to pack up the entire kitchen. A psychological trick I love to use is to overestimate. If I think it will take me one hour, I budget two hours. It is a win-win, because I either finish early or I gave myself the correct amount of time.

Don't bite off more than you can chew. There is no reason you have to pack your entire place in one day. Pack one room a day for a week. When making your plan, don't leave all the physical labor tasks for the same time frame. As an example, a good plan might be three hours total to pack a kitchen. I'll work for 90 minutes, then sit down at my PC and update all the mailing addresses, then work another 90 minutes.

Tip #2: Manage Expectations

If you want to keep your anxiety under control, it is of vital importance to manage expectations. Rome wasn't built in a day and moving is a giant pain in the you-know-what. It is important to understand that moving is going to take time and everything will not always go as planned. From packing to the actual move to unpacking, moving is a process and an unpredictable one at that. Things *will* go wrong.

Understanding the nature of the process allows you to stay ahead of it. If you know that something is going to go wrong, it won't be so bad when it does. Leaving extra time to handle the things that come up ensures that you aren't rushed and have time to make good decisions.

It isn't a bad idea to have backup plans for common moving mishaps. What is your contingency plan if it rains, for example? I always recommend getting extra tape, packing materials, and boxes. Better to have them and not need them than the other way around.

Finally, take lots of breaks. There is no shame at all in sitting down and taking a moment for yourself. Build in time for going out to lunch so you can get away from the situation for a bit. There is no reason to go full-tilt for hours on end without a break.

Tip #3: Use the Buddy System

I'm a lucky man when it comes to using the buddy system to reduce anxiety. My wife is my constant companion and is wonderful. She is helpful, thoughtful, and her presence is naturally soothing. For big projects, like moving, I lean on her heavily to keep me focused and calm. There is nothing more helpful than a well-timed hug or joke. She also notices when I start to get overwhelmed and suggests "an early lunch" or five-minute break.

The flip side to the buddy system is to not ask people to help who cause you anxiety. Sure, your best friend is a great person, but will s/he be helpful in a move? Maybe they are great to catch a movie with, but are extra critical of the dust bunnies your couch ate years ago. Part of using the buddy system is to get the right people around you. Having support is invaluable.

All in all, it is important to keep your eye on the prize. Sure, moving is a hassle, but whatever reason you chose to move should be your mantra. For this move, my wife and I are focusing on the bigger yard, the extra space, and that this is the first house we picked out together (I originally moved in with her). We are excited for the future and that helps keep me calm when I see my entire life put into boxes and carried onto trucks.

While today is stressful, the future is going to be wonderful.

Psych Central, 9/24/15

Managing Depression & Anxiety While Away At College

When I was younger, I saw a poster of Tiger Woods. The caption read, "How do you go from the best to the worst overnight? Turn Pro."

I always kind of thought it was a bit stupid, frankly. Your abilities don't change because of what pool you're competing in. Tiger Woods' golf skills were the same when he turned pro as they were when he was an amateur.

Then, I graduated high school and went out into the real world. The phrase "it's all relative" smacked me hard, right in the face. So much was different. And I finally understood that poster. Tiger Woods was playing the same game, but his opponents were considerably better than those in the amateur circuit. The game may be the same, but the circumstances have changed.

Symptoms of Depression and Anxiety Increase at College

In order to properly manage anything – from auto maintenance to lawn care – one must have a realistic understanding of what to expect. Someone who has a history with depression and anxiety cannot realistically expect *not* to have symptoms flare up.

Going away to college for the first time has all kinds of potential pitfalls. A new environment, new people, and new rules are all things that trip up the most mentally healthy among us. People suffering

44

from mental illness do well with a set routine and when they feel comfortable in their surroundings.

Going off to college ensures that everything will change. Being aware that those changes are coming and setting realistic goals for overcoming them will help ensure success in the long run. Keep in mind, everyone is adjusting; it's the nature of the beast.

Move Slowly and Deliberately Your First Few Weeks in College

My granny, whom I love more than anything, was always trying to slow me down when I was younger. Her favorite phrase is, "Rome wasn't built in a day." All clichéd expressions aside, she is correct. Remember, college is a four-year marathon, not a one-day sprint. It's okay to be slow to adjust. In fact, it's typical. Don't be afraid to slow down or rest when needed.

Before leaving for college, ask friends and family if it's okay to contact them a little more often. In their own way, they are adjusting, too, and will generally welcome hearing all about new adventures.

On move-in day, arrive early. This allows for a slightly less crowded experience. Use the buddy system and bring along a friend, even if that "friend" is mom or dad. Bring along some comforts from home that help you sleep. I've found that sleeping in a strange place can be difficult and lack of sleep can contribute to issues with anxiety and depression.

During the first couple of weeks, leave extra time to get to classes, meals, etc. The day before, walk different routes to important buildings around campus (like the cafeteria, student services, etc.). This will make becoming familiar with the new surroundings much easier. And don't be afraid to get lost.

Also, learn where the campus health center is. If they have a hotline, keep note of it.

The most wasted times of my life were times I spent judging myself for my "failures." It didn't help me, it didn't feel good, and it didn't work. Setbacks are normal and should be expected. Don't allow them to turn into losses.

I always recommend keeping it simple. Focus on the day-to-day and move from one success to the next. Keep that success in mind and keep going forward.

As Dory would say, "Just keep swimming!"

Psych Central, 8/3/16

4 Sure-Fire Tips to Survive the Holidays If You Have Panic and Anxiety

I love the holiday season. I love the music, the lights, and the decorations. As a person who lives with bipolar disorder, I appreciate the subtle "backwardness" of the season: We bring live trees inside, put electric lights outside, and tacky is the goal rather than an unfortunate lapse in taste.

However, as a person who lives with anxiety and panic disorders, there is a lot to trip on. It's a busy time of year, and all of the festivities can become overwhelming. Add in visits from family and friends, holiday travel, and the desire for perfection, and a perfect storm of anxiety can easily happen.

Here are four simple steps to survive the holidays, no matter what they have in store for you.

1. Take breaks

Everyone at this time of year is trying to accomplish a lot. Just because it's the holiday season doesn't mean we can stop living our daily lives — and those lives are already taking up all of our time. So, with the extra things that pop up during this season, it's easy to see how anyone can become overwhelmed.

Allow yourself to take breaks. There is no shame in accomplishing a task and then taking a rest. Go for a walk. Read a book. Play with the dog. Remember, the holidays are a marathon, not a sprint. Set a reasonable pace and don't overdo it.

2. Involve family and friends

This tip has two parts:

a) Ask friends and family for help in completing goals. During the holidays, people are generally willing to lend a hand. Ask those you love for help, advice, or ideas on how to lighten the load.
b) Educate the people around you that sometimes you need a hand from them to help manage your anxiety.

For example, if you visit with family or friends, let them know in advance that sometimes you need to step outside (or into another room, if you live in the snow belt) to gather your bearings. If you'd prefer a hug when you get anxious, let them know in advance that you may be asking for one. Whatever you would like them to do for you, talk to them *before* you need them to do it.

3. Celebrate your success

If you spend the entire holiday season focusing on things that didn't turn out the way you planned, you're in for a pretty crummy December. By not celebrating what you've done right, you're unintentionally tipping the scales to see more of the negative.

Life is a balance of success and failure, and it's okay for things not to turn out how we intended. Be flexible and allow yourself to be less than perfect. Because, nobody's perfect and that's okay.

4. Be realistic and don't overdo it

The most important tip that I can share is to keep your plans realistic and to not bite off more than you can chew. It's easy to *plan* on spending four days with our parents, decorating the entire outside of the house so it can be seen from space, and preparing an elaborate Christmas dinner.

But after you plan it, ask yourself if it's reasonable for astronauts to know you have holiday spirit. It's okay not to do it all. And it's okay not to live up to what other people think you should be able to accomplish. If you can only visit with your family for an hour before you head back to the safety of home, then praise yourself for that hour.

There is no correct way to spend the holidays. If I had to declare any holiday rule, it would be to be merry and joyous and promote goodwill toward our fellow humans.

And spreading goodwill means we have to be nice to ourselves, as well.

Five Tips to Beat Holiday Stress

The holidays can be a difficult time of year. Whether it's depression, family drama, anxiety, or the fear of missing out, the holiday blues can be difficult to beat. Listed below are five constructive ways to help make the holidays happier — or at least more bearable.

1. Take Time for Yourself

The hustle and bustle of the holiday season can quickly become overwhelming, creating the ideal environment for anxiety to flourish. While our minds are preoccupied by plans with friends and family, we often forget about ourselves. Taking a moment to breathe and relax can help reduce anxiety, allowing for a happier holiday.

The holidays can't be enjoyable if your stress meter is maxed out the entire time. In this time of giving, don't forget to give to yourself. Allow time to breathe, relax, and care for your well-being. Even if this means you might miss some opportunities, you'll enjoy the ones you don't miss more.

2. Have Reasonable Holiday Expectations

When the holidays come around, we are often filled with the idea that everything must be perfect, which is literally impossible.

Of course, we want an all-inclusive, no-drama, picture-perfect holiday with family and friends, but sometimes folks can't make it.

The turkey is in the oven too long, your Uncle Fred has an argument with Aunt Janice over politics, and that picture-perfect holiday begins to crack and hang crookedly on your wall of memories.

In an ideal world, these unfortunate events would have no place at the holiday dinner table, but life happens and does not always go the way it was originally planned. Keep in mind that life is unpredictable, even if you have an itinerary prepared.

Remember, we can all enjoy the holidays more if we keep our expectations reasonable.

3. Keep It Affordable

During the holidays, many people find themselves in emotional turmoil as the cost of presents, decorations, food, and parties add up. Let's face it — the holidays can be expensive.

But they don't have to be. It's important to remember the reason you're celebrating and to keep things in perspective. You shouldn't need to take a loan and spend an arm and a leg just to enjoy yourself and feel merry.

Remember, the holidays aren't happier just because you spent more money.

4. Avoid Toxic People This Holiday Season

The holidays are typically spent with friends and family — but that's not a requirement. Let's be honest. Sometimes our friends and family can be triggering and detrimental to our mental health. Not everyone is jolly around the holidays.

The holidays can bring up our own feelings of anxiety, depression, and general stress, so it may be a good idea to avoid those who are constantly spreading negativity. You are not required to see anyone during the holidays, and it's okay to ignore people if their negativity has a harmful effect on you.

5. Be Grateful for the People Around You

Unfortunately, the ones we love are not always around. Often, we dwell on the missing person so much that we forget about the people who are there.

Although others will not fill the void left by your loved ones' absence, it is important to remember that you have other people who love and care about you. The holidays are a time of joy. Be thankful for the friends and family who were able to share the holidays with you.

Along those same lines, be thankful for what you have, rather than worrying about what you don't have.

In Conclusion...

The five tips listed above won't work for everyone, but they may give you some ideas on how to make the holidays more enjoyable. Remember, there is no right way to celebrate, just remember to enjoy yourself.

Psych Central, 11/17/2016

Five Ways to Make the Holidays Less Blue

The holiday season can be a stressful time of year for everyone — but they don't have to be. In a previous article, *"Five Tips to Beat Holiday Stress,"* I offered some suggestions on ways to avoid some of the pitfalls that come along with the holidays.

It turns out five suggestions wasn't enough; so here are five more ways to help avoid the holiday blues.

1. It's Okay to Be Alone

Not everyone has a big family or a plethora of friends to celebrate the holidays with. Due to various schedules or location, it may be impractical to get together over the holidays.

Of course, there is no reason you have to spend the holiday season with anyone at all. It's perfectly acceptable to stay in and celebrate by yourself. Watch a movie, read a book, take a long bath, and take time to reflect. Some folks will buy themselves gifts or go on vacation.

Remember, it's okay to be alone, so make the holidays your own!

2. Make a Holiday Plan

This time of year, the holidays follow one after the other and it is easy for someone to become stressed from last-minute preparations. Planning can greatly reduce the pressure and slow down the typically speed-driven holidays. Rather than frantically putting together last-minute festivities, do as much as you can ahead of time. The more you can complete before the holidays hit "fully jolly," the more time you'll have available to really enjoy the holidays.

3. Don't Be Afraid to Seek Professional Help

If the holiday blues are constant and you think there may be bigger issues at play, you should seek the help of a therapist or other mental health professional. Sometimes, the holidays are when we feel the most alone; scheduling an appointment can help tremendously during this time.

4. Don't Listen to the Media

The media can play an important role in how we view the holidays. Pop culture loves to emphasize images that include large families lovingly gathered around a fire, feast, or other holiday festivity. Don't compare real life with the "picture-perfect" versions of the holiday season.

Doing so can greatly increase our feelings of isolation, while decreasing our self-esteem. Remember, media portrayals of everything are designed to impress; they are not reality.

Finally, please remember...

5. It's Okay Not to Like the Holidays!

Sometimes, we simply do not like something and that's okay! We are allowed to not like a specific holiday or the entire holiday season and it doesn't mean anything is wrong with you.

If you dislike the holidays, you are not alone in your opinion. Many people cringe at the thought of holiday festivities. For some, the holidays are simply too loud, too busy, too expensive, and too obsessed over by others. No one can make you enjoy the holidays, just as no one can make my niece, Nikki, eat her vegetables.

Do keep in mind, however, that if the holidays are not your cup of tea, it's not a sentiment you need to share. Spreading negativity does no good for either party and only adds unhappiness. Some people dislike this time of year, and other people (like me) love it. No one should be made to feel "less than" for their opinion.

Psych Central, 11/20/2017

7 New Year's Resolutions for a Person with Bipolar Disorder

One of the many things I say over and over again is that people living with bipolar disorder are just like everyone else. We participate in the same cultural traditions that most others do, and that means some of us make New Year's resolutions.

In 2016, the number one New Year's resolution was "enjoy life to the fullest," according to *Time* magazine. The article didn't list the top New Year's resolution for people living with bipolar disorder, so I decided to list seven New Year's resolutions for people living with mental illness (and anyone else who is interested).

1. Start a Mood Journal to Track Bipolar Symptoms

I used to think mood diaries/journals were silly. When the idea was first floated to me, I laughed and thought, "Only 12-year-old girls keep diaries." Aside from being a bit sexist, I was also dead wrong. Journaling is something that many people do – all ages, races, and genders – for all kinds of reasons.

In my opinion, the number one reason to keep a mood journal is to literally track moods. Before keeping a journal, I would report to the doctor and/or therapist that my mood for the entire month was exactly how it was on the day of my appointment. In other words, if 29 days were happy and the day of my appointment I was depressed, I would report my symptoms for the last month as "depressed."

Giving a doctor accurate information is a huge deal when it comes to reaching recovery.

2. Take Medications Regularly, as Prescribed

Many people with bipolar disorder have issues with being "medication compliant." Without opening up a can of worms, I'll simply say that medications cannot work unless taken exactly as prescribed and on a regular basis.

3. Make Amends for Things that Occurred Because of Bipolar Symptoms

Bipolar anger, mania, and depression aren't exactly the best traits for a person to have. While these symptoms were very hard on me, they were also hard on my friends and family. Once, during a particularly bad manic/anger episode, I screamed, "I hate you" at the woman I was married to.

It took me years to realize how horrible that must have been for her to experience. I should have apologized much sooner, but better late than never.

Remember, while the things you do because of bipolar disorder may not be your fault, they aren't anyone else's fault, either. Take responsibility and make amends.

4. Create and Keep a Routine (Including a Sleep Schedule)

There is overwhelming data to support the idea that routines are very helpful in managing the symptoms of bipolar disorder. Eating at the same time, going to familiar places, and keeping the same sleep schedule are all excellent tools in achieving and maintaining wellness.

I single out sleep hygiene because most people in the U.S. do not respect sleep enough. *Everyone* should get up and go to bed at a regular time. Sleep recharges the body, relaxes the brain, and is necessary for proper functioning.

5. Exercise More

Exercise has long been proven to help ease the symptoms of depression. Runners, for example, talk about the "runner's high" quite frequently and they aren't incorrect. Simply put, exercise makes a person feel better.

Plus, you can't have a New Year's resolution list without including exercise.

6. Make Time to Do Things You Enjoy

Bipolar disorder is difficult to manage and a person can spend a lot of time on it — time that, frankly, isn't very fun. While that time is necessary, it doesn't mean it's all you have to do. Every day, or at least a couple times a week, carve out some time to do something enjoyable.

Whether it's going to a movie, going to dinner with friends, or relaxing at home with a good book or TV show, give yourself permission to have fun. You'll find it helps with motivation to do the not-so-fun work.

7. Create a Vision Board with Goals Unrelated to Bipolar Disorder

Finally, create a vision board — or just a simple list, if you aren't the creative type — that includes goals having absolutely *nothing* to do with bipolar disorder. Often, I talk with people living with bipolar and all of their hopes and goals surround being well and reaching recovery, and those *are* phenomenal goals. However, we *all* want to get well and stay well so that we can do something other than be sick.

Your entire life cannot be focused exclusively on bipolar disorder, regardless of whether that focus is on being sick with it or living well with it. Having goals such as buying a new car, going on vacation, or getting new furniture (as examples) can make tremendous differences in how we view the world — and how we feel about our place in it.

There needs to be a reason to move forward other than "to not suffer from bipolar disorder." When I created my vision board many years ago, I put some easy items on it, like "eat at a new restaurant" and some difficult ones, like "buy a Rolex watch."

As of today, I still haven't gotten the Rolex, but I've done almost everything else on the list. It was exciting for me to dream about a world past bipolar disorder and, once I started achieving those goals, I felt successful, motivated, and *happy*.

No matter what New Year's Resolutions you make, remember to be kind to yourself and take time to congratulate yourself for your successes.

Bipolar Magazine, 12/6/2016

3 Ways to Manage Bipolar You (Probably) Haven't Thought Of

Before we get started with the three ways to manage bipolar disorder you probably haven't thought of, it's important to note that different suggestions will be more or less helpful, depending on where you are on the bipolar spectrum. Managing bipolar takes a lot of practice, patience, and good medical care. These are great suggestions and I recommend them, but this list is in no way comprehensive.

1. Manage bipolar depression by cooking

When I'm in the throes of bipolar depression, I don't cook, but I do eat. I know first-hand that it's difficult to motivate ourselves to get up and do anything when depression is weighing us down, but there really is a lot of benefit to cooking for ourselves when depressed.

First, cooking has therapeutic value. Feeding ourselves is essential to staying alive. Completing the task of cooking even a semi-healthy meal sends a subtle message to our brain that we still care. There is a pride factor in preparing a meal and when the food is done, there is the reward of enjoying it.

Second, eating foods that are better for us will make us feel better faster. Eating junk like potato chips, fast food, and other processed foods only serves to make us feel sicker, not better, and prolong our suffering.

So this suggestion really is two rolled into one. During bipolar depression, remember to nourish your body with healthy foods that don't keep you feeling bad.

2. Manage bipolar by keeping up with household chores

Dedicating a little time every day to managing our household goes a long way toward managing bipolar disorder. When I was a teenager, I would never have thought that something as boring as doing laundry would have so much impact on my day-to-day life.

Being overwhelmed is something that those of us who live with bipolar need to work hard to avoid. It turns out that life is filled with incredibly boring tasks that, if managed poorly, can cause innumerable headaches. And there is no better deterrent than keeping our living spaces organized and clean.

The level of organization and cleanliness will vary from person to person. Generally speaking, there is no right or wrong. For example, my BFF makes her bed every morning and I never make mine. It's personal preference. It is when we allow our homes to get messier than our comfort zones allow that we get ourselves into trouble.

3. Manage bipolar disorder by volunteering

Giving back is something that I believe everyone should do, not just people living with bipolar disorder. I could write several columns on the general mental health benefits of volunteerism, the rewards of influencing our communities, and so forth. However, for the purposes of this article, I want to keep it specific to managing bipolar.

When I was somewhere in between "very sick" and "in recovery," I didn't have a lot going on in my life. I wasn't working, so I spent a lot of time at home watching TV. I wasn't depressed, but I didn't have the confidence to get a job, either. I wanted to "dip my toe" back into the real world, but with some sort of safety net.

I started by volunteering my time with a local children's charity. They gave me a schedule, assignments, and expectations. They depended on me and I wanted to prove to myself that I could handle the responsibility. The confidence that I built during that time went a long way toward helping me get my first job after diagnosis.

I built up my stamina, gained valuable experience, and was able to work my way back into full-time employment. Without that step, I may have taken on too much too quickly and, at that time, I wasn't in a place where I would have handled failure very well. Volunteering was an important stepping-stone toward rebuilding my life.

Bipolar Magazine, 2/7/2017

Meds

3 Common Psychiatric Medication Side Effects No One Talks About

When it comes to psychiatric medications, certain side effects get all the publicity. Everyone discusses the sexual side effects and the increased likelihood of suicide in teenagers. Weight gain (or even the less common weight loss) is another side effect that is often discussed.

There are literally hundreds, if not thousands, of other possible side effects. If you count the side effects that taking two different medications at the same time can produce, the number soars even higher. However, most of these side effects are exceptionally rare and often avoidable by working with your doctor.

There are a few common side effects that many people who take psychiatric medications live with and manage to cope with. These aren't discussed frequently, but if you sit in a mental health support group, you'll likely find at least a couple participants who tolerate them.

Side Effect #1: Taste Changes

Medication is serious business and is designed to change the way your body works. The point of medication is to help your body do something that it's not doing efficiently on its own. In some cases, certain medications will literally change the way food and drink taste to the person taking them.

This means that a food or drink you loved before taking the medication may now taste different, or even bad. This may seem like an insignificant effect – and often is – but imagine if you woke up one morning and Mom's meatloaf, or other favorite comfort food, tasted terrible? It can be a jarring side effect that causes a lot of confusing, uncertain, and unhappy feelings.

Side Effect #2: Memory Issues

Any medication designed to modify the way your brain functions is also going to impact memory on some level. There is a spectrum of effects that needs close attention.

On the worst end, the medication could cause serious memory loss. Much more common, however, is causing forgetfulness or difficulty in focusing or concentrating. Losing any mental capacity is a big deal, however, and it represents a compromise on the part of the person taking the medicine. It once led me to say that I'd rather have partial control over a working brain than full control over a broken one.

Side Effect #3: Frequent Urination

This common psychiatric medication side effect is actually a two-in-one. There are medications that, for reasons only known to science, make a person urinate more. But, more commonly, these types of medication lead to dry mouth. Dry mouth leads to drinking. And drinking leads to urination.

I've led support groups for people with mental illness for years and I can tell you that, without fail, someone will need to use the restroom during the session. And at least half the room will bring a drink with them citing dry mouth as the reason. Dry mouth is easy to remedy and frequent urination, though annoying, is livable. The worst part, to be honest, is the comments we hear from all of our friends announcing the number of times we get up to head "down the hall."

We get it. You urinate less. No need to rub it in.

Side Effect Conclusions

While none of these side effects have quite the impact of doubling a person's body weight or removing a person's ability or desire to have sex, they do represent a loss. Living with the side effects of medication, even "easy" ones, means the person taking them has to give up something.

No one wants to accept less than 100% of anything and learning to compromise on health issues can be a delicate matter. I never thought that I'd be okay with losing a part of my memory in exchange for less depression. It was a difficult and unfair choice, but it is one that most people living with mental illness face.

For that, we deserve to be commended.

Psych Central, 11/29/15

Mental Illness Q&A: Medication Doesn't Work for Bipolar Disorder

Dear Gabe,

My son is 33 and a college graduate diagnosed with bipolar disorder with psychotic tendencies. He has been on many meds, but none seem to work for him. What was your turning point and do you take any medication? Thank you in advance.

Bipolar Meds Don't Work

Dear BMDW,

I do take medication and the "turning point" took years.

It was at least two years before I started to approach wellness and every bit of four or five before I reached where I am today. There was no "A-ha" moment for me; I just kept moving forward, every day, a little bit at a time. And honestly, sometimes I would go backward. It was analogous to a yo-yo on an escalator.

I was moving up and down, but the escalator continued upward. That was what my progress looked like.

I know firsthand that medication can be challenging. However, when folks tell me medication doesn't work, I point out there are over 300 approved psychiatric medications and people with severe mental illness (such as bipolar disorder) often need to take more than one.

I, for example, am on five different medications. Using 300 as the estimated number and assuming your son also needs five meds, then he has 19,582,837,560 potential combinations before he can be certain that medications won't work at all for him.

It is important to note that medication isn't prescribed randomly.

A doctor gathers data and makes educated choices about dosages, medications, and therapies. The way an individual patient responds to each medication provides a wealth of data for the doctor to use to determine how to move forward. It is highly unlikely that you will need to try more than 10 to 15 different combinations.

However, this is a time-consuming process. Given the limits of medical science as they exist today, it should be. People aren't lab rats and we shouldn't tolerate a system of care that just loads people up with the first medications that come to mind. We want the right medications, not just any medication.

All of this can be overwhelming and that is understandable. This is a complicated and potentially deadly illness. The way medication is prescribed is a long process. It needs to be a long process.

Each medication takes approximately six weeks to reach therapeutic levels in a person. Each medicine needs to be prescribed, typically, one at a time. So, assuming my doctor was able to prescribe each medication perfectly, it would have taken 30 weeks, over six months, to reach the perfect medication combination.

We also have to factor in the time it takes to learn the limitations of the disorder. It also takes time to acclimate to the medication and any limitations or side effects they caused. I also gained valuable insight from experience and therapy.

I believe that many people don't realize this illness has to be fought daily. I sure didn't. The first year of my diagnosis, I was devastated every time a medicine didn't work. I felt personally responsible. I felt like a failure. I was sick, hurting, and desperate and I didn't know what to do. I judged myself. Harshly.

Society is already judging the illness; let's not judge the treatment as well.

There are no easy answers. It takes hard work, determination, and patience. Most people with bipolar disorder and other serious mental illnesses will need medication to reach recovery.

I am aware that the Internet has many stories of people managing bipolar disorder without medication and I wish them all the best; but it is the exception, not the rule. We need to consider the Internet has stories of people surviving sky diving falls without parachutes, as well. I don't recommend it.

We need to consider that discouraging people who are sick from seeking appropriate medical treatments is helping no one.

Mental illness is a medical illness, and it needs medical intervention. What that medical intervention looks like is between the patient and their doctor. It shouldn't be between the patient, their doctor, and society.

I firmly believe it is the judgmental, discriminatory, and stigmatizing actions of our society that are making people wary of treatment. Taking medication is a daily reminder of all that criticism. It is a difficult thing to accept and adds yet another layer of "symptoms" to an already complicated and painful illness.

Elephant Journal, 7/13/2014

Mental Illness Q&A: Anti-Depressant Medication Ruined My Sex Life

Dear Gabe,

I recently started taking medication for major depression. And now I have difficulty just keeping an erection. I am a young guy and I love sex and I still want to have sex, but can't really perform. Depression with sex is better than no depression without it, so I'm thinking of stopping my meds.

Frustrated

Dear Frustrated,

This is a common issue for most people taking anti-depressants. For first time users, such as you, it probably comes as quite a shock. If sexual dysfunction is not the number-one side effect, it is without a doubt the number one reason people want to stop taking their medications. For most of us, anything that gets in the way of our sexual needs is quickly eliminated.

You didn't state your age in your e-mail, but you did include that you were a young guy. Whether you meant to or not, you were making sure I knew that the only solution that was acceptable was for you to regain your sexual ability, and that is perfectly fine. Your goal is to both treat your depression and have a normal sex life; therefore, you must clearly communicate this to your doctor.

Perhaps you don't want to tell your doctor about this for some reason. Sex is, in many ways, a private matter. You have to move past any potential embarrassment and be honest. You cannot get good care without honestly reporting what is going on with your body. Society has conditioned us to feel guilty about sex, but it is important to be forthright with your physician to ensure you get the care you need. Your doctor is there to provide medical care, not judgment.

The two main ways to resolve this issue are to switch medications to one that doesn't have the undesirable side effect or to be prescribed a medication to treat the side effect.

Mental illness medications are not easy to adjust to in the first place. Don't complicate the issue by incorrectly reporting your symptoms or not addressing your concerns. Finally, don't live with depression and risk dying by suicide because you don't want to have an uncomfortable or tough conversation with your doctor.

Lived Experience vs. Medical Advice

There are a few themes that come up time and time again in mental health advocacy and the sexual side effects of medication is certainly in the top five. It is important to consider that the way a person with mental illness looks at treatment and the way a person without mental illness looks at treatment are very different.

To the outside observer, a person who is depressed, delusional or even suicidal has more important things to worry about than his or her sex life. But to the person with the illness, the most important thing is living a happy and fulfilling, even, dare I say, a normal life.

The typical age of a mental illness diagnosis is in the early 20s and it is during this period that the average person begins to fully explore sexuality, sexual desire and sexual fulfillment. For most people, this exploration is an important learning, growing and maturing process.

So when a medicine comes along and halts this process, it is a shock to the system. Typically, the sexual side effect kicks in before the medication has provided relief from the symptoms it was meant to treat. It is seen as a major setback and can be devastating to a person's progress.

Factor in a person's—especially a young person's—difficulty in openly and honestly discussing sex, as well as society's general way of shaming it, and you end up with a whole lot of people going off much needed medication, rather than working with their doctors to resolve this issue.

Lived experience with mental illness has taught me, and many people like me, that part of battling this illness is not running away from difficult conversations, but meeting them head-on.

It has also taught us that the medical community, as well as society, can help by providing a safe, judgment-free space for people to feel comfortable reporting everything they are going through.

Open, honest, and judgment-free communication isn't just the best way to fight mental illness—it is the only way.

Elephant Journal, 7/30/2014

Tips for Caregivers & Clinicians

What's the Difference Between Bipolar Symptoms and Normal Emotions?

Many people don't realize that those of us who live with bipolar disorder have a natural range of emotions, just like everyone else. A bipolar diagnosis doesn't mean that suddenly all high moods are mania and all low moods are depression.

Bipolar disorder exists on a spectrum

Bipolar disorder is a spectrum of moods that covers everything from the lowest of lows (major depression) all the way up to the highest of highs (mania). This range is quite a bit wider than what the average person experiences.

I like to explain the spectrum of bipolar disorder by holding my hands as far apart as possible to indicate how wide the bipolar spectrum is. Then, I move my hands closer together to show how wide the typical range is.

It's important to understand this to tell the difference between a bipolar symptom and typical mood swings. In both instances, the middle part of the mood spectrum is identical whether or not you're being treated.

Bipolar disorder and typical moods exist on the same spectrum

Many people believe that bipolar disorder is a different range of feelings altogether. The belief is that the "bipolar spectrum" replaces a person's "normal spectrum" of moods. This is not the case. Bipolar disorder is a widening of the emotional range that you already have.

People with untreated bipolar are able to travel all the way up to dangerous levels of mania or all the way down to depression. Along the path, there are other mood ranges that are out of the ordinary. Moods like rage, fits of crying, or hypersexuality all exist on this one spectrum. Those of us with bipolar disorder access them more frequently than those who don't. We are also, often, unable to control our emotions.

Medication to treat bipolar disorder helps shorten that spectrum and close off – as best as possible – certain emotions, moods, and feelings. Once moods like depression, mania, and rage are off the table, we are better able to control ourselves.

The primary difference between a bipolar symptom and typical emotions

When it comes to bipolar disorder, any mood *could* be a symptom. Any mood that is very high or very low almost certainly is. Extreme moods, like excessive irritability (rather than just being mildly annoyed), are most likely symptoms as well.

It boils down to frequency, intensity, and control. A secondary consideration is cause. For example, if you are flooded with emotion and the urge to cry after hearing about the death of a loved one, that is expected behavior.

Typical moods have understandable causes. When moods start changing suddenly and without apparent cause, it very well could be a bipolar symptom.

3 Warning Signs of Bipolar Mania

I live with bipolar disorder, but the majority of individuals I associate with do not. In fact, my immediate family and my wife don't suffer from any mental illness at all.

If I expand the circle a little wider to my group of friends, about half of them live with depression, but that still makes me the only one who has experienced bipolar mania. All the people in my life are well aware of my diagnoses, and we all care about each other very much. That said, I find it frustrating when every little excitable gasp I make triggers concern that I'm about to be manic.

To help them help me, I've created this handy list of three warning signs that someone is experiencing bipolar mania:

1. Not sleeping is a big indicator of bipolar symptoms

It's important to differentiate between not sleeping well and not sleeping at all. Most people will experience restless nights from time to time. The big indicator for bipolar mania is being constantly awake, very energetic, and not wanting to go to sleep.

Another way to connect lack of sleep with bipolar mania is that the person appears to not need to sleep. Even though they've been up for 24 hours, 36 hours, or longer, their energy level is still very high.

2. Racing thoughts present as rapid speech and a flight of ideas

If you suspect someone is experiencing bipolar mania, listen to them speak. Are they making sense? When I'm in the throes of bipolar mania, I have dozens of thoughts, ideas, and memories racing through my mind, all competing for attention. When I try to engage in conversation, words from each of these will run together in a jumble of words that make no sense. To me, I'm making perfect sense. In reality, for everyone else, it's mostly incoherent.

It's important to ask someone several questions about a variety of topics to truly get a feel for how the person is reacting. Ask open-ended questions, sit back, and see if they ramble on, jump from topic to topic, or simply answer with nonsense.

3. The stereotypical bipolar excessiveness

The stereotypical analogy for bipolar mania is behaving like a rock star. If the person in front of you is not worried about consequences, doing almost anything to excess with no plan or reason, then mania could be steering the proverbial ship.

Excess comes in many forms. The examples that most people are aware of are spending sprees, sex, and alcohol and drug use. But excess comes in all shapes and sizes. Taking unnecessary risks while driving, overeating, and having unrealistic goals are common in people experiencing mania.

Pursuing a hobby without regard to how it impacts the rest of their lives is another excellent example. It's easy, for example, to think that working out is a healthy choice. But if the person in question is skipping school or work to get in an extra few hours of exercise, it could be a warning sign.

Keep in mind that, in order to do something to excess, there will be a level of obsession that is unhealthy. Take a step back and evaluate the person's motivations. If they can't stop doing something for a period of time and are ignoring everything else to focus on that task, all wrapped up with a high level of energy and enthusiasm, then mania is a likely driving force.

Bipolar mania and excitement can look alike

Before you're tempted to diagnose every person in your life who has bipolar disorder with mania, remember that those of us who have experienced bipolar mania do, in fact, experience a normal range of emotions, as well. We get excited like everyone else over appropriate things.

If you suspect that bipolar mania is at play, but aren't sure, stand back and watch for a couple of days. Mania has a way of being unmistakable after a while.

What Does Enforcing Assisted Outpatient Treatment (AOT) Look Like?

There is a lot of talk in the news lately about "Assisted Outpatient Treatment" or "Forced Treatment," depending on whom you ask. Regardless of what you call it, the purpose of the legislation is to take someone who does not want treatment for mental illness and utilize the court system to compel them. Not every state has AOT laws and those that do have AOT do not necessarily have the same rules governing it.

As a person living with Bipolar Disorder, I have many opinions on this. For this article, I want to focus on what the process actually looks like when it's enforced by the courts and ultimately the police –specifically in the state of Ohio.

How Ohio Handles Assisted Outpatient Treatment

I live in Ohio and a new law recently went into effect that allows for a person with a history of mental illness to be treated against their will via court order. First, this law only works for mental illness. If you have lung cancer, for example, and choose to continue smoking, this law cannot be used to compel you to quit. Same if you are an addict with ten DUIs. Unless it can be proven that the drinking is a mental illness, you would be safe from the courts ordering you into treatment to stop.

Second, there were already laws in Ohio that allowed a person to be committed to a psychiatric hospital if they were a danger to themselves or others. The new law took it a step further and allowed for treatment outside of that scope. It made it easier to force someone into treatment, in other words.

I do feel the need to point out that while mental health advocates and groups all over the country aim to prevent law enforcement, the court system, and the corrections system from being a source of treatment for persons with mental illness, the Ohio government created another level of bureaucracy for people with mental illness to become ensnared in.

Assisted Outpatient Treatment Court Orders Are Enforced by Police Officers

If the judge grants the petition to have a person probated, then that order must be enforced. If the person who is probated is unavailable or unwilling to turn themselves in, then the courts must go find that person.

The police are charged with locating people via court order. So, like anyone who has a warrant out for their arrest, detainment, etc., the person with mental illness is now being pursued by the police.

I work for a drop-in center for people with mental health, addiction, and trauma issues. Last week, the very law designed to help people with mental illness to receive compassionate care resulted in five SWAT officers coming into this safe haven to collect a person on probate. Other people with mental health concerns watched as armed SWAT members looked for someone in order to help them. It was a traumatic experience, whether as staff, a recipient of services, or the person the police were looking for. It is important to note, the officers weren't deliberately trying to traumatize anyone, this is just an unfortunate byproduct of involving law enforcement.

It isn't lost on anyone with mental illness that the method of help being prescribed by the government looks fairly close to the method used to apprehend criminals.

We Need a Better Way to Help People with Mental Illness

The court system, government, and the police are not to blame here. As easy as it would be to blame them, they aren't the problem. When I was first diagnosed with bipolar disorder, I was admitted to the hospital (as I was a danger to myself) and when I called my granny to let her know, she instructed me to keep my mouth shut and she would send a lawyer to get me out.

She wasn't being malicious, arrogant, or egotistical. In her mind her suicidal, depressed, and delusional grandson would be better off at home alone than receiving proper care. She was just uneducated, misinformed, and ultimately wrong. However, had she gotten her way, my story could have ended much differently.

Advocating to send the police, the court system, and the government to help the seriously mentally ill is questionable. The amount of trauma caused to people who are not suffering from an illness, upon being detained by the police, is well documented. The court system is *not* a good place to provide care; it is tasked with the enforcement of laws, not with providing medical care.

We need options that provide and promote wellness and that do not cause additional trauma to the very people we are trying to help. The mental health system of care is seriously lacking in financial resources and using some of that precious money on government bureaucracy is ill conceived. There is no wellness in these methods, only force, trauma, and expense. The police and court system should not be tasked with recovery. They should be an option of very last resort, not a solution to a long-standing societal issue.

We are looking in the wrong places for solutions. Sick people need resources, support, and care. Last I checked, the court system and the police did not provide those.

Psych Central, 4/29/2015

Ask Me Anything: Mental Illness Questions About Suicide & Patient-Doctor Tension

Dear Gabe,

My child committed suicide just over a year ago and the anniversary of his death has brought forth so many emotions, especially anger. I miss him terribly, but I just cannot get over how selfish he was. How could he not even think about what this would do to his family?

Angry Mom

Dear Angry Mom,

Of all the misinformation about mental illness that exists in the world, the mentally ill "committing" suicide is the cruelest one. This bit of misinformation strips the dignity from the dead, vilifies people living with mental illness, and bullies the deceased's loved ones.

Mental illness has no cure. It is a disease, and people do suffer greatly. And, like many severe illnesses, people do die. But unlike when a person dies of cancer, the survivors often blame victims of mental illness for their own deaths.

To be clear: the person who has died isn't faking, seeking attention, or manipulating anyone. They are just dead. Their illness was so severe that it literally ended their life.

The mentally ill do not "commit" suicide. It makes it sound like they did it on purpose or that they had a say in the matter. But they don't, really. Their illnesses were in control.

The entire concept of "committing" suicide, as it relates to mental illness, is nothing short of tragedy. Your son died by suicide. More specifically, he died from his mental illness, which caused him so much torment and suffering that he ultimately succumbed to it. It was not his fault, nor was it his desire. Most importantly, it wasn't his choice.

Your son didn't kill himself; the illness killed him. I understand your desire, even your need, to be angry, but please direct it where it belongs. It is not your son's fault for dying from mental illness any more than it is my grandfather's for dying from cancer.

I can only imagine the emotions that you, and your family, are experiencing because of your loss. I have experienced loss in my life, but I am certain it doesn't compare. Please accept my sympathy and I sincerely hope you can forgive your child.

Dear Gabe,

I also live with a mental illness and I find it frustrating that I am always told what is wrong with me and what medicine will fix it, rather than what I am doing well. I acknowledge that I'm sick. I'm not trying to insult doctors, or medicine, but why is the medical community so quick to dismiss the patient?

A Person, Not a Problem

Dear Person,

Your complaint is common in advocacy circles. There is often a tense relationship between medical professionals and patients.

Ironically, both sides agree that this tension exists, although each side is quick to blame the other.

First, let's dismiss the notion that anything unethical or illegal is occurring. I understand that doctors are human and, as such, make mistakes. But for the purpose of this answer, let's assume we are just dealing with a philosophical difference of opinion and discuss ways to "bridge the gap."

Second, we have many different types of mental health professionals. The negative grumbling most often occurs about psychiatrists, who are the only ones who can prescribe medication and, more often than not, have the least amount of interaction with the patient. Let's focus our attention there.

The lack of time is a huge impediment to positive interactions and outcomes. No one likes to be rushed, especially when sick. People with mental illness want help realizing their hopes and dreams. They don't just want a pill or a diagnosis. They want to be well so they can worry about something other than being sick.

Because we have a definite shortage of psychiatrists in the United States, it's common for psychiatrists to spend an inadequate amount of time with patients, so they are unable to truly understand what the patient wants. They have a small window of opportunity to get the information they need to make a diagnosis, prescribe treatment, and move on. The time you have with a psychiatrist can be as little as ten minutes, and you may have to wait months for an appointment.

To make the best use of your limited time with your doctor, write down your symptoms in advance, keep a mood journal, or perhaps bring a trusted friend or family member to help remember questions or report side effects or concerns.

The best outcomes involve the doctor and the patient working together. If you are frustrated at the amount of time you get with your doctor, there are better than average odds that they are frustrated, too. They want you to be well as much as you want to get well.

Both sides need to realize they are victims of a broken and overloaded system and not put the blame on each other.

Elephant Journal, 6/29/2014

Mental Illness Q & A: Bipolar Family Members & Does Society Care?

Dear Gabe,

My mom was just diagnosed as bipolar.

The doctor said it's severe, but I don't get it. How could she not know she is "severely" mentally ill?

Mommy's Girl

Dear Mommy's Girl,

The major symptom of bipolar disorder is a swing between an extremely high mood (mania) and an extremely low mood (depression). For example, your mother might go from very sad to very happy.

Most people lack education and understanding when it comes to bipolar disorder. From your mother's perspective, she might not have seen being "sad" or "happy" as symptoms. It's possible that she just saw them as normal parts of her personality.

To give you an analogy not related to mental health, many people have moles on their bodies. Most of these are benign, but some of them are cancerous. In other words, many people are walking around right now with a serious disease that has gone undetected, even though in many cases it can literally be seen, simply because they don't know what a cancerous mole looks like.

Understanding the difference between moods, feelings, and thoughts that are "normal" and ones that are not goes a long way to determining if something is or isn't wrong.

Understanding the symptoms of any illness is the key to deciding to seek help. I obviously can't speak for your mother, but many people aren't diagnosed with severe mental illness until they reach a crisis point. A mental health crisis can be as simple as losing a job due to not being able to get out of bed or as critical as a suicide attempt.

For additional insight into why your mother may not have known she was mentally ill, keep reading.

Dear Gabe,

I have a family history of mental illness. I have watched family members struggle to get care and be healthy. I don't understand why they are left to struggle alone. I keep asking myself why our society doesn't seem to care.

Needing to Understand

Dear Needing to Understand,

It is impossible to answer a question about the feelings of an entire country. I can't figure out why society worships celebrities but isn't paying attention to mental illness.

The truth is that many people do care about people living with mental illness. I care, you care and the people battling a mental illness care the most. We have pockets of people all over the country who care deeply.

It is human nature to think there are only two sides to an issue. But there are almost always far more than just two sides. In the case of mental health, two factions may agree on the ultimate desired outcome, but disagree strongly on how to achieve it.

The side I try to focus on isn't the one that doesn't care and I don't need to focus on the side that does. The majority of people just don't know. The limited knowledge they have about mental illness doesn't give them enough information to choose *any* side. They are unaware of the suffering, the loss of dignity, the lack of resources, and the hope that is being lost daily.

It isn't that they don't care; it is that they are unaware.

I was born in 1976 and was diagnosed with bipolar disorder in 2002. Assuming that I can't be held accountable for not understanding mental illness when I was a minor, then I spent about seven years in the "unaware" category.

My ignorance on the subject was so great that my failure to act on behalf of persons living with mental illness almost made me a casualty. Two hours before going to the emergency room for suicidal ideation, delusions, and crippling depression, I steadfastly stood my ground and declared, "I do not need to go to a hospital. I am not sick. Only sick people go to hospitals."

I didn't just think I was right when I said those words; I knew I was right. Nothing in all my years gave me a shred of understanding of what was happening. At that moment, I had a greater understanding of nuclear physics than a disease I had been unknowingly battling my entire life.

Hearing about mental illness, knowing it exists and seeing portrayals on television and in the media isn't the same as understanding it. We are all aware of love, but until we fall in love, we don't understand it. And even then, some of us understand more than others.

Our society lacks education, understanding, and empathy about mental illness. The knowledge about mental illness and the people who live with it and suffer from it is almost nonexistent in the minds of the majority. Misconceptions outweigh facts and those misconceptions often lead to fear.

Society will help people with mental illness; but first, they need to understand our struggle.

Elephant Journal, 6/18/2014

3 Things Every Psychiatric Practitioner Should Remember

As both a mental health patient and an advocate, I hear a lot of complaints from patients about providers. Each side sees things from their perspective and a power struggle often emerges.

There are many things I wish psychiatric practitioners understood about living with mental illness. Much of this, however, is taught in medical school and many practitioners do understand and incorporate them into their practices. When discussing an entire profession, spread across an entire country, who work with a variety of different people, it is impossible to offer advice that benefits everyone.

That said, here are the top three things that every practitioner should keep in mind to help their patients achieve better results. If you are already doing them, thank you. If not, please consider adding them to your routine.

1. What Is the Goal for Your Patients?

Whenever I give a speech to providers, I always start by giving the group index cards and pens and asking them to write the number one goal for their patients.

Answers like "med-compliant" and "miss less appointments" and "follow my instructions" are always the most popular answers. I use this to illustrate the divide the between patients and providers because almost no one ever writes "live well" or "go to Hawaii" or "get back to work."

Being med-compliant, missing less appointments, and following medical advice are *steps* to reach goals, along with many others. If your goal for your patients is that they go home, swallow pills, and come back – on time – then your goals are the wrong ones. The fact that many practitioners feel this way becomes very obvious to patients very quickly.

Work with your patients to understand the *benefits* of following these steps. We all have goals in life and you are in the position to help someone achieve theirs. When your patient understands that your objective is to help them achieve their goals, they will be much more inclined to follow your lead.

2. Ensure That Your Office Staff Understands the Needs of Your Patients

The phrase, "You never get a second chance to make a first impression" is important to remember. Most times, that first impression isn't created by the provider, but by the provider's staff. Office staff sets the tone for a practice. Even things as simple as rushing a patient through check-in or not thoroughly explaining the process can be troubling to a patient who is particularly vulnerable.

Visiting a mental health provider can be scary for many reasons and the office staff is on the front line. If a patient is anxious, feels threatened, or feels isolated, and the office staff behaves in a way that is deemed threatening, the patient could become defensive and combative.

This extends to the waiting room, as well. Crowding, noise, and uncomfortable temperatures can all trigger people suffering from mental illness issues and side effects. Depending on your medical specialty, your patients may spend more time in the waiting room and with the office staff than they do with you. Creating an environment where the patient feels immediately safe and supported will go a long way toward improving the effectiveness of care you can provide.

3. Medication without Understanding Limits Compliance

Medication is an important tool for reaching recovery. It's also very misunderstood by patients and, given the confusing nature of a mental health diagnosis and the lack of knowledge surrounding these disorders, misinformation often becomes fact in a patient's mind.

Realize that a patient is not refusing to be medication compliant because they are difficult, malicious, or even ignorant. It's because they are scared of something. More often than not, it is a side effect they are suffering from or a *perceived* moral value in the taking of psychiatric medications.

All of this can be remedied with education. Psychiatric medication classes should be offered by medical practices. These classes would cover exactly what different medications are for, the appropriate expectations of taking them, and the patient's responsibility — more than what a pharmacist is tasked with providing, but specific information for psychiatric patients. People need to stop believing that pills work instantly and without side effects, and that doctors always prescribe the correct pills and the correct dosage on the first visit.

Medications, as all doctors know, don't cure everything. Therapy, support groups, and experience, in conjunction with medication, lead to wellness. If a patient mistakenly thinks that a single pill, taken twice daily, will solve all of their problems, they will often stop taking *all* medications when that doesn't happen.

When people understand how difficult it is to find the right combination of medications, and feel like they have input into that search, they will become motivated to work *with* the process instead of *against* it. Managing expectations and fostering an understanding of the process improves the patient experience and, therefore, compliance.

In Conclusion...

This list could easily be a top ten list. Patients, myself included, wish that providers had more time to spend with us, that the waiting list wasn't so long, that providers asked better questions, assumed more, or assumed less.

We wish providers knew that it can be intimidating telling our stories to a stranger. Along those lines, it can be hard for a patient to remember four, eight, or more weeks' worth of moods since the last visit. We often just answer how we feel in that moment.

It is important to discuss diet, exercise, and sleep with us, because our bodies are connected to our minds. We want you to celebrate small victories with us. Getting out of bed for the first time in two weeks is a big deal to us.

But, more than anything, we want our providers to understand that mental illness can be pure hell. We want to know you are dedicated to helping us lead great lives and are taking our issues and concerns seriously. Living with mental illness means a lot of people in our lives don't take us seriously. We need to trust you, and for you to trust us.

gabehoward.com, 7/27/2017

Advocacy & Working in the Mental Health "Industry"

My Path from Bipolar Patient to Mental Health Activist

Editor's Note: This was written after Gabe was the second-place winner of HealthCentral's Live Bold, Live Now *Photo Contest.*

My name is Gabe Howard and I live bold every day with bipolar and anxiety disorders. That phrase, along with the hashtag #voteforgabe, became my rallying cry for the three weeks voting was open in Health Central's *Live Bold* contest...

...a contest I had *no intention* of entering.

I didn't intend to enter the *Live Bold* contest simply because people with mental illness don't often do well in these types of things. I'm just a regular (if redheaded) guy living in Ohio. I do manage a chronic illness, but not one that people find inspirational to overcome.

Americans have been celebrating overcoming disabilities and illnesses for as long as I can remember. We celebrate someone who, in spite of their circumstances, lives bold. We love an underdog, and want them to win.

We live in a society that isn't very open about mental illness. When it is uncovered in a person, the whispers start. The person with the illness often tries to hide it. When people do find out, they don't show up with food and compassion. Outside of mental health

92

circles, we rarely see anyone celebrated for overcoming mental illness. I thought the contest was interesting and inspiring and overwhelmingly positive.

As a mental illness activist, speaker, and writer, I spend most of my time educating the public. I stand in front of groups and boldly proclaim that people with mental illness are just like everyone else, only with a chronic illness to manage. The misinformation about mental illness greatly outweighs the truth, and that isn't acceptable. I have made it my mission to tell the entire story.

I entered a national contest designed to show people living boldly, despite a health challenge. The day voting started, I took a deep breath and thought, "What possible chance does a guy with mental illness have at placing at all?"

Over the next few weeks hundreds of people would answer that question for me. The outpouring of support was nothing less than amazing. It may be my name on the ballot, but this victory belongs to *all* of us.

My Journey to Activism

Looking back, I had the symptoms of bipolar disorder starting in my early teens. I was either talking a mile a minute and bouncing off walls or so tired and depressed I couldn't move. As far back as I can remember, I thought about suicide every day. I did not see any of this as abnormal, but as part of my personality.

I was bullied as a teenager and had a difficult time relating to my peers. I felt isolated and misunderstood. I did not understand how others could live with the weight of these emotions and not be burdened by them. Many of them seemed happy and I felt terrible and worthless.

The symptoms continued into my early 20s, but no one noticed. Or if they did, they neglected to say anything. The older I got, the worse the illness was. Mania became a life-threatening ordeal with drugs, alcohol, hypersexuality, and taking other unnecessary risks. Since I was an adult, there was no one to slow me down.

Depression became a life or death struggle and my inability to control my emotions estranged me from friends and family, including my wife. As my wife and I divorced, my mental health finally reached a breaking point. I was depressed, suicidal, delusional, and no longer able to manage without help.

The symptoms I was exhibiting would be very obvious to anyone with even a tiny bit of knowledge about mental illness. The people in my life, myself included, had no idea what the warnings signs of mental illness were. I wasn't violent, shaking, psychotic, or acting crazy, so no one thought I was sick at all.

Fortunately for me, a woman I was casually dating at the time did have a working knowledge of mental illness and knew that I needed help. She took me the emergency room, where I was admitted to the psychiatric hospital. It was during that hospital stay that I was diagnosed with bipolar disorder. About a year later, the anxiety disorder was diagnosed.

After I was diagnosed, however, I started to experience firsthand what society thinks of people with mental illness. One co-worker told me killing myself wasn't that difficult and, had I really wanted to die, I would have been successful. People who used to respect me started to avoid me. I had been at my job for over three years and suddenly I was an outcast. I was trying to utilize the resources afforded me by my job to manage my illness but, after a period of time, I was terminated from my position.

Battling bipolar disorder, managing symptoms, and dealing with the discrimination and stereotyping of people living with mental illness is a difficult thing to do. Standing up to discrimination helps bring mental illness out of the shadows. It helps reduce stereotypes and provides society with the opportunity to be educated.

There is no cure for mental illness, just recovery. I live with bipolar and anxiety disorders every day. Living well is difficult, but possible. It took me over four years to achieve the level of wellness I have today.

But I did it and, because of my efforts, I can now say, with absolute certainty, I live bold.

Stigma Fighters: Gabe Howard

According to the Internet, my friends, and mental health groups all over the world, I am a stigma fighter. I'm an elite, mentally ill stigma fighter looking to change the perception of mental illness in a single bound. I, of course, am not an elite anything, but I am a person with knowledge, lived experience, and knack for getting myself into situations where providing a little context goes a long way. Having the ability to provide such information is the true power of all stigma fighters.

I was born with mental illness, hit my crisis point in my mid-twenties, and was diagnosed while in an inpatient psychiatric ward of a local hospital. When I was diagnosed, what I didn't know about mental illness greatly outweighed what I did know. Even what I did know was almost entirely wrong – a tidbit of fact wrapped in multiple layers of fear, stereotype, and misinformation.

It took me many years and many setbacks, but eventually I was able to use therapy, medication, experience, and sheer determination to reach stability. After people found out about my diagnoses, I noticed some strange behavior in the people around me, both in how they acted and how they treated me.

People Became Tongue-Tied

They no longer knew how to talk to me. People I had known for years suddenly were unable to communicate with me.

They Treated Me as a Scapegoat

People were now able to blame everything on me! Is there a problem and you are unsure who's to blame? It must be the man with bipolar!

I Became an Advice Magnet

Before being diagnosed with mental illness, no one felt the need to offer unsolicited advice. Thanks to the magical power of severe and persistent mental illness, all of the advice someone has been holding in is now appropriate for me! Do you have the wrong idea, impression, or love to play on stereotypes? Come find me. I want to sit back and listen to you explain to me what I am going through.

Because of all of the misinformation out there, I honed my ability to explain to people what living with mental illness really means, replacing their fear with facts. I am a mental illness myth buster by day and a stigma fighter by night! Or vice versa – I show up when and where I'm most needed.

I have bipolar and anxiety disorders and I freely acknowledge this to anyone who cares to know. Does owning my mental illness and sharing it with others help me as much as it helps others? Absolutely. There is an incredible amount of value in being who I am, and being secure enough to share. There is a subtle confidence boost in being called brave, inspirational, or amazing.

There is a downside, however. Not everyone feels the same. To many people, admitting you have a mental illness is proof your mental illness isn't "under control." They let stereotypes, fear, and personal bias get in the way of seeing me as a person. They judge me, and often harshly. They see it as something I should be ashamed of.

I know I am changing the way people see mental illness. I see great value in being open and honest and talking to as many people as I can about what my life is like, about what I have been through and what it took to reach the point where I am now.

I am proud to be a stigma fighter and to be on this stigma fighting team!

StigmaFighters.com, 9/12/2014

Three Easy Steps to Becoming a Mental Health Advocate

I receive a lot of e-mail, direct messages, and phone calls asking me a variety of questions. With the exception of specific questions about living with mental illness, the questions most asked have to do with my advocacy work or how to become an advocate themselves. While there is no guarantee what part you can play in the advocacy world, literally anyone can become a mental health advocate by following these three easy steps.

Step #1

The first step toward becoming a mental health advocate is to remove all expectations. I truly mean all expectations. Don't expect to become the next Patrick Kennedy, Pete Earley, or even a well-read blogger like many others or me. You simply cannot know where you will fit in or how long it will take to reach any level.

If the sole reason you want to be a mental health advocate is to help people, then losing expectations is easy. Ask to help at a local consumer-operated service, fund-raise for a mental health charity, or sign up to volunteer for the suicide hotline. Doing any one of those things will make you a mental health advocate. Beyond that, you can just enjoy the journey and see where you end up.

Step #2

Many people, myself included, are not satisfied just volunteering for a local mental health charity. In fact, we aren't happy until being a mental health advocate has taken over our identity. In addition to my full-time job, I am a professional speaker, writer, and a volunteer for the cause. I work in mental health, volunteer in mental health, and use every moment to advocate on behalf of people living with mental illness. People like me.

If step one doesn't satisfy you, then step two is the acknowledgement that you don't want to be *just* a mental health advocate. You want to be a *paid* mental health advocate. There is nothing wrong with this. This kind of work is expensive and time consuming. It costs a lot of money to maintain this level of output. Internet, office space, and transportation costs add up. Plus, we need to eat and pay rent. It's important to approach this as a business. It's easy to get sucked into working for free, and there is nothing wrong with that. However, your landlord and creditors will probably not care *why* you don't have money.

Step #3

The final step to completing your mental health advocacy transformation is the hardest one. Be prepared to fail. Not just fail, but fail *publicly*. I have often speculated that the term "epic fail" must have come from someone watching a mental health advocate at work.

When I was a young and naive advocate, I thought I could affect real and lasting change in a matter of weeks. I would just explain to people that they were wrong, enlighten them to my way of thinking, and be home in time for dinner. I have been at this for almost a decade and, while certain things have improved, we still have more work in front of us than we do behind us.

Advocacy at this level needs to be your life's work and you must learn to celebrate the tiny victories because there is more failure on a day-to-day basis than there is success. There isn't enough money, understanding, or education to change the minds of an entire country overnight. Brace yourself; this is a going to take a while.

Failure comes in all shapes and sizes, as well. I get e-mails telling me I am a war profiteer because I charge for services, get called names by those who cannot respectfully disagree, and a grieving mother once wrote me an e-mail that said people like me led to the suicide of her son because of my position on Assisted Outpatient Treatment (AOT). It is impossible not to take these things personally. The frequent failures, the suffering of those we are trying to help, and our own emotions will often overwhelm us.

The truth of the matter is that if you truly want to reach the highest levels of mental health advocacy, then you need to believe in what you are doing so deeply, so passionately, and so thoroughly that you are willing to sacrifice your own personal well being for a *chance* to make a difference. If there is something inside you that makes you want to fight, you are exactly what mental health advocacy needs.

Psych Central, 5/20/15

The Adversarial Nature of Mental Health Advocacy

In addition to being a writer and speaker, I am an advocate for persons living with mental illness. Advocating, in its purest form, is essentially debating. It requires me to engage a person, institution, or society as a whole and try to convince them that they are wrong. It is an adversarial relationship. They are looking to continue without changing and I am looking to get them to change. There are many things people don't understand about mental health advocacy, but there are a couple big ones.

In mental health advocacy, someone "wins" and someone "loses," right?

Wrong.

Despite what the media and the "winners" tell you, there is a third option. I won't go as far as to call it compromise, but it does represent a certain mash-up of various ideas, concepts, and thought processes. Some people refer to these as "silver linings," some as "small victories," but what they represent is a change from the original thought process to a different one.

In mental health advocacy right now, the biggest debate is involuntary versus voluntary treatment. This has played out all over the country in various ways, and is a component of "The Murphy Bill." I, personally, am against most forms of involuntary treatment, for a variety of reasons. So, if these laws pass, it means I lost, right?

Not exactly. It does mean that I didn't get everything I wanted. It also means the "other side" can claim victory and, since the winners write history, this will be seen as a loss for my side of the debate. But, life is messy.

All Mental Health Advocacy Has the Same Goal in Mind

All advocates have the same goal, even if they vary on how they think this is best achieved. Over the last couple of years, I have met a great many people on both sides of this particular debate. For the most part, we have all gotten along. We are all good people, with various ideas to contribute. We have learned a great many things about each other and, while we have not always agreed, we have achieved a mutual respect.

I do not have a crystal ball. I cannot promise you that these new laws will have all the negative consequences I fear any more than a reasonable person can promise they will have all of the benefits they hope. But I do feel that our open dialogue now, and into the future, will keep us working together for the goal we have in common: making life better for people living with mental illness.

It is difficult not to get angry with people who disagree with you, especially when the disagreement is so personal. I'm not going to tell you I've never gotten angry with someone or that someone hasn't gotten angry with me. I'm also not going to tell you there are organizations or people that I don't wish would just stop it. Because, as sure as I'm writing this, there are.

Fighting each other, however, is not going to make life better for anyone. We need to come together for a common goal – but, short of that, we each, as individual advocates, need to spend as much time as possible promoting what we love, instead of bashing what we hate.

As the great Dr. Martin Luther King, Jr., said: "Darkness cannot drive out darkness; only light can do that. Hate cannot drive out hate; only love can do that."

Psych Central, 8/13/15

What All Mental Health Advocates Need to Do

I have the solution to changing the negative way society sees people with mental illness:

Stop it.

Stop yelling at people. Stop trying to make people feel badly for not understanding our circumstances. Stop being disrespectful, condescending, and angry toward people who don't know what it's like to live with mental illness. It isn't helping our cause and is, in fact, *hurting* it.

The general population believes that people with mental illness are unstable, erratic, and potentially violent. So when they encounter a person with mental illness who treats them poorly, it reinforces that belief. They don't see the people we are; they see the angry people we present. And, frankly, no one looks their best when angry.

I'm not saying *not* to be angry. In fact, if you aren't outraged, you aren't paying attention. What I am saying is that anger is better used as motivation. As such, it needs to be crafted into productivity. Anger fuels action and the *appropriate* action inspires change. What we want– what we need– is for more people to join our cause. That will happen a lot faster if we remember that society isn't the enemy. Most people are just uninitiated. It isn't that they don't like us; it's that they don't know us.

Society Sees People with Mental Illness at Their Worst

Because of the media, pop culture, and the way bad news spreads faster than good news, society sees people living with mental illness at their worst. When I walk down the street on a normal day, no one sees a man with bipolar disorder minding his own business. However, if I were in crisis and running down the street crying because I was being chased by something only I could see, society would notice that. In turn, that would become the basis of their opinion of those with mental illness.

What we want is for people to openly discuss mental illness. We want people to share their thoughts, concerns, and opinions. Because they have such little understanding and such little knowledge, I can almost guarantee they will say something offensive.

Believe it or not, saying even the wrong thing out loud is progress. Don't give them a reason to stop talking. Don't give them a reason to disengage. We *want* them to talk openly and we want them to talk to *us*. We want people to feel comfortable asking us anything. We want the opportunity to change their minds and, if we respond with anger, they won't listen. They will continue believing, maybe even more so, the misinformation they have been fed.

One by one, we need to show society that we are just people. We are people with individual stories, personalities, with hopes and dreams. We laugh, we cry, and sometimes we make mistakes. We are people living with a chronic illness that does not define us and many of us lead amazing lives in spite of our health challenges.

We often assume that people are saying hurtful things out of malice, but more often than not, they are saying offensive things out of ignorance. They aren't trying to be mean. They simply don't know what they are saying is offensive. We have an opportunity to change their minds, to educate them, and to make them our allies. Explaining our anger rather than expressing it opens the door to educating them.

And that opens the door to making them our allies.

We need to remember above all else that we, with all of our experiences, are the best counter to all the negative stereotypes that exist in society.

We can't expect society to change its opinion because of what we say. Only when society understands the truth of who we are and what we advocate for will opinions change.

Psych Central, 6/3/2015

Integrity in the Face of Adversity

When I was younger, my mom had a daily calendar on her desk in the living room. She almost never peeled back the dates, and it sat there for years among a pile of papers and other clutter. One day, when I was bored, I picked it up and read through each day's quotes and one stuck in my mind:

"I didn't say it was going to be easy; I said it was going to be worth it."

I like this quote for a number of reasons. It's short, inspirational, and vague enough to apply to just about any difficult situation. As I look at the situation I am in now, with all the positive potential and all the possible negatives, I keep repeating the last part of the quote in my head:

"I said it was going to be worth it."

Doing the Right Thing Doesn't Mean There Aren't Negative Repercussions

Over the past few weeks, I have found myself in a tough spot. As part of my responsibilities to an agency where I volunteer, it is my job to help prevent mismanagement and fraud, and ensure the integrity of the organization.

In a perfect world, everything would hum along without issue and that position would be relatively unnecessary. In essence, it would be the human version of a smoke detector – sitting around waiting for something to happen and hoping the battery didn't die.

However, the position I hold is invaluable if something is amiss and, just like a smoke detector, it's my job to warn people of danger. In order to do this, I must first draw the attention of others, and then report what I saw.

And, unfortunately, that kind of thing puts a giant target on a person's back. It doesn't matter if you are a corporate whistleblower, witness in a court case, or exposing any other sort of injustice – when you stand up against wrongdoing, it's going to elicit some sort of response. In a perfect world, the truth would stand alone. However, the world is complicated and often the person reporting the issues becomes the enemy of the person they are reporting.

The problem with exposing the misdeeds of people who lack integrity is that they will often say and do unseemly things to protect themselves. Truth is of little consequence to them. The standard game plan is to attack the person exposing the wrongdoing in the hope that this will cause people to not take that person seriously.

Doing the right thing can cause the most stable among us massive amounts of anxiety and stress. Doing the right thing is complicated further when living with an anxiety disorder or other mental illness. Being attacked for standing up for what you believe in is extra stressful because, while the truth will eventually set you free, first it'll drag you through hell.

The Truth Doesn't Change, Even When You're Being Threatened

I can't change the truth just because I'm being threatened. As much as the attacks on my personal character hurt, the truth remains the truth. As an ethical person acting with integrity, I don't alter the facts just because my feelings are hurt.

It's horrible having to watch all I have built be called into question. I suffer the consequences of sleepless nights, sadness, and a damaged reputation. I hear the whispers, field the questions, and get stuck with the negative aspects of having my integrity disputed.

Knowing the only reason this is happening is because I did the right thing makes the entire thing incredibly unfair. Would I have been better off to have kept my mouth shut? My anxiety disorder and paranoia kicks into overdrive, making me wonder whom I can trust and who believes the lies they've heard about me. I watch as people who used to be friends pull away and am put in the awkward position of not knowing what circumstance led to that distance.

During my darkest hour in this entire mess, all I can really think of is that damn smoke detector. It "sees" smoke and it chirps – loudly. It doesn't consider the politics or wonder if it should get involved or consider if the timing is right. Smoke equals chirping and the detector stands by its decision until it's literally incapable of carrying on. Our integrity must be as unwavering as a smoke detector's.

We've all gotten into a fight with a smoke detector. We wave our hands in front of it, open windows and doors, and attack it with a broom handle. And when we finally silence it, one thing is undeniably true:

It's *absolutely* certain we know there is smoke in the room.

Psych Central, 2/11/16

I Have Bipolar and Anxiety Disorders and I'm a Hypocrite

Being a mental illness advocate, blogger, and speaker is a fascinating career. For the most part, I enjoy it and I am quite good at it. I like challenging people's perceptions of what it means to live with bipolar and anxiety disorder, I like providing education and insight, and I like the change I see in people when they have a better understanding.

Openly discussing mental illness, including my own lived experience with bipolar and anxiety, has a great benefit to society. More often than not, the public sees people with mental illness at their worst. The media leads with examples of the mentally ill acting bizarre, being arrested, being violent. In short, they show us in crisis. The common stereotype portrays us while we are at our sickest points, when everything that could go wrong has.

My message is, and presumably always will be, a message of realistic optimism. I don't deny that the worst-case scenarios occur. I embrace them. I own them. I talk about my own worst-case scenarios and all of the many times I failed to be the person I wanted to be.

And then I leave people with the impression that I will never go back. And it gets worse. In my writing, speeches, interviews, and so forth, I leave the impression that I beat this terrible illness and I am home free, free of symptoms, setbacks, and mistakes. One time, I came right out and said, "I don't think about bipolar and anxiety every day. I just lead a perfectly normal life." This is, almost entirely, an *outright lie.*

I Am NOT an Example of Perfect Bipolar Recovery

Without actually saying it, I am saying, "Look at me! I am an example of perfect recovery from bipolar and anxiety disorder!"

But I'm not and, since I don't believe myself when I say it, I can't imagine that my audience is fully on board, either. But, like me, they want to believe me. They want it to be true.

There isn't a cure for bipolar and anxiety disorders. I am honest about experiencing symptoms. I explain I have highs and lows and struggle with anxiety, but I am equally quick to offer a joke, "hey, it's just life, it's just me, and it doesn't affect me negatively." My favorite phrase to help sweep it all under the rug is, "It is what it is."

And when I am well, I mean every word of it. I see nothing but sunshine. I take my medicine, I go to therapy, and I live my life. I work hard to educate, motivate, and inspire. I want to show people the other side of the spectrum with mental illness, that there is something other than the negative stereotypes.

To combat the very negative stereotypes, I aim to be very positive. There is wisdom in this plan; I know this. The media and rumors aren't working to make negative stories more positive, much in the same way that I'm not making my positive story more negative.

Even when I am in a bad way, I will pretend I am not when I interact with the public. I am generally honest with my friends and family, but I keep my current struggles with bipolar and anxiety very private most of the time.

My Bipolar and Anxiety Disorders Aren't About You

Because they're about me. They're about convincing society that there is hope and that people deserve dignity and respect. It's about letting people know that those of us with mental illness achieve great things in spite of our struggles.

Some days, however, I sit alone with my thoughts, staring blankly, shutting out the public world, and only interacting with a few close friends. Sometimes, I cry and beg the universe to make it stop. I get agitated, annoyed, scared, and the occasional suicidal thought pops into my head. The paranoia grips my body and I am paralyzed mentally and somewhat physically. It is the opposite of who I am when I am on stage.

The world needs hope and understanding about mental illness and I want to be one of the people who provide it. It isn't just my chosen career; it is my life's work.

I know my audience isn't fooled. I know they aren't, because I wouldn't be. And because no one – even those without mental illness – is ever positive all the time. We all have bad days, self-doubt, and bad moments.

But more than that, I think my audiences understand why I put on a game face. I do it because it's necessary for everyone to see something other than that standard media version of mental illness.

And if that means I have to hide my real feelings for a time, if that means presenting a Gabe Howard that is, at that moment, utterly fake, then I have to own that. I'll be a hypocrite as long as something good comes out of it.

gabehoward.com, 1/21/2017

Confessions of a Depressed Mental Health Advocate

I'm a mental health advocate who also lives with mental illness. I experience the symptoms of bipolar disorder just like anyone else would. Bipolar and anxiety disorders cause me to feel depressed, manic, anxious, and a host of other less-than-fantastic symptoms. Because of my status as an advocate, I almost never discuss the negative aspects of the disease as it relates to myself. When I do, I discuss it as something from the distant past. I have blogged before about how I have bipolar and anxiety disorder and I'm a hypocrite and why I feel that is acceptable. Today's article is going to be a bit different from my usual hopeful, inspirational, and educational offerings. Today, I am going to air my dirty laundry, because I am depressed and I need to share what that feels like to me.

I'm Depressed and I Hate Everything

The other night, I slept for two hours. Two. Hours. I considered this an improvement because the previous two nights I slept for two hours – combined. During the insomnia, I sit on my couch, mindlessly watching television and texting other people to tell them I'm depressed. Despite my understanding of my illness, I still believe that telling enough people I'm sad will make me feel better. I update my Facebook status around midnight with a polite and caring message. I post a cute picture and type out, "Night-night, smooches

113

on your heads." "Smooches on your heads" is my social media sign off. I do mean the sentiment as I type it. Even in my misery, I still deeply care about others, but it provides no relief to the swirling emptiness in my head.

A while back, a friend suggested, during one of my "I hate my life 2 a.m. text messages," that I make a list of all my accomplishments. This way, when I feel like a failure, I can look at the list and see that I am not. A good idea, in practice, but as I read the list of awards I've won, I quickly come up with reasons to consider them failures. My writing stinks. I just got lucky on that one. None of these awards have led to fortune and fame. In fact, by accepting these awards, I'm an attention seeker, a braggart, and this is proof I'm not trying to help anyone. I'm using other people's misery to pad my resume. The list quickly became *proof* I'm a terrible person.

I'm Depressed and I Deserve to Be, Because I Am Bad

I view this as punishment from the universe. As the day drags on, almost in slow motion, I see all my failures stack up. At work, I wanted to complete a certain task last week and I'm still working on it – failure. My wife should have married a man who wasn't mentally ill, who could achieve something and make something of his life – failure.

I deserve to feel this way. This isn't an illness. I'm lying to myself and to everyone else. This is a *result*. I feel this way because these are the feelings I'm supposed to feel, given what a horrible person I am. I'm a liar, thief, hypocrite, con artist, and I am hurting people simply by living. My very existence is proof of my failure.

The world moves slowly around me, and every sense is heightened to ensure the worst possible outcome. If someone says hello, I hear the insult in their tone. Sight, smells, and even touch annoy me, offend me, and cripple my ability to focus. My thoughts begin to race with multiple, fast-moving insults. I know all my buttons and my thoughts begin to press them with impunity. I'm a bad son and husband, I'm unworthy of love, I've ruined people lives, and I'm a fake. I'm worthless and need to be put in my place.

Feeling depressed is a soul-sucking, never-ending pit of self-hatred, darkness, and mental torment. I'd rather be stabbed, because the body heals easier than the mind.

I only tell you this and write it down because, even during my worst depression, if you walked up to me and asked how I was, I would smile, make you laugh, give you a giant hug, and say I was great. Because, after all, I'm a liar and you shouldn't trust me.

Being Depressed Today Doesn't Mean I Will Be, Tomorrow

The struggle I face (that many depressed people face) is to remember that being depressed today doesn't mean I will be, tomorrow. Not the easiest task to accomplish when racing thoughts are pulsating through my subconscious the way light pierces darkness. In a way, pretending to be happy and mentally healthy around people has the benefit of reminding me that it feels good to be happy.

Perhaps the old adage, "fake it till you make it" has some merit. Or maybe I do it because I don't want to bring the world down with me. Perhaps I am modeling good behavior, or maybe I am just afraid of the world seeing a man with mental illness actually "act" mentally ill. My quest to be a shining example of recovery could have the downside of preventing me from being truly vulnerable.

Most likely, though, it means something different to every person witnessing it. My life is seen as an inspiration to some, as a failure to others, and is totally unknown to far more. Underneath the depression, the anxiety, and all the darkness, there is a little ray of something. I believe that *something* is me.

Psych Central, 5/13/15

My Bipolar Isn't Severe Enough

When I got into advocacy work, public speaking, and blogging, I knew there would be people who disagreed with me and even disliked me altogether. I am familiar with pop culture references to "haters" and I know the comment section can be a difficult place to get opinions about my work.

Much of the feedback I receive is easy to deal with. Compliments give me confidence, disagreements give me knowledge, and insults give me motivation. I am not against any type of feedback; talking to people is how I grow. Even the meanest feedback I have ever received has taught me something.

However, there is a type of comment, criticism, or statement that I don't fully understand. I am not always certain the motivation of the person saying it and I am not sure how to respond. I am told, with some frequency, that my bipolar disorder isn't severe enough.

This statement always follows the same line of thinking: I don't look sick, I can pass for someone who doesn't have bipolar disorder, their loved one was sicker, they are sicker, and having bipolar disorder didn't prevent me from being successful, so how bad could my illness be?

Most illnesses are on a spectrum, including bipolar disorder. There are many levels of severity and many things that affect how severe a particular case is. Being treated, for example, often results in a much lower level of severity than being untreated. Even something as simple as the age of the person can change the outlook completely. But more than anything, the day you come in contact with me can change how you feel about how severe my bipolar is (or isn't).

The day I woke up in a psychiatric hospital for suicidal ideation, delusions, and crippling depression was not a day that anyone would think to say to me that my illness wasn't severe. But years later, after many medication failures and successes, much therapy, and experience, I am doing very well.

These comments are some of the rare instances where I am left not knowing what to say. Do I try to convince them that I do, in fact, have severe bipolar disorder? That I have been through hell with this illness and what you see today is me overcoming a crippling, debilitating, soul-sucking illness?

Do I put myself in their shoes and consider all the reasons they may be saying this to me? It is more likely than not that the comment has little to do with me and says more about how they feel about themselves or their loved one. After all, if I am doing well and they are not, it could be because they can't do better. It takes the pressure off them, or their loved one, and puts it back on the illness.

This is a slippery slope, and a dangerous one. I cannot just go around telling people with bipolar disorder that they all can reach the same level of success as I have. For starters, some folks can reach a higher level of success. I am not done fighting symptoms, cycles, medication side effects, and the like. I want to continue to minimize the impact of bipolar on my life.

Additionally, as bipolar disorder exists on a spectrum, some do have a more severe case than I do. I also have co-occurring general anxiety disorder and panic disorder diagnosis. So, in that way, my mental illness could be more severe than someone with only bipolar disorder. Even then, that isn't certain.

I do my best not to compare my journey with bipolar disorder with another person's. At the same time, I want to send a message of hope, wellness, and recovery to anyone I come into contact with. I want people to understand that, with the right combination of medical intervention and personal fortitude, they have a good chance of leading a successful and productive life.

There are many discouraging stories about people suffering with bipolar disorder in the mainstream. Let's work together to add stories of people overcoming bipolar disorder.

International Bipolar Foundation Online, 6/6/2014

Why Are Mental Illness Advocates Fighting Each Other?

Mental illness advocates are used to debating. This is not surprising as all advocacy involves a lot of debate. We live in a society that has yet to agree on whether the toilet paper goes over or under, so it isn't surprising that something as complex as being a mental illness advocate often brings out the claws.

We only have to look to Facebook to see the anger that some folks show toward political candidates they disagree with. Democrats and Republicans will be in conflict from now until the end of time. And, without muddying the waters with political debate, that makes sense. Those two parties are on different sides, with sometimes wildly different views.

But what about the massive disagreements of people who are, in theory, on the same side, who *should* have similar views?

Mental illness advocates deal with serious issues. They are life threatening. But more than anything, they are personal. The outcomes fill a spectrum from inspirational to devastating. I work in an industry where the typical advocate is either a person living with mental illness or a person who has had a loved one, most often a close family member, suffer from or die from this illness.

Most of us have, on some level, watched someone we love suffer. The most affected of us will carry the emotional scars of someone we love having died. The loss is only compounded by the idea that, had we done something differently, this tragedy would not have occurred.

But most of us have no idea what it's like to be that person living with the illness, experiencing the discrimination, managing the disease, being terrified of what is next, and suffering at great lengths due to not being healthy and worrying about how we are negatively affecting our loved ones.

One size certainly does not fit all, even in the above cases. My mother's experience with me is not identical to other mothers with their children. But family members quickly find common ground. And the same is true for people living with the illness. We find common ground with folks that have similar lived experiences.

All advocates started out on the same side on day one. We wanted better outcomes for people living with the horrors of this terrible disease. But, unfortunately, the fracture soon begins. People take their emotional journeys as powerful motivators, and consider them as inviolable truth. They say, "If I had only had done X, I'd be fine." Or, "If my loved one had only had X, they would be fine."

That may well be true. But personal experience does not public policy make. There is a big difference between the thought process of mental illness advocates and the thought process of people with a vested emotional connection. Let's be honest, this is a complex social issue. In our society, what people do not know about mental illness greatly outweighs what people do know.

Instead of coming together, we fight each other. We don't focus on our similar views; we fight about our differences. And we fight publicly.

Far too often, mental illness advocates hide the similarities, and publicly display our differences.

The biggest fracture is people living with mental illness fighting the loved ones of people living with mental illness. In the community, this is known as family members versus consumers.

The family member side is considerably better funded, at least in Ohio. And, given the public stereotypes of the mentally ill, they have an easier sell: "The mentally ill don't know any better and we need to help them."

The consumer movement has an uphill battle because the first step is to convince the public we aren't all violent and/or helpless. We need to show the public that there are positive outcomes, and that people living with mental illness can and do live productive and meaningful lives.

The mental health community is divided. We should be on the same side, but we're not. Not really. And we are asking the public to choose which of us to listen to.

We need to focus on what we all agree on: the mentally ill deserve care, dignity, respect, and a chance to live well.

This is something everyone can relate to, not just those involved in the debate, but the people watching, as well. And we need to lead by example...

...or nothing will ever change.

gabehoward.com, 1/21/2017

Peer Support

What Is Peer Support in the Mental Health System?

In the U.S., there is a growing trend of using peer supporters to help people suffering from bipolar disorder, depression, and other mental health issues. There is a general misconception, however, about the role of peer support in recovery. In some people's minds, peer support is a *replacement* for traditional medical treatments and therapies.

Before I explain how peer supporters can help a person have better outcomes when managing severe and persistent mental illness, I want to explain exactly what peer support is and is not.

What Peer Support Is Not

When first hearing about peer support, people wonder if or outright assume that these services were designed to replace traditional medical treatments. There's a presumption that people with mental illness believe they can help each other reach recovery and therefore no longer need/want therapy provided by a psychiatrist, psychologist, or other licensed mental health professional. Some people go so far as to believe that peer support is designed to replace medication treatments.

Nothing could be further from the truth. Simply stated, peer support is *not* a replacement for medication, therapy, or visits to your doctor.

So, if it doesn't replace any of those resources, then what good is it? What function does it serve?

What Exactly Is Peer Support?

Peer support was designed as a complementary service to fill gaps in our system of care, much in the same way that cancer support groups were designed to help people living with cancer to cope – not to replace oncologists.

Per Wikipedia, peer support is defined as:

> *Peer support occurs when people provide knowledge, experience, and emotional, social, or practical help to each other. It commonly refers to an initiative consisting of trained supporters (although it can be provided by peers without training), and can take a number of forms such as peer mentoring, listening, or counseling.*

More specifically, peer supporters facilitate support groups, answer basic questions, and provide a listening ear when people need someone to talk to. Because peer supporters are not medical providers – and therefore are not seen as authority figures — most people find it generally easier to make a connection. The relationship between them is based on a mutual understanding of one another's shared perspective.

Real World Example of Peer Support

Peer supporters are being used more and more frequently in emergency rooms, where long waits are, unfortunately, quite common. When someone walks in feeling isolated, scared, and/or suicidal and then is asked to wait alone for a long period of time, the outcome is often less than ideal.

Instead of asking that person to wait alone, they are paired with a peer supporter who not only listens to that person and provides much needed reassurance, but also explains hospital policies and procedures. When the patient does see the doctor, they are less anxious because they have this better understanding, as well as a trusted ally in their corner.

The benefits to the patient are obvious, but consider the benefits to the hospital. Emergency room doctors report that they spend considerable time calming patients before they can even begin to provide actual medical care. Since the peer supporter has already done that, doctors can focus more on treatment.

Additionally, the overall time a medical provider will need to spend with a patient to gain an accurate assessment will decrease, which means others will spend less time in the waiting room.

Peer Support is Not a New Concept

Peer support has always existed in our society. People with similar experiences have always gotten together to support each other, whether formally or informally. As an example, there are peer support groups for public speaking, weight loss, small business owners, and just about anything else you can think of.

It's only now getting to the mental health community because, for the longest time, society didn't believe that people with mental illness could offer much of anything.

Thankfully, that is changing.

Psych Central, 1/23/17

How Peer Support Can Help You Manage Bipolar Disorder

Back in 2003, I wasn't *Gabe Howard, mental health speaker, writer, and activist*. I was a very sick man sitting in an emergency room with untreated bipolar disorder. A woman I was dating at the time had brought me there because I had told her that I planned to kill myself.

It would be years before I would truly grasp what it means to live with bipolar disorder, before I would hear the word "stigma," learn the ins and outs of the mental health system, and become an advocate. In that moment in 2003, I was just a depressed, delusional, suicidal man sitting in a hospital with no understanding of what was happening.

Accidental peer support

Even before I heard the term "peer support," I'd been unknowingly using it for years. The woman who had brought me to the hospital was, by all accounts, my personal peer supporter. She lives with depression, so she understood treatment options. She helped guide me in those early days.

When I met with doctors and social workers, she helped me set up the appointments and explained to me what was going to happen. The first year I spent managing bipolar disorder, I understood very little. I was sick, scared, and confused, and having someone I trusted to guide me was incredibly beneficial.

Purposeful peer support

Eventually, when I started doing advocacy work and volunteering, I officially learned about peer support. It was then that I realized the extent to which I had been leaning on those around me to advance in my recovery.

In those years, I had been going to classes and support groups led by people living with mental illness. I was also reading first-hand accounts of my peers' journeys online. I would talk to peers and get helpful advice about services in my area. All told, these resources were an incredibly helpful part of my journey.

Peer support isn't a complicated concept. Since that frightening day in the hospital in 2003, I have found support among my peers. Find someone who has gone through what you are going through and utilize their knowledge, support, and experience to make your recovery easier. There's no need to blaze a trail on your own; not when so many people have walked the path before you.

Mental Illness Crisis at 35,000 Feet

While on a cross-country flight recently, I witnessed a woman with mental illness, who was clearly in crisis, try to enter the cockpit of an airplane. The chain of events that led to this started in the back of the airplane, where I was sitting. This gave me a clear vantage point to witness a young woman walk from the front of the plane to the back lavatory and attempt to enter. She struggled with the door for a moment and the flight attended let her know the bathroom was occupied and she needed to wait her turn.

The woman, clearly confused, responded that no one was in there and the door was just stuck. I looked up and could see the anxiety in her eyes, the confusion and fear radiated off her as clear as day to someone, like me, who has experienced panic and anxiety attacks before. The flight attendant let her know that the front lavatory was open. The woman started to cry, gasp for air, and whimper unintelligibly, but headed for the front of the airplane.

Mental Illness Can Cause Confusion

This confusion, coupled with desperation and fear, can lead to frightening outcomes. When she reached the front, she started to grab various handles in an attempt to gain entry to the bathroom. One of those handles was the cockpit door.

Since 9/11, people aren't allowed to form lines at the front lavatory, let alone try to open the cockpit door. It is a federal crime and the flight attendant told her to stop immediately. She refused, saying the door was stuck and she just needed to use the restroom. The flight attendant immediately stood between her and the cockpit door and gently pushed her away from the door. The woman yelled, cried, and slumped to the aisle floor. People began whispering quickly, confusion set in, and I realized this young woman was suffering from more than a panic attack. She was clearly delusional.

Keeping Mental Illness at Bay

While some staff was defusing the situation in the front of the plane, another flight attendant came back to try to find a seat in the back to reseat the woman. Seeing this as my opportunity, I introduced myself as someone who works in mental health and offered my assistance, which was gladly accepted.

Much of her story was clearly not grounded in reality. She spoke of an ex-boyfriend she claimed she lived with for two years, but could produce no photos of them together, despite having several hundred pictures on her iPhone and Facebook pages. No one knew where she was, and no one was expecting her. She cried and apologized for her behavior often, saying she was bad. I comforted her and told her she was not bad; she was sick. There is a world of difference. Listening to her speak made it clear this was a woman who was sick and needed help.

The remaining four hours were uneventful. I reassured her that illness today does not mean wellness is impossible tomorrow. Through listening to her, I was reasonably certain her parents lived in the destination city, and that is what prompted her to choose to fly there, of all the available choices. Even in her delusional state, she wanted her parents.

Once we landed, I stayed with her through the questioning that happened on the ground and, along with the incredible airline staff, helped her find her father and ensure she wasn't left to wander the airport alone without help. She was safe, and the part of her story involving me was over.

It Takes a Mentally Ill Person to Help a Mentally Ill Person

I am a peer supporter, a person living with mental illness who has taken the classes and passed the appropriate tests to provide certain services and support to others living with mental illness. No one could have provided better services to that woman that day. Not a psychiatrist, psychologist, or therapist. It isn't to say they couldn't have done an equal job, but certainly not a better job.

In those moments, what she needed was compassion and understanding, but, more importantly, she needed someone she trusted quickly. Peer support isn't about excusing behavior; it is about understanding and commiserating over shared experiences. She trusted me quickly because I was, in many regards, the same as she was. While my "boarded an airplane without warning" moments are hopefully in the past, they still happened. We were able to make a quick connection and build rapport.

At 35,000 feet in the air, on a plane with 144 passengers and a four-person flight crew, we didn't need anything other than to defuse the situation quickly, for the safety of my new friend as well as everyone else.

Psych Central, 4/1/2015

Bipolar Support Groups: Why It Pays to Keep an Open Mind

I am almost 40 years old and have attended many bipolar support groups. Like everyone, my life experience forces me to see things in certain ways – even if just subconsciously. As an example, while I fancy myself to be an enlightened male, I'm embarrassed to admit that I still trip over certain gender stereotypes.

Most support groups – whether for bipolar disorder, addiction, or grief and loss – operate on two basic premises:

1. You must be in touch with your feelings and be willing share them in a public space.
2. You must be willing to change your behavior and try new things.

Bipolar Support Groups Have a Lot of "Bad" Suggestions

The vast majority of what I heard in the various bipolar support groups I both attended and facilitated *felt* incredibly stupid. The most ridiculous suggestion I've ever been given is something called a mood journal.

Remember those gender stereotypes I told you tripped me up at the beginning of the article? Sitting in a room with a bunch of strangers and discovering that a "mood journal" is really just writing down my feelings was a mental disaster for me. I immediately recalled that my baby sister kept a diary of her feelings – in elementary school. It felt to me at the time like I was being infantilized and marginalized.

I didn't mean to feel this way. That is just where my mind went at the time. I thought of my blue-collar upbringing and the culture that surrounds masculinity. Sitting on my bed writing down my feelings seemed *wrong.*

But I did it anyway and, while to a lesser extent over time, I still keep one to this day. Because, as it turns out, mood journals work for me. Keeping a daily record of my moods, successes, and failures allowed me to realistically evaluate progress, show my psychiatrist a day-to-day accounting of my symptoms, and allowed me to move forward in a positive way.

In other words, I was wrong. The very thing I thought was stupid when I first heard about it is one of the best tools I use to stay well.

Bipolar Support Groups Have a Lot of "Good" Suggestions

Bipolar support groups just have a lot of suggestions, period. Some are good and some are bad. Or so I thought at the time. But the more I thought I about it, I realized there really weren't good ideas versus bad ideas at all.

When I first started attending groups, I had decided that if an idea wouldn't work for me, or I didn't want to try, it was a bad idea. This is the equivalent of saying that, since I prefer vanilla ice cream, chocolate is "bad" ice cream.

Although I did not realize it at the time, removing those "bad suggestions" would hurt my recovery. Even though I never used those ideas, other people with bipolar did. People who were living well with bipolar made themselves available to support me or simply give me hope that recovery was possible.

All those ideas floating around also attracted a diverse group of people who all, in some way, helped me move forward, whether by safety in numbers, showing me what not to do, or giving me ideas that I did use. The system isn't setup to give me a single perfect answer.

Everyone with bipolar disorder is a person with their own likes and dislikes and what is stupid to me could be perfect for someone else. I'm fond of saying that support groups are like the buffets my family would go to when I was a kid. Mom ate salad, Dad ate steak, my baby sister ate cucumbers dipped in ranch, and my brother and I ate nothing but desserts.

In other words, we all took what we wanted and left the rest. And we all went home happy.

Bipolar Magazine, 10/4/2016

What Makes an Online Peer Support Group Helpful?

As someone who lives with bipolar disorder and often feels disconnected from the "real" world, it's no surprise I've spent a lot of time in online support groups. All of this was long before I reached recovery, became a writer, or even heard the term "peer support."

For me, it was simply about finding other people who could commiserate with me and understand what I was going through. Overall, I had good experiences in many of the online support groups I joined. However, not all such groups are created equal.

Are All Peer Support Groups Helpful?

When I began my career as a writer and speaker, I didn't intend to start critiquing the mental health community. I wanted to focus on explaining mental illness to people who didn't understand it.

However, the more mentally healthy I became, the more need for improvement I saw inside the various unmoderated support groups I was a member of. Many groups seemed to focus on complaining about their situations, rather than seeking solutions.

I even noticed that some people were playing what I dubbed the "Suffering Olympics." No matter how sick, traumatized, or desperate a person was, someone would "one up" them and claim to be worse off.

In many support groups, the groupthink mentality was trending negative, instead of positive. It made me feel hopeless and sad. So, I did the only thing I could think of and started my own online support group, *Positive Bipolar/Depression Happy Place.*

Can We Discuss Mental Illness Positively?

It's evident that I went a little overboard in naming my group. Depression and bipolar disorder are serious and the name can be a bit off-putting. It's not that we don't take these diagnoses seriously; it's that, in spite of the obvious negativity, the group strives to move forward in a positive manner.

Our mission statement says things a little better:

"The mission of the Positive Bipolar/Depression Happy Place is to stimulate and nurture positive conversations surrounding managing and living with bipolar disorder, depression, and other mental illnesses through the power of acceptance and positive engagement with our peers."

Recently, a conversation took place in the group that I thought really illustrated just how important strong, positive support really is to reaching recovery.

First, this question was posed to the group:

I thought everything was going good with my meds but sadly I ended up developing some bad side effects. So now I'm going to be starting a new one. 4th one to be exact. Has anyone else had this many problems finding one that worked?

Within 24 hours, 50 comments were posted about the struggles of finding the right medications with a mental illness diagnosis. Here's a small sample:

- "Yes. It's been over a year since my BP1 diagnosis and we're still searching for the right combo to treat the BP depression."
- "it's been 14 yrs... over 25 diff meds..... don't give up"

- "It is a hard process to find the right combo, but worth it in the end. Don't give up."

People shared stories of the difficulties and even complained about the process. But there was information and hope exchanged between the participants. The overall focus was on moving forward and reaching recovery. Yes, it is hard, the group agreed, but it's worth it and it can be done.

We don't minimize each other's experiences or pretend that this is easy. We don't ignore the horrors of our illnesses, but work together to eliminate them. The groupthink, overall, is how to give something as devastating as mental illness a positive note, how to encourage each other to move forward, and how to help each other stay in and/or reach recovery.

I didn't invent the power of positive thinking. To be honest, I learned it from the overly optimistic people in my life, like my wife and my mother, who see the best in people and situations. I can't help but find them incredibly annoying, but I can't argue with the results of being open to the idea that we can do and be better.

Psych Central, 9/9/2017

135

3 Things All Certified Peer Supporters Need to Know

I have been an official peer supporter (completed course work, passed the test for the state of Ohio) for almost a year. Before that, I was trained to facilitate support groups and teach certain courses, and before that, I was a volunteer for a mental health charity. I've been an unofficial peer supporter for many years, which is to say I used my lived experienced with bipolar disorder to help other people reach recovery.

Recently, while on Stigma Fighter's Facebook page, a friend posted that she was working toward becoming a certified peer supporter for her state and wondered if anyone had any tips. I immediately thought of about a million tips, but Facebook tends to frown on million-word comments. So I narrowed it down to the top three:

1. A Certified Peer Supporter's Opinion is Often Irrelevant

Many of us are opinionated people and eagerly share our opinions with others. But when doing peer support, it's important to remember our opinions are largely irrelevant. It really doesn't matter what *we* think; it matters what the people we are helping think – and people tend to think differently from each other.

Recovery looks different to everyone. Just because therapy, medication, and talking to my friends helped me doesn't necessarily mean it will help the next person. People reach recovery in all types of different ways and find different things valuable. I like to think of myself as a tour guide in an art museum. It's my job to show people the art, not tell them which art they are "supposed" to like.

2. Certified Peer Supporters Need to Have Thick Skin

Taking fewer things personally is good advice for all of us, but it's very important not to take anything personally in the role of peer supporter. People need support when they are hurting. It's not uncommon for them to become upset and take it out on the person standing in front of them.

As professionals, it's vital to stay calm and set strong boundaries. A large part of a peer supporter's job is to deescalate out-of-control emotions, comfort people when they are fearful, and help them reach a place where they can more effectively participate in their own recovery.

Mental illness (and addiction and trauma) can lead people down dark paths. People are often untrusting and are very vulnerable when they begin seeking help. As peer supporters, we need to build rapport and trust. This doesn't mean be a pushover – no one is saying to take abuse – but it does mean staying calm and setting clear and consistent boundaries without escalating.

It also means forgiving people when they make mistakes. Just because someone crossed a line last week doesn't mean they will this week. Be quick to forgive when people show remorse. Forgiveness and understanding are very importation in this line of work.

3. Peer Supporters Can't Help Everyone

Beyond being literally impossible for any of us to help *everyone*, I also mean that peer supporters can't help everyone due to limitations on what we're permitted to do. We can't prescribe meds, for example. We aren't therapists. There are many things that are simply outside our scope of work.

Also, there will be times when, despite our best efforts, we will need to walk away. There are people with whom we won't "click" and we need to be professional enough to hand them off to someone else. That person may interact better with someone older, younger, of a different gender, or just with different lived experience or personality traits.

Remember, it isn't about *us*; it is about the people we serve. Our feelings, emotions, and desires aren't the goals of providing peer support. The goal is to support our peers. It is crucial to remember that.

The biggest hurdle for me was managing my personal expectations. To this day, I need to remind myself that my job is to meet people where *they* are and help them get to where *they* want to be. While I wish that people were in a different place, or behaved differently, or listened better (or whatever), that isn't the reality of the work I chose.

As long as a peer supporter remembers to put the client's needs first, everything will be fine. If this were easy, the world wouldn't need us.

Psych Central, 10/1/15

Suicide

If you know of someone who is suicidal, please call the National Suicide Prevention Lifeline at (800) 273-8255. If a person is in immediate risk of suicide, call 9-1-1.

Suicide Isn't About Wanting to Die

There are many misconceptions when it comes to suicide. People believe that it is selfish, egotistical, and even immoral. To stipulate, I am speaking of suicide in the context of mental illness. I am not speaking about assisted suicide in the context of choosing not to fight a terminal disease or cases like in old spy movies, where the captured spy takes the cyanide pill.

As someone who has been suicidal and has worked with a lot of suicidal people, I can tell you with authority that the biggest misconception is that people who are contemplating suicide want to die. But if death isn't their primary motivation, what is?

What Makes People Think of Suicide?

Wanting to die by suicide is almost never normal. Most people never contemplate suicide. I was surprised to learn this, at 23 years old, because up until then, I had contemplated suicide most every day of my life, as far back as I can remember, at least. On good days,

I thought, "I don't want to die," and on bad days, I thought, "Maybe today is the day I end my life." But if thinking of suicide is so abnormal, what would make someone do it?

Pain, loneliness, and hopelessness can make people desperate and, in those desperate moments, a person's thoughts become distorted. It becomes easy to believe that the feelings of those moments will *never* improve, and suicide seems like the answer.

As the isolation builds and depression starts to overwhelm even happy memories, everything they have ever done becomes tainted. While the reality is that they were happy before and will likely be happy again, their minds become clouded and heavy with one thought and one thought only: the pain felt in this moment will never end.

I have fought off the urges to die by suicide; I am here to assure you that there are other options.

The reasons people think about suicide are misunderstood because, to the average person, it makes no sense. Our bodies instinctively protect themselves from danger. We immediately pull our hands back from something hot. It's without thought; our bodies do it automatically.

Furthermore, how could anyone give up the chance to get better? The answer is very straightforward: people who are contemplating suicide do not believe it will ever get better.

Depression is Temporary; Suicide is Permanent

The reality is that people who are contemplating suicide aren't looking for reasons to die, they are looking for a way to make the pain stop. Since the depression, emptiness, and loneliness are clouding a person's thought process, suicide seems to be the *only* way to make the pain go away.

The problem, of course, is that the assumption is wrong. Depression, even the worst depression ever, is temporary. The feelings ebb and flow, and while suicidal people may be tired of the cycle, they are aware it exists. Even without medical intervention like therapy or medication, depression will get better.

It is important to remember that these feelings *will* pass. Tomorrow is another day and you need to hang on and fight, quite literally, for your life. Suicide doesn't end pain; it ends life. There is no feeling of relief because there is no ability to feel. But the pain remains. It's transferred onto the people left behind. Many suicidal people believe that no one will miss them, or that others will be relieved that they are gone. Ask anyone who's lost a loved one to suicide and you'll know just how untrue this is.

While it may be obvious to others that a suicidal person has a lot to live for, to them, there is nothing left. They don't need to be reminded that they have a nice car, friends, or family and they won't believe they have "a lot to live for."

Instead, they should be encouraged to fight for *tomorrow*. They need to understand that what they are feeling is temporary and suicide is permanent.

Things *will* improve. It may require counseling, medication, or both, but it *will* improve. Suicide, however, removes any possibility of this happening.

Always take talk of suicide seriously. It's a myth that those who talk about it do not attempt it. On the other hand, suicidal people often do not reach out to others, so it is important to be aware of the signals that could indicate that a person is considering self-harm. Acting withdrawn or agitated, sleeping too much or too little, and reckless behavior are common signs of someone who may be suicidal.

Psych Central, 5/27/15

Their Son's Suicide: "We Did Everything Right."

A few weeks ago, I gave a speech at a National Alliance on Mental Illness (NAMI) fundraising dinner. The event was designed to give different perspectives on the challenges our society faces related to mental illness and suicide.

I was there to speak about living with bipolar disorder. Additionally, there were a couple family members, a comedian who lives with depression, a public health official, and a man running for local political office.

I attend many of these types of functions and hear similar stories literally hundreds of times. As a mental health activist and someone living with bipolar, I'm intimately familiar with this subject. I don't want to go as far as to say I'm desensitized, but I'm no longer surprised.

Suicide Doesn't Discriminate

My speech was first and I told my story, a tight 15 minutes that ended with a standing ovation. I was pleased that I had done a good job and shook hands with audience members as I made my way back to my seat.

A little later in the evening, it was the politician's turn. He walked up with his wife and I cynically assumed I was in for a five-minute stump speech about how, when he's elected, he'll cure bipolar and prevent traffic jams.

He quickly introduced himself. He stated that he was running for prosecutor, obviously was married, and summed up his impressive resume. He was a polite, well-spoken, well-dressed, African-American man. Then he said that his wife had something to say that they weren't planning on saying, but felt compelled to share after hearing my speech.

She told the story of a young man who excelled academically, competitively, and socially. He was handsome, funny, and his smile lit up a room. He was the life of the party. She spoke of her belief that his future was going to be amazing. I could feel the love and pride she had for him.

She told us this young man was her son and that, at 19 years old, he died by suicide.

The room was so quiet, you could hear a pin drop, and I was staring at her like I'd never heard a story like this before. She and her husband went back and forth describing the aftermath of what happened to their son – and to them.

Choking back tears, her husband stepped forward and said, "We did everything right. Two-parent household, good schools. We were involved with our son. I work hard and have a good job. We live in a nice house."

His voice trailed off and his wife added, "We loved our son. We didn't know."

Our Best Defense Against Suicide

And that's when it hit me. I started to tear up. I realized that, had my life turned out differently, this could have been my parents talking.

I could see my mom telling people how much she loved me and how my smile lit up a room. My dad would explain that he went to work every day and made sure I had a stable life and was involved in activities.

My dad is a retired semi-truck driver, a stereotypical blue-collar white guy with a limited education. The man speaking at this conference was an incredibly well-educated African-American man. It seemed unlikely the two of them would have much in common. Yet, at the moment, I could see my dad in this man's eyes. Those eyes were filled with fear, regret, and sadness so deep there appeared to be no bottom.

I looked into the faces of this crying couple as they told a room filled with strangers about their son. They spoke of how preventable this tragedy was, if only they'd had knowledge, resources... *anything* other than the *nothing* they were equipped with.

I realized how *lucky* my family was that I got the help I did and how devastated my family would have been if I hadn't. I could feel in the pit of my stomach my family's anguish, had I died. And as I sat there crying, I realized how lucky I was that someone found me and took me the Emergency Room that evening when I was depressed, delusional, and suicidal.

As I watched the mother and father of the young man who tragically died regain their composure, my mind focused only on one fact: Luck should not be our best defense against suicide.

Society needs to stop ignoring mental health. We should not be afraid to have tough conversations surrounding mental illness and suicide. We need to be just as aware of our mental health as we are about our physical health and, therefore, mental health education should be required curriculum in our schools.

Educate yourself and others. Knowing the warning signs of suicide could literally be the difference between life and death.

Psych Central, 8/12/16

What Does Being Suicidal Actually Feel Like?

Suicide is the all-too-frequent outcome of a complex web of distorted views, depression, and delusional thinking. It's the result of a person's mind operating in ways that are counter-intuitive to a person's natural desire for self-protection. That said, I've been suicidal many times in my life, but can't really explain how it feels because I don't know how to explain emptiness.

Suicide is a Process – of Sorts

Being suicidal isn't one specific feeling; it's more a collection of events that leads you down a dark path. It generally begins with depression, and that leads to thoughts of suicide. Most people consider themselves to be suicidal when they are seriously considering acting upon the impulse to kill themselves.

Suicidal thinking generally involves rationalizing and action. A person living with mental illness is very susceptible to the idea that they are better off dead and/or that they won't be missed.

Rationalizing comes in when the suicidal person begins to think that he or she is a burden to loved ones. Suicide (this sort of thinking goes) would improve loved ones' lives. The suicidal person rationalizes his or her death as "a good thing."

Depression is very painful and it's easy to believe that suicide is the only way to make that pain stop. Suicidal people are typically unable to see how their lives can improve, and therefore see suicide as the only option.

Some people do plan to die by suicide. But this is a lot less common than popular culture would lead us to believe. That said, people don't generally attempt suicide out of the blue. They have been tormented by a distorted thought pattern for some time. Then, in a moment of crisis, they act on those thoughts. The "crisis" doesn't have to be something huge, either. It's often just "the straw that broke the camel's back." To a person in this state of mind, even small things can be overwhelming.

It's important to realize that, while it only takes someone a moment to decide to end their life and then act on it, it also only takes a moment to intercede and save someone's life. It's important that if you think someone is contemplating suicide that you say something to them.

To go back to the question posed at the beginning of this post, if I had to choose any word to describe what being suicidal feels like, I'd pick hopeless. When I've felt suicidal, it was because I felt like life would never improve. I believed that what I was feeling in that moment would be how I'd feel for the rest of my life.

In those moments, I'd do anything to stop that feeling; to stop my suffering. It's irrelevant that my feelings were unreasonable, because they felt so incredibly real. Feeling suicidal feels like eternal hopelessness without the benefit of foresight to realize that things can – and will – improve.

Suicide Prevention Should Be Taught Everywhere

Do you ever wonder what you would do if your house caught on fire? Do you see yourself rounding up the children, pets, and photo albums and hustling out the front door? Maybe grab a cell phone to call the fire department and then wait for help to arrive on the front lawn? Most people don't wonder about this. They have an actual plan.

What if I told you there was an epidemic in this country that is largely ignored by all levels of society? This epidemic is eight times more likely to kill you than a home fire, yet the vast majority of the country is not talking about it at all.

In 2016 (the most recent year for which data are available), nearly 43,000 suicide deaths were reported in the United States, making suicide the tenth leading cause of death for Americans. That year, someone in the U.S. died by suicide every 12.3 minutes.

The effects of the suicide epidemic are far-reaching. For every person who dies, it is estimated that six people will be intimately affected. Scores more will have known the person in passing. The victims aren't the only ones who suffer. The ones they leave behind suffer, as well.

Suicide affects everyone equally and is very misunderstood. Healthy, successful people are just as likely to be affected as the poorest. This is an epidemic that knows no boundaries. Ignoring suicide has only helped it become more prevalent.

Suicide is misunderstood because, in order to comprehend it, the instinct for self-preservation must be overcome. People who die by suicide have already lost their own biological programming to stay alive. One could argue that those who fail in their attempts saved themselves at the last moment. But attempting suicide once dramatically increases the chances that it will be tried again.

Society pays little attention to suicide. Sure, there are whispers. But, ultimately it is thought of as someone else's demon, someone else's family. Most of society is not able to recognize the warning signs and cannot tell if someone is reaching out for help.

This knowledge is more likely to be useful than "stop, drop, and roll." How many people do you really think catch on fire in a given year?

The Warning Signs of Suicide

Some possible warning signs of suicide:

- Major Depression that lasts for more than two weeks
- Loss of interest in things/activities one cares about
- Making arrangements; setting one's affairs in order
- Giving away possessions

The single most offensive thing that is often said about suicidal people is that it's just a cry for help. Yes, it is a cry for help, which is why we should give help to the people who are asking. Suicide isn't about wanting to die; it's about wanting the pain to stop. Sources of that pain include feeling abandoned, hopeless, and alone. If a person is reaching out for help and is ignored, it confirms what they already believe – that no one cares about them.

Another common misconception is that asking if someone is feeling suicidal will put the idea of suicide in the person's head. As a mental health advocate, this one surprises me. Equally surprising is the notion that if a person is talking about suicide, they aren't serious about going through with it. Nothing could be further from the truth.

Talking about or even hinting about suicide is one of the ways people ask for help. Every threat of suicide or mention of suicidal feelings should be taken seriously.

It amazes me that we don't see mental illness as a life-threatening disease in this country. We take murder much more seriously, yet there are more suicides than homicides in the U.S. every year. There are more suicides than traffic fatalities, as well. We tell our loved ones to be careful in dark alleys and to drive safely, but we ignore something far more dangerous. We must have the tough conversations and educate ourselves about suicide and mental illness.

We must be willing to ask people if they need help and know how to assist them if they do. The value of doing so is priceless and will literally save lives.

Psych Central, 7/2/15

How to Handle a Teen's Dramatic or Manipulative Suicide Threat

Teenagers have a tendency to be dramatic. Many of us don't like to admit it, but we were dramatic at that age, too, at least to some extent. Now that we're parents (or other relatives, mentors, caregivers, or friends) to a teenager, the universe is giving us a taste of it from the other side. Most teenage angst is typical. I remember the first time my mom insulted my favorite band. What she said was, "I don't like this band."

What I heard was, "You're stupid for listening to them and you have awful taste in music."

When teenagers get angry, watch out. We've all said things we regret when angry and the minds of teenagers aren't fully formed. Many life lessons that we adults take for granted have not yet been experienced by the average teen. When angry, they lash out and will say whatever it is they feel will hurt you.

Threatening to "commit suicide" is a fairly typical escalation point for an upset teenager looking to lash out.

Don't Ignore Any Suicide Threat, Even If You're "Sure" They're Lying

Our society is deficient in mental health education and suicide prevention. The fact is that many adults don't know what to do when *anyone* threatens to commit suicide, let alone a kid. Our natural tendency is to ignore things that make us feel uncomfortable or that we don't understand. However, ignoring teenagers when they threaten suicide is a bad idea – even if you are sure they are just being dramatic.

There are only two reasons for individuals to say they are contemplating suicide:

1. They are considering ending their lives and are in need of medical care.
2. They are trying to manipulate you and, in doing so, (unintentionally) making it harder for people who aren't lying to be taken seriously.

Either reason needs to be taken seriously. Addressing the first reason is obvious; addressing the second ensures that your teen doesn't minimize the experiences of people who truly need help. Crying wolf doesn't just hurt them; it causes a ripple effect that prevents people who need care from getting it.

That's not okay.

What Do You Do When Someone Says He or She Is Considering Suicide?

If someone says that he or she is considering suicide, you immediately get the person medical help. Call 9-1-1, take them to the emergency room, or take them to the doctor's office or local health department. Do not ignore the comment and do not try to handle it on your own. Mental illness, mental health crises, and thoughts of suicide are medical issues that need medical intervention.

Even if you are sure the teen is "just being dramatic," seek medical help anyway. Suicidal threats are not something to take lightly. Many people don't want to "waste their time" or "waste a doctor's time" with something that they believe is just an adolescent being manipulative.

And they would be wrong to think that. Suicide is permanent. Would you want to take that risk if there is even a 1% chance that you're wrong? Also, a teen learning the lesson that threatening suicide isn't a weapon to be wielded in a disagreement or a tool for manipulation is a very valuable lesson.

So, your teen gets life-saving medical care or a life-changing experience that will make him or her a better person. There is no downside.

For all the manipulation, teenage angst, and dramatic rantings out there, I still take all threats seriously. I'm 99% positive my six-year-old nephew can't get, and doesn't have, a gun. But, if he walked up to me and said he had a loaded gun under his bed, I'd still go look.

Wouldn't you?

Psych Central, 4/21/16

Society's View of Mental Illness

The Benefits of Bipolar Disorder

I am often asked, both in person and online, about the benefits of bipolar disorder.

This isn't an ignorant question. The media is filled with examples of mental illness making people better detectives, artists or creating other "super powers." The people who ask this question are varied, as well. Family and friends, the inquiring public, and even people living with bipolar disorder all want to know the upsides of this illness.

And it's a very easy question to answer:

There aren't any.

The Benefits of Cancer

My grandfather spent several years dying of cancer when I was a teenager. It was a long process and it took its toll on my family. It was the first time I saw my father cry and it was the first time I watched a person go from strong and healthy to practically nothing, and finally succumbing to disease.

My grandfather fought cancer daily and, even though it finally took him, there were some bright spots during those years. Cancer made him humble, it gave him time to slow down and talk with his family. Over the years, he got weaker and weaker and we would all come rushing to be with him when we thought the end was near. This would not only allow us to visit with him, but with each other.

Ultimately, cancer took my grandfather from us.

If I credited cancer for the bonds we formed and the togetherness of family, people would be appalled. They would give cancer zero credit in this scenario.

They would credit the love we share, the strength of my family, and they would see that cancer got in the way of our relationships, rather than helping us.

Bipolar Doesn't Have an Upside; People Do

Bipolar disorder is a terrible burden.

I have suffered greatly because of it and will probably continue to do so.

I have a fantastic life. I love my wife, friends, and career, but this is in spite of bipolar disorder, not because of it. The good things in my life are not benefits of bipolar disorder, but of my hard work, my triumph over circumstance and my dedication to recovery and wellness.

Nothing good comes from bipolar disorder, only negatives. The way a person fights the disorder, the success of treatment, or the togetherness of family isn't because of bipolar disorder, but because of the person fighting it. The silver lining is spun entirely from the amazing people living with the disease.

Bipolar disorder takes a lot from a person. Let's not give it credit for all the good things that happen to us. We earned our success, our wellness and fought through the darkness and now bipolar wants credit for that? All of the amazing things that define us as people are exactly what bipolar disorder is trying to take away.

A good thing coming from a bad situation is not a benefit. I have never been one to stand by and say the benefit of a child dying is that the parents will have more free time and disposable income. While that statement may be true, let's not put a positive spin on something so tragic.

Bipolar disorder is the same way. The disorder does not cause happiness, it prevents it.

People with any mental illness need to take credit for success because *they earned it*. That perseverance is a testament to who we are as people. Our illnesses didn't gift us anything.

We are the sum of our experiences and, while bipolar disorder certainly plays a role in defining who we are, the credit for living *well* goes to us. Allowing bipolar disorder to share in that success ignores all that this illness takes away.

When we spin that suffering into something amazing, it's because we are amazing. We triumphed in the face of despair.

Elephant Journal, 2/10/15

Magical Mental Illness Syndrome

Living with mental illness is a tough experience under the best of circumstances. Dealing with people's ignorance of the disease, managing symptoms, and paying for treatment can cause even a person without a health challenge to snap.

Once I was well into recovery from bipolar disorder, like so many others, I started doing advocacy work. I currently make my living as an activist, speaker, and writer and it is my job to openly discuss what it means to live with mental illness. I'm not shy about sharing the difficulties of managing bipolar disorder or the unfortunate mistakes I've made along the way. Does simply having mental illness make me an inspiration? Shouldn't I have to do something?

Mental Illness Makes Everything I Do Inspirational (Not!)

I've noticed that some people believe everything I've done is inspirational, for apparently no reason other than my mental health status. Further, I've begun running into throngs of people who believe everything they do is inspirational simply because of their diagnosis. It's as though having a mental illness has made us magical.

I watch some of my peers expect special treatment for their illness while at the same time demanding equality. The idea that having mental illness means we can do whatever we want because we are brave and inspirational doesn't sit well with me. I want to be judged on the same level as everyone else. This means if my speech is boring, I get the same polite golf clap as every other boring speaker in history.

It also means that when I make a mistake, I have to own up to it. Requesting a pass because of an illness gives the impression that we want, even expect, special treatment. There is no equality in people making excuses for our behavior, especially when they come from us. If my panic attack damages your car, I owe you an apology and payment to repair your car. The rules of society don't change simply because we are sick.

All Mental Illness Stereotypes Can Be Damaging

All mental Illness stereotypes can be damaging, even positive ones. Even if we use a stereotype to somehow escape consequence, rest assured there is a catch.

The stigmatization of people with mental illness is a multi-headed beast. If a person truly believes that just getting dressed in the morning makes us an inspiration, they clearly don't see us as equals.

While it is nice to be recognized, let's set the bar higher and let people know that not drooling on ourselves doesn't make us inspirational; it makes us normal. Frankly, many of us *are* inspirations for the success we've had helping others and leading accomplished and normal lives. But we can't all be incredible advocates helping educate the public on what mental illness is and is not. Let's be inspirational because we are being judged on the same scale as everyone else.

Let's be inspirations because we *achieved* something, not because we were *diagnosed* with something.

Psych Central, 4/8/2015

Gun Violence vs. Mental Illness: Facts Don't Matter

More and more, facts seem to take a back seat to feelings when it comes to what society believes. This is especially true when it comes to things we are afraid of. Currently, there is a lot of discussion about gun violence in America. We see images of dead children, dead parents, and grieving families and it affects us deeply.

Because we are scared, we want answers, and, since we can't find any readily available, we go with how we feel.

Mental Illness is a Gun Violence Scapegoat

Recently, Speaker of the House Paul Ryan (R-WI) expressed his concern about "people with mental illness that are getting guns and are conducting these mass shootings." But, like most people, he says nothing about the population of people without mental illness doing the same thing (a much larger percentage). And, more disturbingly, doesn't appear to be looking.

People with mental illness can be violent. That is a fact and not one that I have any interest in disputing. But are they (are *we*) the sole issue? Not even close. Violence on any level is unpredictable, despite what the media often says and what the average person believes. The real world isn't like an episode of a TV police drama. Violence is equally represented across the spectrum because it is committed by random people – randomly.

And those people seldom have common traits. One they do share is that they are most often male. Yet, strangely, there is no talk of curbing the "man issue." Because people aren't generally afraid of men. They don't *feel* all men are dangerous in the same way they *feel* all mentally ill people are violent.

So the stereotype holds up, even though the facts don't support it at all.

Mental Illness Advocates Are Aware of Gun Violence

Mental health advocates, like myself, are aware of gun violence within our communities. For example, six out of ten shooting deaths are suicides. We sponsor suicide hotlines, education, and trainings to prevent suicide and naturally, that includes suicide by gun.

If you ask advocates whether they believe a person experiencing psychosis, hallucinations, or erratic behavior should be handed a loaded weapon, we would say no. Because we aren't stupid. We understand that people who are a danger to themselves or others shouldn't be handling firearms. That is just common sense.

Even though persons with mental illness are only responsible for 3-5% of *all* crime in America, we in the mental health community still self-police and promote appropriate and safe standards for handling guns. In order to make any improvement, however, we need the other 95-97% to do their part.

In other words, even if all mentally ill people went away tomorrow, 95% of all the crime – including violence – would remain. Because everyone is looking at people with mental illness to solve this problem, they aren't looking anywhere else. For what it's worth, mental health advocates are diligently doing our part to make everyone safer.

Which makes people with mental illness a very responsible group when it comes to guns and violence in America.

Think about *that* for a moment.

Psych Central, 12/3/15

Do Positive Stories About Living with Mental Illness Hurt People?

I love hope-filled stories of recovery from mental illness. Living with bipolar disorder has led to many instances of triumph over my circumstances and I often write about them. As anyone who lives with or knows someone with mental illness is aware, it's a horrible disease.

Do Positive Experiences Glorify Mental Illness?

As a writer and speaker about my experience with bipolar and anxiety disorders, I'm often accused of glorifying mental illness, and of not telling the full story or giving the public an incomplete picture. Many people — and national mental illness advocacy organizations — believe that the only way to truly advance mental illness advocacy is to make sure the public knows just how terrible it is. And there's no question — these illnesses *are* terrible.

Some of these organizations have gone so far as to tell me that I'm "ignoring the seriously mentally ill" and, my personal favorite, that my bipolar disorder is not serious, so I simply don't understand.

I once made a video for a charity in which I told my story. It was short, less than three minutes, and I started with my behavior before diagnosis, discussed being admitted to the psychiatric ward, and then talked about reaching recovery and how my life was now going well.

As it played in front of 100 people at an advocacy dinner, I discovered it had been edited to remove the part where I reached recovery. It stopped at the worst part of my life — where I was sickest. All the positivity was gone and it played like a sad, hopeless story.

When I asked why it was altered, the executive director told me that it wasn't very realistic and they didn't want to give people false hope. I quickly added that if no one can recover, what's the point? If the only possible outcomes are violence, suffering, and/or suicide, then why advocate at all?

Does Anyone Live Well with Mental Illness?

The truth is that many people do live well with mental illness. For the most part, I'm one of them. It wasn't easy and it took a long time, but I got there. I'm proud of that. All that said, I don't talk about recovery to hurt those who are suffering. I do it to help them. Because our culture loves to spread bad news, I do my best to tip the scales with positive messages of recovery. Frankly, I don't need to tell negative stories. The media and gossip channels do that for me.

I remember when I was diagnosed with bipolar disorder and felt so helpless and alone. More than anything, I was scared that I'd never be happy again. The very first thing I thought was, "I need to quit my job, sell my house, and move into a group home."

My entire understanding of what it meant to be mentally ill was based on the horrible outcomes I'd heard about. Because I'd never heard about anyone getting better, I assumed that meant no one did.

Thankfully, I started to meet people who told me recovery was possible. In addition to the positive stories, they gave me practical advice. I worked with doctors, therapists, and support groups. All of them provided valuable assistance on my road to recovery.

I'm not sure how people got it in their heads that promoting recovery equals ignoring the seriously mentally ill. I'm not ignoring anyone. Trying to balance the conversation is a positive advocacy step.

If the general public believes that nothing can be done, they aren't going to be inspired to get involved. And if someone believes they can't get well, they aren't going to try.

Both of those scenarios are incredibly damaging to our efforts.

gabehoward.com, 5/20/2017

'Normalcy': The Most Problematic Issue with Bipolar Disorder

I believe the most problematic issue with this illness is that no one realizes you're sick.

The official definition for bipolar disorder – a psychiatric illness characterized by both manic and depressive episodes – is, in my opinion, misleading. The general public understands the two main symptoms stated in the definition, but are mostly unaware that bipolar exists on a spectrum. Simply stated, an individual with bipolar disorder isn't just either depressed or manic, but experiences all the moods in between the two extremes.

In addition to having the normal emotional range that every human has, we also have all the moods created by cycling back and forth. In all honesty, I have no idea what to call the five-minute period in which I go from incredibly happy to unreasonably irritated to melancholy, and end up crying.

However, even that emotional mess isn't the most problematic issue in living with bipolar disorder. The single biggest issue that I see is when everything is just fine. In other words, the biggest issue is being entirely symptom free.

The problem with being "normal" while bipolar

First, "normal" is an annoying concept. In America, for example, it's normal, acceptable, and encouraged to bring dying trees into our homes every December. For the purpose of this article, we have to consider that, whether we embrace the concept of normal or not, society has behaviors that it collectively views as normal and abnormal.

When a person with bipolar disorder is manic, society recognizes this behavior as extreme. The same holds true with suicidal depression. Even the lesser-known symptoms of irritability and grandiosity are widely recognized by the general public as abnormal.

As a person living with bipolar moods that travels back and forth along the spectrum, I can say there is a distinct period of time when I am "normal." I'm in control of my emotions, symptom free, and able to fully use all of my mental faculties.

It's during this period that a person with bipolar will complete projects, solidify relationships, and accomplish the typical things that society expects. But, there is a dark side to everything being just fine and having no abnormal issues to speak of: people around us think the more extreme symptoms of bipolar disorder are simply bad behavior we can control. After all, they *know* we can control ourselves if we wanted to. They have seen us do it on multiple occasions.

The burden of society's misconception falls on people with bipolar disorder

If you're living with bipolar disorder, it's a well understood fact that society's misconceptions become our problem. When I had my first long depression spell as a teenager, my father pulled me out of bed and ordered me to go to school. When I explained I was sick, he told me that "being sick of school" was not a real illness. He told me I was too smart and capable to refuse to get an education.

In his defense, why wouldn't he think that? He personally witnessed me excel in academics. He knew I was intelligent, so this behavior *had* to be laziness. In his mind, there was simply no other explanation.

I liken the symptoms of bipolar disorder to an intermittent car issue. Have you ever taken your car to the mechanic and the problem you're having can't be replicated? It's frustrating beyond words, but at least the mechanic believes that there is a problem.

Imagine if instead of working with you to fix your car, the mechanic instead looked at you and said, "Hey, I saw you drive it in, so there obviously isn't an issue."

Or, perhaps more analogous would be if the car wasn't running at all and the mechanic said, "I saw this car running yesterday, so I know you can start it if you wanted to."

There are many things that make life hard for someone living with bipolar disorder, but the biggest issue I've ever faced is that people remember me when I'm at my best when they see me at my worst. Since they don't believe I'm sick, they tell me snap out of it and make better decisions.

If I were always sick, the people around me would have a better chance of realizing it. But because they didn't realize I needed help, they didn't offer any. Instead, they focused on what I could be instead of what I was. And I can't blame them, because I did the same thing.

I believe the most problematic issue with this illness is that no one realizes you're sick. Because, just like the car at the mechanic, bipolar disorder's symptoms are intermittent.

Bipolar Magazine, 1/3/2017

Mental Illness is Not an Invisible Illness

Working as a speaker and writer in the mental health field, I hear a lot of things over and over. Stigma, for example, comes up a lot, as do various analogies for different diagnoses. Obviously, I don't agree with everything I hear, but sometimes I don't realize I disagree until years later. This is the case with mental illness being an "invisible" illness. When I first heard this, I thought to myself, "That's true. Mental illness is invisible. It can't be seen by the naked eye and there is no definitive test."

Today, however, I feel much differently. Mental illness is *not* an invisible illness – and I can prove it.

Why Do We See Mental Illness as Invisible?

The first question we have to ask ourselves is, why we see mental illness as invisible in the first place. What about this particular collection of illnesses makes the average person assume they aren't detectable to the naked eye? Further, why are people with mental illness (any one of the many mental illnesses) so quick to agree with this assertion?

Stigma.

I'm not a fan of the term stigma. It is overused and the average person doesn't understand exactly what it means. Sadly, more often than not, if you know what stigma is, it is because you've been stigmatized. In other words, someone has discriminated against you because you have a mental illness. Nevertheless, we believe our illness is invisible because people can't see it.

Sadly, that isn't the case at all. People *can* see it. They just don't know what they are seeing. The public's ignorance has become the responsibility of people who are sick. It isn't their fault for not knowing, after all. The illness is invisible. Nothing to see, nothing to do, just blame the illness and carry on.

I call poppycock.

Mental Illness is Far from Invisible if You Know What to Look For

Mental illness isn't invisible; it is just difficult to spot without a basic understanding of what it is. I walked around for years with untreated bipolar disorder and no one noticed. Family, friends, and associates all witnessed the highest ends of mania and the lowest levels of depression, but quickly dismissed it.

They "knew" what mental illness looked like and I wasn't displaying any of the signs. I wasn't violent, wasn't trying to blow up a mall, and wasn't hearing and/or seeing things. Since that was the limit to their knowledge, they saw no danger. But the danger was obvious. Just because we couldn't see it doesn't mean it was invisible.

My symptoms were there, plain as day. They were no more invisible than a cancerous mole on someone's back. Just because everyone else sees it as a weird looking pimple doesn't change the fact that, to an educated eye, it is something to be concerned about. Depression, just as a quick example, *is* noticeable. In general, we can tell when there is something *different* about the people in our lives. Asking someone if they are okay, if they are thinking about harming themselves, or if they need help can save someone's life.

But, if we believe that mental illness is invisible, we don't have to bear any responsibility or guilt for not seeing it. In my case, this allowed everyone, myself included, to easily move on from the fact that our collective ignorance could have resulted in my death.

Mental illness can be a like a polar bear in the snow, too similar to its surroundings to see easily. I, personally, hide in my home when I'm depressed so no one can see me. When I'm doing well, the illness is still there, but much harder to detect. Some might say that I am able to hide it so well, and have recovered so well, that the illness isn't *always* visible.

But invisible? No. Mental illness can be seen if we, as a society, better educate ourselves on what to look for. This education will lead to understanding and both reduce stigma and save lives.

It is time we stop pretending mental illness is invisible and instead open our eyes.

Psych Central, 8/12/15

Has Bipolar Disorder Become a New Fad?

The number of people with a bipolar diagnosis has nearly doubled over the past 10 years. There are many ways to interpret this information. Given the sensitive nature of this discussion, I want to remind people up front that I am *not* a doctor, researcher, or therapist. I am a person living with bipolar disorder who works in mental health advocacy and education, and this article is written from the standpoint of how it affects me, a person living with the disorder. In other words, please read more than one point of view on the reasons for and consequences of the rise in diagnoses. That said, here is why I think bipolar disorder is becoming a new fad.

Bipolar Disorder Is Starting to Be Seen as Desirable

Through observation and personal experience, I've noticed two distinct types of people with the bipolar disorder diagnosis. The first type includes people who have suffered greatly. They are people who have had suicidal thoughts, have been manic to the point of blacking out, and those whose lives have been deeply negatively affected. In general, this group sees bipolar disorder as a horrible illness they wish would go away forever.

The second group contains people who feel or think differently from the rest of the world. They have felt depression and have even been manic, although the spectrum from low to high isn't as wide for them. In general, they see bipolar disorder as a gift that makes them stand out, gives them a unique perspective on life, and makes them

169

special. They associate themselves with artists, geniuses, and free thinkers. While they do acknowledge some downside to bipolar disorder, they see it as a fair balance of positive and negative attributes.

At the most basic level, those in the illness group want a cure, while everyone in the gift group doesn't think a cure is needed.

However, more and more, bipolar disorder is starting to be seen as hip — albeit in certain circles. People who see the world differently, are quirky, and possess nontraditional skills are beginning to seek out the diagnoses or are self-diagnosing themselves with bipolar disorder. Since bipolar is diagnosed by self-reporting symptoms to a doctor and more and more general practitioners are diagnosing, this *could be* a contributing factor to the rise.

Some people are being diagnosed not because they are seeking treatment for a medical condition, but in an effort to cement the idea that they are different and special. In these cases, the diagnosis becomes "proof" of their special status. It confirms that they have not been lying about experiencing deep sadness and vast highs. But, more often than not, this is a group of people who feel no need to treat the illness.

In this way, bipolar disorder becomes a positive stereotype. Although, I do need to point out that even in the "gift" group, bipolar disorder is often used as an explanation (or excuse) for negative behaviors. This makes me believe that, on some level, there is understanding that bipolar disorder is an illness.

Bipolar Disorder is Not Trendy, Fun, or Desirable

Since I am a member of group one, I don't see bipolar disorder as trendy, fun, or desirable. I find the idea that this disorder is anything other than a medical condition incredibly frustrating. Because bipolar disorder *isn't* a gift. Currently, the suicide rate for those with bipolar disorder is 15%. I can't imagine the families of those who have completed suicide think bipolar disorder is a gift and we can no longer ask the person, because they aren't around anymore.

Where does this come from? As a society, have we become so jaded that just thinking differently has become some form of mental illness? Can't someone be mentally healthy *and* quirky? It seems to me the two are not mutually exclusive. Why does behaving, thinking, or acting different *have to* be equated with madness?

I see no pride in having bipolar disorder. I see no pride in having dandruff, either. I'm not proud of any illness I have ever had. I'm proud of myself for whatever part I played in recovering from bipolar. I'm proud of the hard work, dedication, and personal resolve it takes to live well in spite of a chronic disease.

But, do I think the reason I had the ability to put in the hard work, be dedicated, and find the personal fortitude to live well in the face of a debilitating illness was because the illness made me stronger?

No. That's literally nonsense.

Bipolar Magazine, 8/25/2015

Why Do People with Bipolar Disorder Lie About Their Issues?

One of the accusations that people living with bipolar disorder constantly face is that we are "faking." This accusation persists in a number of ways, from stating that we are being "dramatic" to being told, "Stop it; it's not that big of a deal."

Most people, even those of us who have never suffered from mental illness, have heard some variation of "pull yourself up by your bootstraps."

When depression (typically the most common bipolar symptom) pops up, caring friends and family will no doubt explain to us in great detail how we have nothing to be depressed about because we have a home, car, family, TV, clothes, food, or whatever else they can throw at the wall to see what sticks.

These hopefully well-meaning people are right – just not in the way they think they are. Many people living with bipolar disorder are skilled actors who are constantly playing a well-rehearsed part when it comes to our feelings, moods, and thoughts.

Where the accusers get it wrong is that we are *minimizing* our feelings and symptoms, not exaggerating them. We aren't seeking attention; we're trying to avoid it.

Why hide the symptoms of bipolar disorder? Simply put, hiding the symptoms of bipolar disorder is common because we want to fit in. Many of us employ a "fake it 'til you make it" strategy or are trying to protect our relationships so as to not drive anyone else away.

It's similar to being at a funeral. The people grieving put on a brave face and try to make those around them more comfortable by "controlling" their emotions, rather than just letting them out.

People living with bipolar disorder know that allowing true emotions to run free would drive people away. It's similar to how society accepts that crying at a funeral is okay, but crying at work is not. So, if you're still sad by the death of your loved one when you return to work, you hold it inside. Because that is the expectation.

Most people don't have bipolar disorder. So while some people will understand certain symptoms of the illness, such as depression, asking a person to truly understand what it is like to live with bipolar disorder just isn't possible.

Like everyone else, we want to fit in and belong. We want to share our experiences, but we also know the damage bipolar disorder can cause a relationship. So we hold back as much as we are capable of, in that moment.

It's the social contract. When a clerk or server asks us how we are, we say, "Fine." Not because we are, but because that's the polite formality of an answer to a polite formality of a question. We don't tell the truth because they're not actually asking for it. For people living with bipolar, it's the exact same principle, just on a much larger scale.

So the next time you think someone is exaggerating or being dramatic or faking for attention, consider all the times they may have hidden their true feelings from you.

For many of us managing bipolar, we are faking it frequently. Because we are controlling our emotions, managing our symptoms, and protecting our relationships. We are, in essence, giving the polite formality instead of the truth. We are working hard to fit into our surroundings.

Even if that means being actors in our own lives.

Bipolar Magazine, 2/23/2016

Should You Tell Your Employer That You're Bipolar?

Bipolar disorder is considered an "invisible" illness. This means that while there are potentially visual clues, you generally can't ascertain just by looking at someone whether they have it. This is especially true when that person is symptom-free.

People living with bipolar disorder who work are generally people in recovery and are, especially while at work, symptom-free. Thus, most people living with bipolar disorder can hide their diagnosis from their employers.

Is Your Bipolar Disorder Your Employer's Business?

The simple answer is "no." You are not legally required to tell your employer that you have *any* medical condition. However, there are some exceptions that should be noted.

- If you are requesting an accommodation under the Americans with Disabilities Act, you must disclose.
- If you have a prolonged absence and need the job protections provided by the Family and Medical Leave Act (FMLA), you must disclose.
- If you are using employer-sponsored, short- or long-term disability, you *may* be required to disclose at some level.

If you are being treated the same as everyone else and not asking for anything outside of what the typical employee is getting, then there is no reason that you are *required* to disclose. This doesn't mean there isn't any reason to. It just means there is no legal requirement.

Can You Be Fired for Having Bipolar Disorder?

There are two answers to this question: the legal one and the practical one. Legally, in the U.S., you cannot be fired for any mental health-related diagnosis that does not directly interfere with you meeting your job requirements.

Practically, it is expensive, time-consuming, and often difficult to prove that the reason a person was fired was directly related to them having a mental illness. Further, there is no definitive medical test for bipolar disorder, making it easy for an employer to argue that the employee is committing fraud. These are realities that most employers are well aware of. And, depending on the size of the company, their legal representatives and HR departments are frequently skilled at protecting their interests — and the company's bottom line.

It's important to be aware that, while there should not be repercussions for disclosing bipolar disorder at work, there often are. There is risk involved and each person will have to decide whether disclosure is worth it to them.

The decision doesn't always boil down to what we want, but the difference between having a job or not. This, of course, translates into having a place to live, being able to eat, and even having medical insurance. Stability is something we all need in our lives, but it's extra important for someone managing bipolar disorder.

Why Would Anyone Disclose Bipolar at Work?

There are benefits to disclosing one's bipolar disorder at work. For example, educating your employer may make your work environment less stressful. It could help your employer account for any changes in your behavior. Also, having knowledge of your condition may enable your employer to assist you in the day-to-day management.

For many, myself included, it feels wrong to not disclose. The secret can feel like a burden. In my case, I felt like I couldn't connect with the people around me because I was having to constantly police my words and actions. I was terrified of the truth being discovered and it was exhausting. Every day, while at work, I was terrified that this was going to be the day I was found out.

I disclosed to my employer because, for me, the pros outweigh the cons. I wanted to be myself everywhere, including during work hours. I couldn't live with the fear of being "found out," and I wanted to be an advocate and show society what someone with my illness can achieve. I found an employer that worked with me and is supportive. Other employers weren't so supportive, and that made it difficult. Fortunately, I was able to find a good arrangement that works for both me and the organization I work for.

Even with the risks, I believe that living openly with bipolar disorder is a powerful thing and will help make life easier for those who haven't yet been diagnosed. It isn't always easy, but it was the right choice for me.

Can a Person with a Bipolar Spouse Win a Presidential Election?

As the primary season winds on, many conversations about who is – and who isn't – electable continue to dominate the news cycle as well as interpersonal conversations. We, as a society, should probably be focusing on the issues that most affect our lives, but we're not. As a general rule, my friends, family, and I don't spend a lot of time discussing politics. It isn't that we aren't political people, it's just that we all make up our minds on our own and either already agree with one another or we are willing to bare knuckle box to defend our positions.

What we do discuss a lot is living with bipolar disorder and what that truly means. The other day, someone said to me (and I'm doing my best to quote exactly), "Man, your wife could never be president. America would never be okay electing someone married to an actual crazy person."

Is Being Married to Someone with Bipolar a Political Liability?

At first, I dismissed him. Poppycock, I thought. I've certainly faced a lot of stigma and discrimination, being so open about my illness, but that won't extend to my wife. After all, bipolar disorder isn't catching. After a couple well placed verbal jabs, he clarified his position further by stating that my bipolar disorder is a bigger barrier to the presidency for her than anything else he can think of.

I looked at him, startled. Listen, I'm not naïve. I understand that a person with a history of mental illness has about as much chance of becoming president as my dog – and I don't have a dog. But, given the overall role of the spouse of a president, what difference does it make what illness I may, or may not, have?

The discussion went on for a bit. It is, of course, nearly impossible to quantify what is truly a political liability. Back in 2007, for example, many people were positive that an African-American could not rise to the highest office, and then Senator Obama's race was considered too big of a political liability to overcome.

As the discussion went on, my friend brought up the criticism faced by presidential hopeful Ted Cruz's wife for suffering from depression — over ten years ago. I learned, via Google, that Mr. Cruz's campaign felt the need to explain what her issues may – or may not – be. I was sort of dumbfounded. Is this even remotely relevant? I'm curious as to Mr. Cruz's blood pressure – is it high? Do the American people have a right to know?

Politically Speaking, Would You Rather Be Married to a Bipolar or .. ?

My wife has zero political ambitions and is under the age of 35, so I'm currently not preventing her from being the President. I do worry that my openness about living with bipolar disorder will hold her back. It has already caused her a problem or two, inter-personally.

Mostly, though, it has been smooth sailing. She came into our marriage with her eyes open because I made sure she understood the consequences of being married to a person with a chronic illness – and one that has so much stigma attached to it.

Still, I never thought that, because of me, she couldn't be president. I certainly never thought that my having bipolar disorder would be seen by the country as a reason my wife wouldn't be a good leader. I'm still stuck on the idea that my illness has any bearing at all on her job performance.

This discussion was, of course, completely hypothetical. But, the best discussions often are. I want to be clear that I don't care about the gender, race, sexuality, age, or fashion choices of the president, or their spouses (or lack thereof). The purpose of this article isn't to support or criticize any candidate. Frankly, I wish them all well and encourage everyone to vote for the person they feel is most qualified.

As my friend and I continued to verbally spar, we realized that, ultimately, our discussion boiled down to one basic question:"How much of a political liability is a spouse's mental illness?"

And, what does the answer say about the state of mental health advocacy in our country?

Bipolar Magazine, 4/5/2016

What People Living with Mental Illness Fear

At least once a week, I stand up in front of a group of people, most often strangers, and say, "My name is Gabe Howard and I have a mental illness." Sometimes I mix it up, to prevent my own boredom, and say I have bipolar and anxiety disorders, but the single message is always the same: I publicly confess to having mental illness, which is a disorder most people not only don't understand, but actively fear.

I have been called brave and people shake my hand, give me hugs, pats on the back, and tell me that I have given them valuable insight, hope, and understanding. It is a wonderful feeling, and one of my primary motivators, but even with all of that, it doesn't come close to erasing my fear about living with mental illness.

In order to fight my fear of being mentally ill, I do have to be brave. As a person living with mental illness, I am afraid. I fear for myself because the reality of relapse, pain, suffering, and even death is very real.

Fear of How Society Reacts to Mental Illness

When you consider the very public debate over involuntary treatment, the undermining of privacy rights, and the elimination of due process, it is easy to see why I am afraid. The outcomes of these debates have very real, and potentially negative, consequences on my life.

Society openly talking about what is best for me, as if I have nothing to offer the conversation, is frightening. There are countless stories of people just like me being denied jobs, services, freedoms, and opportunities because of an illness we didn't ask for and absolutely don't want.

The media uses people like us as scapegoats for violence, disruption, and chaos, and this misinformation causes my friends and neighbors to worry about what I, and others with mental illness, might do. While the vast majority of people with mental illness do nothing wrong and lead normal lives, we are held accountable for the small percentage that does.

Everywhere I look, the loudest voices for mental illness advocacy are not people living with the illness. They are the friends and family members of people with mental illness. They are concerned community members, politicians, and directors of mental health charities. More often than not, they are people who have been affected, often negatively, by others living with mental illness, not suffering themselves. The conversation, for the moment, is heavily slanted to what can be done *about* the mentally ill, instead of what can be done *for* us.

We Need to Fight Mental Illness; Not People

People with mental illness are *not* problems to be dealt with. We, as people, are not the problem; the illness is the problem. And, make no mistake, our illness is a nasty one. But society is blaming people for having mental illness instead of trying to provide treatment for it. The conversation is going in the wrong direction. This should not be a debate about how to protect society from persons living with mental illness, but a debate on how to help the people living with mental illness reach recovery.

We should be preventing suicide, providing education, providing treatment, and approaching the mentally ill as people with an illness. Far too often, the debate focuses on how society can make a person with mental illness do what society thinks they should do.

Treatment and medical intervention are often incorrectly seen as the goals for people living with mental illness, rather than the mentally ill having an equal quality of life as those without mental illness.

Mental illness takes so much from a person. Please, don't allow it to trick society into taking our humanity as well.

gabehoward.com, 1/21/2017

Santa Claus as an Analogy for Bipolar Mania

I love the Christmas season. The lights, the tackiness, and amazing stories of a fat man flying through the night sky all make me smile. I love that cutting down a tree, dragging it into my house, and putting lights and baubles on it is not only acceptable this time of year, but encouraged.

It occurred to me the other day that the Christmas season, in all its grandiosity, is the best analogy for mania I've ever thought of. As someone who lives with and writes about bipolar disorder, I am always on the hunt for the perfect way to help people without bipolar disorder understand the various aspects of living with this illness.

Bipolar mania is a particularly hard one to explain. It would be easy to say that, at its core, mania is simply being "too happy." But that isn't accurate, just as it's not accurate to say that depression, at its core, is simply being "too sad." Either way, simple explanations really don't offer much in the way of understanding. Hence, analogies and longer explanations were born.

What Do Christmas and Bipolar Mania Have in Common?

The Christmas season and bipolar mania have quite a lot in common. Think about all of the extravagant traditions we love. The base premise, from a purely non-religious viewpoint, is that a jolly fat man delivers presents to children all over the world in a single night.

183

But, let's not be stupid about this, he can't do it alone. He has an army of helpers – elves – who work around the clock at amazing speed to assemble all the gifts. He obviously can't walk to every child's home, needing much faster transportation, so he enlisted the aid of reindeer. Specifically, magical flying reindeer that pull a sled big enough to hold all the gifts.

It goes on from there because Santa is no fool. He expects all of us to carry our weight. First, all the children have to be nice. And Mr. Claus knows if you've been bad or good. (During the rest of the year, I suspect he works for the NSA.) In addition to being good, the children must decorate a dead (or fake) pine tree, hang stockings by the chimney with care, and it doesn't hurt to put a couple hundred lights on the outside of your house. Finally, on Christmas Eve, you must remember to put out cookies and milk for Santa – and, for bonus points, the reindeer like carrot sticks.

Everything from the sparkling lights to the magnificent story of Santa to the majestically tacky decorations makes up the splendor which is Christmas. And I love Christmas with all my heart.

It's utterly ridiculous and its grandiosity knows no bounds. Each story is more glorious than the last and we celebrate the awe-inspiring nature of the entire season. We buy into the stories and we act them out. Those who love it most triple their utility bills with decorations only an electrical engineer and an artist could pull off. We sing, we laugh, and we "believe" in the magic that is Santa Claus.

Most of all, we love it. We love all of it because it's fun and amazing and an escape from the pressures of the real world. We play along with our friends and family because we know, deep down, that this is all make believe. Santa, his reindeer, and his magical elves all live in our collective imaginations.

And we all love it, together. Bipolar mania is like the entire Christmas season, in all its grandiosity and amazement. It's a fun, joyous, and magical celebration for everyone. Much in the same way mania is seen by bystanders as exciting, the people following along and celebrating are excited to be part of it. Everyone is having fun – *almost* exactly like the person who is actually manic.

But, unlike all the people around them, manic people don't know it isn't real. They aren't pretending to believe in Santa Claus and there is no recognition that this is all in fun. By the time they realize it's all just amusement and make-believe, it's already too late.

And that is why bipolar mania feels amazing while causing incredible amounts of damage. You can wait all you want for Santa to come down the chimney, but he won't. Because feelings don't make things real.

No matter how much we believe they will.

Bipolar Magazine, 12/15/2015

Crying, Depression, and Being a Man

Society has the backward notion that men aren't supposed to cry, even when depressed. Sure, men get a pass at their daughter's wedding or the funeral of a loved one, but even then we are expected to cry in a manly way. We are expected to choke back the tears and fight the emotions instead of displaying them. This denial of our basic emotions does nothing to make things better and, in fact, makes things worse. Now we have the emotions we are feeling *and* guilt about our reaction.

Even as I write this, I want to tell you I am a 275 pound, six-foot-three-inch tall, *big* guy. I feel the need to tell you my favorite sport is hockey. I watch boxing, UFC (mixed martial arts), and football. I play the drums, and I was raised in a blue-collar neighborhood by a father who drives an 18-wheeled semi-truck.

I also swear a lot, once writing a blog called "Mental Illness is an Asshole." I'm telling you this because society has conditioned me to convince you that I am still a "man," even though I just admitted to crying. That is how deep this goes.

Society Says as a Man I'm Not Supposed to Cry

It is okay for *everyone* to cry. It's a smart idea, too. To think that crying somehow makes a guy less of a "man" is utter nonsense.

To be clear, I am saying that even though I am a man – and in many ways a stereotypical man – depression makes me cry and beg for help. Literally cry. Not quiet sobs with a couple streaming lines

186

of tears, but full-fledged, whole body wailing, with snot streaming from my nose, tears blurring my vision, and guttural sounds that can only be described as coming from the darkest pits of my soul. I'm saying that is not only okay, but recommended.

Unfortunately, a lifetime of social conditioning prevents me from publicly crying in any way other than the aforementioned, manly-approved way. I need to change that, but at least I am able to cry alone and in front of people I love.

I'm a man and I cry. Not honoring my basic human emotions would make the isolation of depression so much worse. When I am depressed, I hide, but need people. When I am crying, I hide out of a backward sense of self-preservation. The end result is the same: I am alone, crying like a *<fill in inappropriate stereotype here>*, and sinking deeper and deeper into the abyss.

Depression is ugly and crying isn't the worst part. There are so many stages below crying. I'm not writing an article about how I am a man who cries because I woke up with the desire to open myself up to ridicule. I'm specifically writing this blog to tell men that being able to cry – period – is a good thing. In fact, it is a powerful thing.

Crying is a natural way to reduce emotional stress that, left unchecked, has negative physical effects on a person. Yes, even men. Allowing ourselves to experience our natural response has immense value, as well. Crying releases tension, lowers blood pressure, and stimulates production of endorphins (natural pain-relievers). In short, crying makes someone feel better. Owning all my emotions and asking for help were, even in retrospect, two of the most powerful weapons I had to beat depression and, in the worst cases, stay alive.

I didn't reach recovery from bipolar disorder (including the depression) and anxiety disorder in a way that was pretty or spectacular. Crying was, and is, part of the equation. Crying simply means a person is experiencing a strong emotion – and nothing more.

Psych Central, 7/16/15

That's Not Bipolar

In my role as a mental illness speaker and blogger, I receive a lot of comments and questions. The one item that stands out is that there is a lot of confusion over what bipolar disorder is and what it isn't.

Many folks believe that bipolar disorder is just a more socially acceptable form of depression. Many people who have experienced severe depression do return to a "normal" state and are then happy. Why isn't that bipolar? Bipolar disorder isn't described as multiple mood states. Bipolar disorder is, specifically, cycling through extreme lows to extreme highs, from suicidal feelings to a high that is well beyond "regular" happiness and falls into the range of clinical psychiatric disorders.

Bipolar disorder can be a confusing illness because it encompasses so many things. It mirrors major depression, as an example, because that is the "low." The difference between major depression and the bipolar low is that bipolar disorder also contains a "high," which is clinically described as mania. It is the "high" that causes people to arch an eyebrow in my general direction. "What do you mean you are too happy?"

It isn't the feeling of mania that is the issue. Truthfully, mania feels fantastic. I describe it as a consequence-free environment, with no burden of thinking how decisions I make today will impact other people or how I'll feel about them tomorrow. This freedom feels euphoric and, frankly, pretty damn good. But while mania feels consequence-free, it isn't. It is the bipolar equivalent of saying, "Speeding never killed anyone; stopping did."

The highs and lows of bipolar disorder are not dished out in equal doses. When I was untreated, I was manic around a quarter of the time, relatively "normal" 50% of the time, and severely depressed the rest of the time. Depending on when you came in contact with me, you would consider me happy-go-lucky, laid back, or a total downer.

And even within the various mood states, there is a variance. I have been depressed, seriously depressed, and I have been suicidal, all of which are markers that are considered, diagnostically, as depression, but are incredibly different feelings.

Bipolar disorder is difficult to understand. This shouldn't be all that surprising, as it is a complicated web of feelings, emotions, and symptoms. The journey between my lowest points and my highest points is a long one and one that I have trouble fully comprehending, myself. So I completely understand when my friends and family have a hard time grasping it.

It would be nice if bipolar disorder were easier to explain. It would be equally nice if bipolar disorder were better understood by both those diagnosed with the disease and those around us. Every conversation is an opportunity to educate others. And, like the illness itself, some of the conversation will make us feel low and some will make us feel high.

International Bipolar Foundation Online, 5/1/2014

Depression & Anger

What Does Depression Feel Like?

I've lived with depression my entire life. As far back as I can remember, I thought about suicide every day. On good days, I decided that I wouldn't commit suicide and on bad days, I would think about how I would do it.

When I was younger, I didn't realize this was abnormal. I assumed everyone thought about suicide daily. I just thought it was part of the human experience to weigh the pros and cons of living on an ongoing basis. I did recognize that I was sad — mostly because I recognized that others were happy.

I didn't know I was depressed, however. I just thought I was bad at life. I believed that I just hadn't found what I needed to be happy. I spent the first 25 years of my life feeling as if I was always one step away from happiness.

All of the accomplishments that I thought would make me happy didn't. They would provide temporary happiness, of course, but a couple weeks of feeling as if I was on top of the world would quickly decline into depression. When that would happen, I'd just choose a new something I needed in order to be happy.

In many ways, depression is like running on a treadmill. It takes a great deal of effort — along with a physical and mental toll — but you don't get anywhere. But, unlike when on a treadmill, you don't have any positive outcomes. No calories burned or smaller waistline. Just frustration.

It's difficult to explain depression to someone because it feels like emptiness. Depression is best described as feeling completely numb, rather than feeling badly. And for people with chronic depression, it feels normal, because chronic depression has a way of wrapping itself around a person and taking control of all emotions.

It feels like swimming with someone who is trying to pull you under and not being sure you care whether they are successful. At first, you try to swim away, but after a while, you become comforted by the fact they are there.

You start to relate to the person trying to drown you and wonder if they are right to pull you under. Subconsciously, you start swimming in areas where it's easier for them to grab your ankle. The fact that they are trying to harm you becomes irrelevant, because you're so used to that feeling that you can't function without it.

I don't know that depression can ever truly be understood by someone who hasn't experienced it first-hand. When I'm depressed, I see no way forward. It's an all-encompassing killer of emotions.

Depression is not darkness without hope for light. Depression is being pulled into darkness and forgetting that light ever existed.

Psych Central, 2/25/2017

How Does Depression Make Me Feel?

I don't want to be depressed. It feels weird that I need to say that, but sometimes I have to remind people, myself included, that I didn't choose this feeling — if "feeling" is even the right word.

"Disorder" or "disease" would be more accurate, but even I have trouble accepting depression as an extrinsic influence. I've had it, off and on, my entire life. It's like an absentee parent who shows up to be disruptive and tell me the parent who stuck around is bad.

I've accepted it so thoroughly that it really feels more like a personality trait. It's as seamless in my mind as my sense of humor. It's just there. And, on some level, it is a personality trait. People know that I'm "prone to depression" or that I "get this way, sometimes." And I agree with them.

Depression Isn't Sadness

I'm not "sad." Depression isn't a "sad feeling." Sadness has a specific cause and people experiencing sadness can be cheered up. Sadness is a feeling. Depression is not. In many cases, it's a complete void of emotion. The worst depression I've ever experienced is as close to being unconscious as I believe a person can get and still be awake.

Depression exists from mild to severe, and all points between. All depression is debilitating and takes a toll on the sufferer.

Depression Makes Me Feel Trapped

Depression attacks on all fronts. It takes away my ability to care about anything or anyone – including myself. While technically alive, my mind might as well be dead to me. Involuntary actions continue, like breathing, but depression takes control of the voluntary functions.

I can still think about what I want to do, but become powerless to actually do it. I am aware that I need to go to work, and aware of the consequences of not going, but I just can't do it. Not physically or mentally.

Depression strips out rational thoughts and replaces them with lies and twisted truths. Our brains hold everything about us: our fears, our pasts, and our desires. All of that is warped and used to convince me that I'm utterly worthless and no one cares about me. Depression tells me that my very existence is meaningless.

As the depression consumes me, I use all the mental resources I can muster to hold on. I somehow have to find the light in blackness and a way to go mentally toward it so that I can physically follow. I can't give up; because this is the only me there will ever be and I have to hold on to the idea that I have some sort of purpose.

I have to remember that the mind pulling me into the darkness is the same one I'm going to use to pull me out of it. If it has the power to hurt me, it has the power to save me.

As long as I'm alive, I'm winning.

Psych Central, 6/21/16

Does Depression Physically Hurt?

Over the past couple months, I've been suffering from depression. I'm managing, but it takes a mental toll. People aren't surprised to learn about the mental effects of depression. After all, it's a mental illness.

What people are surprised to learn – and I often forget – is that depression is physically painful. I'm not speaking in analogies, either. Depression literally hurts. Anyone who has experienced depression already understands this, but for the rest of you, I will explain.

Depression Has Physical Symptoms

Emotions – all emotions – have physical sensations. Folks experiencing joy often laugh and the term "belly laugh" isn't just something people say; it's a literal description. People experiencing extreme sadness often cry. Finally, being nervous can lead to butterflies taking up residence in your stomach.

Depression is serious and, unlike the common mythology, it's far from all in someone's head. During a depressive episode, a person's body becomes heavy and movement very difficult. I've described it as running in concrete shoes, except no one can see the shoes.

Aside from extreme lethargy, other side effects of depression can include insomnia or excess sleeping. Both are equally disruptive to a person's physical health. Our culture doesn't give sleep the respect it deserves, and we've all succumbed to the effects of poor sleep hygiene at some point in our lives.

Co-Occurring Symptoms of Depression

Depression's primary symptom slows down peoples' thinking and makes them believe they are worthless. Those in this state often make poor decisions when it comes to eating, hygiene, and general self-care.

While not technically a symptom of depression, attempting to exist on a diet of cupcakes, chips, and soda isn't a healthy choice and carries with it unpleasant physical consequences.

Additionally, per the CDC, 48% of women and 40% of men with severe depression smoke cigarettes. Nearly twice as many depressed smokers as non-depressed smokers average more than a pack each day (28% vs. 15%). The poor health consequences of cigarettes are well understood and the link between depression and smoking is clear.

Yes, Depression is Physically Painful

For a moment, ignore all the examples above and consider this: depression makes a person feel alone and worthless. In many cases it, causes someone to consider that suicide is a reasonable decision.

That kind of emotional turmoil doesn't just exist inside a person's mind. It radiates through the entire body. I, personally, have been awake for over 48 hours crying, lying in my own sweat and drool, and literally dripping snot all over myself.

With my throat sore, my head pounding, and my vision blurry, I've cried out for people who never answered and have experienced emotional trauma so devastating that it can no longer be described as a feeling, but as a lack of feeling altogether.

To think that kind of mental anguish doesn't have a physical consequence isn't reasonable. Depression is an entire body disorder and it's far from all in someone's head.

Psych Central, 7/20/16

Depression Symptoms or Sadness – What's the Difference?

Of all the mental illness symptoms that exist, the one that is the most understood and misunderstood is depression. Depression and sadness share similar traits, like feeling down, low, or a loss of energy. Everyone, at one point or another, has experienced this. One should also consider that depression, as a word, has different meanings. It is reasonable to say, "I am depressed that my team lost the game" and it is reasonable to say, "I am depressed and I can't get out of bed." Using layman's terms, I'll explain the difference.

What is Sadness?

The difference between sadness and depression lies primarily in the cause and duration. Sadness, generally, has a logical reason to exist and there is a direct link to something that will make it stop. It isn't about the intensity of the feelings, but more about the reasons the feelings exist in the first place.

As an example, losing a job is likely to cause sadness, even intensely so. The cause is clear and logical. It is reasonable to feel sadness during that experience. Additionally, there is something that will make the sadness stop. If your boss were to re-hire you, the sadness would immediately turn to positive feelings. But even if that were not to happen, with time, the sadness will abate and life moves forward. This is where the phrase "time heals all wounds" comes from.

197

What is Clinical Depression?

The primary difference between depression and sadness is that clinical depression has no external cause and there is no obvious way to make it stop. A person experiencing the symptoms of major depression will not cheer up except perhaps temporarily if something positive happens. Even if that something is amazing in nature, like winning the lottery, depression remains.

While people with depression may experience moments of happiness, depression is not something that will be cured "with time." Clinical depression is a disease and follows a disease process. The circumstances of a person's life do little to effect the feelings.

Clinical depression is all-encompassing and leeches into a person's thought process. Living with depression is quite difficult and even things the person found pleasurable, like going out with friends, watching movies, or reading, will be affected. The symptoms, even slight ones, can ruin otherwise positive moments. Once, while depressed, I won a contest and my friend asked how I could possibly be depressed by winning an award. In his mind, the depression was small and the award was monumental.

I explained that having depression is like putting a ketchup packet on a slice of pizza. I love pizza, just as I love winning awards. But the addition of even a little ketchup – depression – completely ruins the taste.

Psych Central, 4/22/2015

What Does Living with Depression Feel Like?

Almost everyone has experienced what they believe to be depression. While many people are aware that depression is more than run-of-the-mill sadness, others truly believe that, for instance, grief and depression are equivalents.

They're *not*.

Depression is Much More than Extreme Sadness

My family doesn't understand depression very well. This is partly my fault, because when trying to describe my depression I sometimes use analogies like, "How you feel after the death of a loved one." While it is certainly possible for depression to develop because of something as traumatic as someone's death, what the typical person in that scenario is experiencing is grief, not depression.

It's true that grief and depression have similarities, but so do taking a shower and standing in the rain. Sharing common traits does not make two things – or experiences – the same.

Depression erodes a person's self-worth and makes them feel insignificant. Feelings of lethargy and a sense of their bodies feeling physically heavy are common. All of this can crush a person's will to live and make completing everyday tasks, like showering and getting dressed, seemingly impossible. It's as if a giant weight is strapped to your back – a weight that also whispers insults in your ear.

Depression affects every area of life. No thought is untouched by it. Favorite activities become uninteresting, or even physically painful to experience. People with depression often feel they are a burden to friends and family.

How Does Depression Make You Feel?

I've heard – and used – a hundred adjectives to describe how depression makes someone feel and most of them aren't wrong. They're just incomplete. I have described depression as soul-sucking, physically painful, and horrific. But if I had to choose one way to put it, I'd say my depression makes me feel utterly empty.

But, here's the thing. As awful as feeling empty is, it's still a feeling. When I feel empty inside, I recognize that I'm not supposed to feel empty. Something is supposed to fill that emptiness.

The difficult part in describing depression is that you can't actually feel nothing. And I'm left wondering if I need to find a new way to describe depression. But for now, "empty" truly feels like the right word, even if "numb" might, in fact, be a more clinically accurate adjective.

For me, though, "numb" feels like a word that implies hope. "Empty" feels like a word devoid of anything positive. In the end, that is what depression feels like to me.

9 Questions About Living with Depression

A few months back, I was asked to fill out a questionnaire about living with depression. It took me a while to get to it and by the time I did, I was too late to submit it. I figured that since I took the time to fill it out, I might as well publish it as a blog. So, without further ado, a depression questionnaire blog!

1. How long have you had depression?

Looking back, I have had depression my entire life; I just didn't know it. I thought I was lazy, physically sick, or just really tired. I pretty much thought it was anything but depression.

I didn't understand what "medical depression" was, so it didn't make sense to me. I understood sadness, but what I was experiencing was deeper than sadness.

Once I learned what depression was, it became obvious that was what was going on. It wouldn't be until my mid-20s that I would really learn about mental illness – including depression.

2. Does depression or other mental illness run in your family?

Not really. I'm special that way.

While it is fortunate that other members of my family do not suffer from depression, it did lead to my suffering not being noticed. My family didn't get me the help I desperately needed because they were unaware I needed help.

3. What are your symptoms?

I have bipolar and anxiety. My symptoms range from feeling worthless, suicidal, and hopeless all the way to feeling god-like, invincible, and indestructible. It is a whiplash effect. The depression feels physically heavy and exhausting. All my limbs weigh 50,000 pounds. Accomplishing anything is impossible. I wrestle my own mind and my body feels like heavy spaghetti.

4. Do you feel friends and family understand?

Everyone in my life now does understand, for the most part. The friends who didn't understand left. It hurt, but they didn't want to be around me when I was sick.

Overall, my family is pretty supportive. They, to this day, ask a lot of stupid questions, but that is okay. Asking a question means they want to understand and asking me means they want to understand FROM ME. So that has a lot of value. They are past the point of assuming they understand and we have created an open dialogue.

Creating an open dialogue was as much on me as it was on them. If I got angry with them every time they asked something that hurt my feelings, they would naturally stop asking. In the beginning, the conversations were uncomfortable. However, we must have uncomfortable conversations. They could not read my mind.

5. Have you ever been suicidal?

Yes. I was hospitalized because I had a suicide plan and was hours away from enacting it. I was lucky that someone intervened and got me the help I was unaware I needed.

6. Please describe your very worst bout of depression and how long it lasted.

The very worst was when I was planning my suicide. I just couldn't manage any more. The pressure, the physical pain, the mental pain, and my brain constantly showing me that no one cared about or loved me. I couldn't stand it anymore. Every second of every day, I was being assaulted by my own mind. There was no escape. No way to shut off the darkness. Every feeling I had was horrible. I didn't feel joy, I didn't feel pain; I felt intense loneliness and hopelessness.

It is the closest I have ever come to truly "experiencing" nothing.

7. What makes your depression better? Worse?

Time, more than anything makes it better. The love of people around me. Sometimes I just want a hug or an acknowledgment that I have value.

As far as worse? It feels like everything makes depression worse while in the moment.

I do want to say, first and foremost, that medicine and therapy have really helped me prevent depression. That's not to say I never experience it now, but it's not as bad as it was before I got help.

8. What is the biggest thing about depression that you would tell the world if you could?

It is somewhat sad to say that the biggest thing I would tell the world is that it is real. It is an illness. It sounds like a stupid thing to say, but it isn't. Many people think it is fake, including many who suffer from it.

People who don't take mental illness seriously are going to suffer needlessly, whether that person has depression or they are unable to help someone they care about. Standing outside and pretending it isn't raining doesn't prevent a person from getting wet.

9. Have you isolated yourself for very long periods?

I am a very social person. *I LOVE PEOPLE.* I don't like to be alone for more than a couple hours a day. I like to hear people while I am working. I like to people watch. If I go an entire day without interacting with people, that is a huge amount of time.

My grandfather, who has no mental illness, has gone 3-4 days without talking to another person. Because he likes it that way. So, people are different.

But for me, going a day without people is an eternity.

gabehoward.com, 1/21/2017

Can Someone Without Depression Understand It?

I spend a lot of time struggling with how to describe what depression feels like. Partly because I'm a writer and partly because I want my loved ones to understand me, I'm constantly trying to find the perfect explanation. I feel as though I've come close using darkness as imagery and trying to build on what people understand about sadness and grief.

I'm always left wanting, though. The intended audience appears to have some level of sympathy, but I never really feel like they have any understanding.

Sympathy Toward Depression vs. Understanding

Once, during a speech, I told the audience that feeling heavy, hopeless, and alone isn't even the halfway point of a depressive episode. Even though all of those things feel horrifying, they are still feelings. Being able to feel that suffering meant I was still able to feel something. Even though what I was feeling was painful and terrifying, it still meant I had a connection with my humanity.

The true horror of depression isn't in feeling bad; it's in not feeling anything at all. That level of suffering isn't caused by being taken to a dark place. It's caused by realizing that my mind is the dark place.

Becoming aware that my torment was internal was more than my fragile mind could handle and that's when the real trauma began.

205

I had mistakenly believed my suffering to be caused by an external force – something outside of myself. I was left trying to wrap my broken brain around the idea that the mind I had to use to find an escape from the pain was the very same mind causing my misery.

It's the equivalent of trying to use a broken tool to fix itself. It quickly became nonsense that demoralized me and the end result left me apathetic and unemotional. My deepest depression leaves me practically oblivious to my own consciousness.

When I finished speaking, I looked at the audience and many people had tears in their eyes. I was so pleased because I thought I had finally made people understand depression.

After the speech, many people came, hugged me, and told me how sorry they were that I had to go through such a horrible ordeal. I realized, then, that they still didn't understand depression – but they did now have sympathy for what I had gone through.

And maybe that's okay.

In some ways, understanding is overrated. Just because someone understands something doesn't mean they care about it. Besides, it's not really possible to understand truly something unless you've experienced it yourself. So, while I do wish people understood what I go through when I'm depressed, I wouldn't wish it on anyone.

Understanding Depression Isn't Necessary

To answer the question posed by the title — no. Someone who hasn't experienced depression can't understand it. That doesn't mean people can't be caring, sympathetic, and compassionate. We don't need to understand the exact plight of another person to be kind.

While a person without depression may not be able to understand exactly what I go through when I'm depressed, I'm sure they do understand what it's like to be scared, to suffer, to be lost, and to be alone.

Their understanding may be incomplete, but it's not non-existent.

Psych Central, 9/7/16

Trauma and Anger and Depression, Oh My!

"You didn't kill the baby, Gabe. It was already on life support when you got there and you tried."

I want to assure everyone we aren't talking about an actual baby. No children were harmed in the writing of this column. The analogy was just used by someone I was venting to.

It was a supportive thing to say, but he said it while asking me not to discuss the situation with him anymore. Turns out I was bringing him down by rehashing the events over and over again. It was at that moment I realized that what I was going through wasn't just a run-of-the-mill event. It was a traumatic event, even if only to me.

What I'm going through is personal, and I am angry and deeply saddened by it. I needed help and he was available as a sounding board for as long as he could be. But my relying on him was starting to negatively affect his mental health. He had to draw the line for his own well-being. "It isn't personal," he said, "It's just self-care."

Traumatic Experiences Can Cause Depression

I really feel that people – myself included – don't fully acknowledge the amount of trauma that we go through. We have this pie-in-the-sky idea that a traumatic experience is only war or death. Nothing could be further from the truth.

Like many things, trauma exists on a spectrum. Just because something is relatively minor by comparison, doesn't mean that it hasn't altered behavior or thinking. A minor car accident, for example, causes most people to drive more carefully, even if just for a short period.

Job loss, divorce, or the end of anything we care about all exist on the trauma scale and traumatic experiences can – and do – cause depression. How we deal with that depression determines how much of an impact it has on our lives. Not dealing with it can lead to loss of relationships, loss of pleasure, and even suicide. It's important to acknowledge the role trauma plays in our lives so we can properly heal from it.

Traumatic Experiences Can Cause Anger

Trauma doesn't always lead to depression. In fact, trauma leading to anger is common. While I don't have exact statistics, I'd wager that traumatic experiences lead to anger more often than depression, especially long term. Many of us personally feel that way about something and most of us know someone who is angry about a past experience.

Not honoring that anger can lead to depression, or more anger – and that leads to more isolation. It's a vicious cycle. The traumatic events I'm experiencing have left me angry and hurt, and by constantly involving my friend in that, I was wearing him down.

Luckily, my friend understands trauma very well and knows what I am going through. When he told me that he couldn't be my sounding board any longer, he also suggested I seek counseling, reassured me that I had done nothing wrong, that he was on my side, and reminded me of all the things I was missing out on by not moving on.

Many people just start avoiding people who are experiencing trauma. The anger is perceived as negative behavior and, by abandoning a person who is, at his or her core, suffering, more trauma is inadvertently inflicted.

In my situation, I was letting what was happening control me and prevent me from experiencing joy. By admitting I was traumatized, seeking help, and working to move forward, I can minimize the impact of these events.

That's what it means to be mentally healthy. It isn't preventing bad things from happening; it's not allowing them to keep you down. It's working to move forward instead of rehashing the past. Moving past traumatic events and healing from all the bad things in our past is the only way to lead emotionally stable, productive, and happy lives.

That's a goal worth aiming for.

Psych Central, 5/6/16

Anxiety or Anger? How Can You Tell?

One of the harder parts of living with anxiety is dealing with how the people around us perceive the various outward manifestations of the disorder. As an example, when I'm having a panic attack, I become sweaty, incoherent, and my heart races. Some people are likely to think I'm having a heart attack, rather than "just" having issues with anxiety.

Heart attacks aside, people often see the physical characteristics of anxiety as anger – or, at the very least, they think the anxious person is annoyed with them. It's not hard to see why people would reach that conclusion. When I'm anxious, I become withdrawn, irritable, and am quick to snap at those around me. This misunderstanding turns people who should be allies against each other. The person suffering from anxiety now has to contend with a defensive – and possibly angry – person. And instead of helping their anxious friend, they themselves are upset. Anxiety has a way of compounding problems and pulling people in – and that is a cycle worth breaking.

How Can You Tell the Difference Between Anger and Anxiety?

In order to tell the difference between anger and anxiety, it helps to understand what the terms actually mean. First, anxiety is defined as an unpleasant state of mental uneasiness, nervousness, apprehension, obsession, or concern. Anger is defined as a strong feeling of displeasure, hostility or antagonism towards someone or something, usually combined with an urge to harm (physically or verbally).

As you can see, just because the outward symptoms may look the same, the motivation behind each is vastly different. Another way to look at it is that anxiety makes a person retreat and anger pushes a person to advance. This motivation provides clues to help you differentiate.

When it comes to dealing with people who are behaving in some atypical manner, it's always best to take a few moments to assess the entire situation before getting involved. By observing, you can see if someone is trying to "get away" or trying to "start something." If they are trying to get away, it's a safe bet that anxiety is driving their actions.

The Very Best Way to Discern Between Anger and Anxiety

My grandfather often says that the simplest solutions are usually the most effective. The best way to discern between anger and anxiety fits that aphorism perfectly: ask them.

Eliminate guesswork, don't jump to conclusions, and keep your own emotions in check. Just look the person directly in the eye and calmly say, "Is everything okay?"

Then sit back and listen to their answer. We can all learn a lot by just talking to one another.

Psych Central, 2/13/17

What is Bipolar Anger?

There are many types of anger associated with bipolar disorder. Putting aside stereotypes is difficult, however. Not every single angry episode can be attributed to mental illness. Just as people who like football have varying degrees of fandom – some paint their faces and attend every game, while others listen on the radio while they mow the lawn – anger is the same way. That said, the majority of people with bipolar disorder have experienced "bipolar anger," a level of rage and hostility outside of the "normal" range. But, what exactly is "bipolar anger?"

The Difference Between Anger and "Bipolar Anger"

Everyone gets angry. Anger is a normal human emotion and one that serves a valuable purpose. As an example, anger triggers the fight or flight response, which can help a person survive danger. During the fight or flight response, a person will automatically respond to a threat without conscious thought.

Much like bipolar disorder, anger exists on a spectrum. From annoyed to enraged, all intensities of anger exist, to some extent, in the typical person. Anger, in and of itself, is not an issue.

Bipolar anger, on the other hand, is a different animal entirely. Appropriate anger has a general cause and a clear way to defuse it. Using the fight or flight example above, once the danger has been removed, the anger will begin to dissipate. When the cause of the anger is due to the symptoms of bipolar disorder, there is no clear reason for the anger and no clear way to defuse it.

In other words, since a person isn't sure what the danger is, they won't know when they have successfully fought it or escaped it. The intensity of the anger can only escalate as people become more and more desperate to defend themselves. At this point, the anger becomes uncontrollable and can be dangerous to the person and to those around them.

You can replace "danger" with "cause" and the person will be in a similar position. Since they don't know what is causing their anger, they can't resolve it. Finally, it is possible that what is angering a person has been distorted or "imagined" entirely. Since the anger isn't based on something concrete, the path to resolution becomes very unclear.

Why Bipolar Anger Needs to Be Taken Seriously

Like it or not, anger can be a symptom of bipolar disorder. Just like depression and mania, anger is relatively common. In my opinion, it is one of the most destructive symptoms, as it relates to interacting with other people, especially friends and family.

Many people with bipolar disorder describe a feeling of abandonment by loved ones. This is an excellent example of how anger can be a very destructive symptom. Whether the anger pushes a person away or we are angry with someone who isn't as prominent in our lives as we'd like, anger can rot a person from the inside out. Ignoring anger is foolish for anyone, but it is especially foolish for someone with bipolar disorder, given what is at stake. Unchecked anger can lead to self-harm, irreparable damage in close relationships, and, in rare cases, can lead to violence.

Managing the symptoms of bipolar disorder is a full-time job and part of that job is to take an honest assessment of all symptoms, even the taboo ones. From hyper sexuality to suicidal thoughts to uncontrollable anger, pretending that a symptom doesn't exist often leads to devastating consequences for everyone involved.

You can't flee any of the symptoms of bipolar disorder, so your only choice is to fight.

Bipolar Magazine, 8/11/2015

Bipolar Disorder, Anger, and Self-Loathing

Anyone who has a basic working knowledge of bipolar disorder knows all about the extreme highs (mania) and extreme lows (acute depression) that a person with the disorder experiences. Anyone who knows someone with bipolar, or has studied the disease, knows about some of the other common symptoms, as well.

There are literally hundreds of symptoms to manage, including hyper sexuality, uncontrollable anger, and even self-medication (such as with drugs or alcohol). One symptom, however, that doesn't get discussed often is self-loathing. Bipolar disorder creates an incredible amount of self-hatred. It's like a voice in someone's head that incessantly beats them down.

Self-Loathing and Bipolar Disorder

Most of us understand the basics of self-loathing. We all know people who have doubted themselves at some point in their lives and self-loathing is the extreme of that. People with bipolar disorder often hate themselves.

In other words, we believe we are worthless, incapable, and can't succeed. We are angry because of our misery.

And, if it wasn't bad enough that we believe it about ourselves, society reinforces that belief. We live in a society that very much dislikes open displays and/or discussions of anger.

When the average person observes someone with bipolar who is angry, they assume the anger is directed at them. Angry people in

216

our culture our looked upon as being bad. Anger is considered a negative emotion because we tend to classify emotions in this way. Adding moral judgement to feelings often creates more problems than it solves.

Since most people are uncomfortable with anger, they become anxious around angry people, considering them a threat. Add on our culture's misconceptions about both bipolar disorder and anger and it's unsurprising when negative outcomes occur.

A person in crisis is perceived as bad, no help will be forthcoming, and that self-hatred will be reinforced. Those who witness the outburst often distance themselves from the person suffering. This further isolates an already desperate individual, often sinking them deeper into depression and preventing them from getting well.

The fact remains that most people don't live with bipolar disorder. It is, thankfully, relatively uncommon, affecting about 4% of the population. Given America's lack of mental health education, it isn't remotely surprising that these "misunderstandings" occur.

If we are honest with ourselves, we must admit that these "misunderstandings" are purely due to our own ignorance, which is far too often due to not wanting to understand.

Just for a moment, imagine how much better the lives of people living with bipolar disorder would be if we did.

Psych Central, 7/8/2016

Myths About Mental Illness & What You Should Know

Forget 1 in 4: Everyone Has Mental Health Concerns

A few weeks ago, I got a call from an older male family member asking me about panic attacks and anxiety. Turns out he has been experiencing them for the first time in his life and was confused and concerned. One of the first things he told me was that he has no history of mental illness. He's family and I can assure you that he is correct; he doesn't have a severe and persistent mental illness. So how can we explain his panic and anxiety attacks?

Serious Mental Illness Versus a Mental Health Issue

One of the biggest issues we have in mental health/mental illness advocacy is the difference between severe and persistent mental illness and smaller, generally situational, mental health concerns, such as the distressing levels of anxiety experienced by my relative.

He didn't realize that he could have a panic attack with no history of anxiety issues. He's certainly been under stress before. He's married with children and parenthood is a stressful experience in the best of circumstances.

Being told that anyone could have a panic attack, at any time, made sense on a logical level; he just never thought about it before.

218

It didn't occur to him that, given his circumstances at the moment, anxiety was *normal*.

He called me because he wanted to know what to do. These attacks freaked him out and he was fortunate enough to have someone he trusted to ask. A little information goes a long way, after all. And misinformation is very damaging.

This is why mental health education is so valuable. His situation may have turned out differently had he been left to fend for himself using only the stereotypes he's learned along the way.

The Correct Mental Health Concerns Statistic is 1 in 1

Most people, most of the time, have good mental health. Even so, they are susceptible to bouts of anxiety, depression, or psychological trauma. This is just like how most people, most of the time, have good physical health, but are nonetheless prone to catching colds, the flu, or chicken pox.

And just like physical illnesses, some mental health issues are more serious than others are. I have bipolar disorder, which is a "severe and persistent mental illness," analogous to someone who lives with diabetes, as an example.

The "1 in 4 mental illness" statistic is misleading as it is often presented. First, according to SAMHSA, the number is 1 in 5. Further, the exact statistic says in a given year, 1 in 5 people will experience a mental health issue. That isn't the same as saying, "1 in 4 (or 1 in 5) people have mental illness."

So forget the 1 in 4 statistic that everyone loves to throw around and focus on this: Everyone has mental health and therefore anyone can have a mental health issue.

Anyone.

Psych Central, 1/21/16

Do People with Mental Illness Really Die 25 Years Younger?

A common statistic quoted by almost every expert is that people with mental illness will die, on average, 25 years younger than those without mental illness. Some mental health advocates even misquote the study completely and say, "People with mental illness die 25 years sooner," leaving out "on average."

When I first heard this, as a person living with bipolar and anxiety disorders, I felt helpless. The average lifespan for a male in the United States is 76 years. The thought of dying at 51 bummed me out – a lot.

As I continued to hear this statistic quoted everywhere, people started offering their inferences as to why mentally ill people were dying. One group blamed psychiatric medications, another group said it was because people with mental illness *don't* take medications, and another group blamed psychiatric hospitals and medical malpractice. None of these groups offered anything that should pass as evidence.

This made me curious, and so I investigated this commonly-held belief, myself.

People with Mental Illness Don't Die 25 Years Younger

First, it's important to point out that the 25-year statement is *technically* mostly true. Although, I could argue that it's false because the majority of the studies quote a range from 10 to 25 years, not just 25 years. Aside from that, however, the way people are using this statistic is incredibly misleading and is causing a lot of confusion.

To begin with, the original study is stating averages. It does *not* state that *every* person with a mental illness dies 25 years younger. The devil is very much in the details, here.

Consider this: according to the Center for Orthotic & Prosthetic Care, approximately one in 250 people in the United States is missing a leg. Let's say, for the sake of argument, that all of these people represent the loss of an entire leg. (I do realize this isn't true, but bear with me.) That means that, in America, the average number of legs per person is approximately 1.95.

Now, imagine you don't live in America. You live in Japan and you read an article stating that statistic about American legs. Wouldn't it be reasonable to expect to come to the United States and see a bunch of people with one full leg and one leg with a piece missing?

It's unreasonable to believe that everyone with mental illness will die 25 years younger – just as it's unreasonable to believe that everyone in America is missing part of a leg.

However, far more importantly than the misunderstanding of how averages work, these studies also list a specific set of comorbidities. In other words, what reduces a person's lifespan isn't necessarily mental illness by itself. It's mental illness *combined* with something else. For example, smoking cigarettes, drinking alcohol, drug use, or homelessness. All of these things are considered common comorbidities for people with mental illness.

Researchers have concluded that a person with mental illness is taking part in these life-shortening activities *because* they are mentally ill, therefore dying from one of them and dying because of mental illness become intertwined. One other factor that must be taken into account is that some mentally ill individuals will become victims of suicide. While most people with mental illness will *not* die by suicide, the ones who do lower the *average* life expectancy for everyone else diagnosed.

If You Have Mental Illness, You Can Live a Normal Lifespan

After I read all the studies myself, I felt much better. The way these studies are presented to people makes it sounds as though people with mental illness *will* die 25 years younger. It's incredibly dangerous to present information so wildly out of context and leave people living with mental illness believing there is nothing they can do to change their fate.

It's important to note that researchers aren't the ones misleading the public. Their research methodology is very clearly stated, continually updated, and, when applied in the appropriate context, is very relevant in determining public policy and treatment options. To sum up, if you are diagnosed with mental illness and you take care of yourself physically, don't abuse drugs and alcohol, have a stable living environment, and are receiving proper treatment for your illness, your odds of living a normal lifespan become comparable to everyone else's.

As you can see, it is a bit difficult to answer the question of whether people with mental illness really die 25 years younger, but I feel confident in saying, "No, as a general rule, we do not."

Psych Central, 3/16/17

3 Common Myths About Depression

Depression is one of those things that everyone has heard about, but few understand. I often joke that depression is like panda bears in that everyone is familiar with them, but most people have never seen one in real life and even fewer have touched one. Yet, we all *feel* as if they are commonplace. Because of misconception, stereotype, and just plain old lack of education, our society knows precious little about depression. Sadly, this doesn't stop people from believing that they know all about it.

I *hate* being depressed. Not exactly an earth-shattering admission. I don't really think there are many people who enjoy being sad, let alone feeling the soul-sucking emptiness that is depression.

I do, believe it or not, appreciate the attempts of my loved ones who try so hard to "pick me up" when I'm down. However, I think their attempts might be more successful if they stopped accepting a few common myths about depression.

1. I'm Depressed, Not a Toddler

Just because I'm depressed doesn't mean I'm suddenly not an adult. In layman's terms, I want to make it clear: depression does not equal regression to childhood.

I say this because, almost without exception, people will talk to me as if I'm a 4-year-old once they discover I'm suffering from depression. I wish this illness was so insignificant that a couple of well placed "atta boys" and maybe a little condescending baby talk could snap me right out of it. But, consider this:

If it's so easy to cure that the random musings that soothe an infant worked to "fix it," why are doctors, scientists, and researchers working so hard all over the world to find treatments? Just hire someone's granny to wander around tickling depressed people and, voilà, problem solved.

2. I'm Depressed, Not Stupid

Just because I'm depressed doesn't mean I'm no longer intelligent. I will acknowledge that depression does cause some cognitive impairment in the form of slower thinking, being unaware of my surroundings, and so forth.

However, it doesn't mean that I don't understand what you are saying. Condescending tones, language, and treatment will upset me just as much when depressed – if not more so – as it would when I'm perfectly well.

It's rude not to talk to me like an adult, because I *am* an adult. I'm just sick. Treating me as if I'm stupid is not only unhelpful, but it makes me feel more isolated and more stuck. I'm also less likely to believe you when you remind me that I'm wanted, needed, and loved.

3. Depression is Not Sadness

The biggest, most persistent, and most common myth surrounding depression is that it is the same as common sadness. It's understandable how people can make this mistake. We use "depressed" in common parlance to indicate sadness. We relabeled "manic depression" to "bipolar disorder" and it would be helpful if we either started saying "clinical depression" or changed the diagnosis name to "unipolar disorder." This, in my opinion, would clear up some of the confusion.

I'm guilty of spreading this misconception myself. When I describe bipolar disorder, I say that it "exists on a spectrum from very sad to very happy." This is my shorthand way of explaining depression and mania to the general public. (FYI: mania is not very happy, either.)

At best, I'm using a poor analogy and, at worst, I'm straight up wrong. Sadness and depression have about as much in common as a gentle rain and a hurricane. Just because both are weather events and both contain water doesn't make them the same. The same can be said for sadness and depression.

Sadness is a component of depression and both are moods, but the similarities pretty much end there. This is important to know because if you suggest a person "just grab an umbrella" and head out in a hurricane, you've done that individual a great disservice. People suffering from depression can't "just cheer up" and it's frustrating to be told we can.

Educate Yourself About Depression

If you want to help someone who is suffering from depression, then you must first educate yourself. This can be as simple as going online and learning more or asking the person what you can do to be helpful.

You can also make an appointment with a psychologist or therapist and discuss ways to be an ally in your friend's fight against depression. The best advice is often the simplest:

Don't assume you know what to do. A little knowledge and effort goes a long way.

Psych Central, 3/24/16

Why Do People with Mental Illness Self-Sabotage?

There is a lot of talk about why people with mental illness self-sabotage. The other day, while reading online, I saw this quote: "I am afraid of two things equally – success and failure." I took notice when I read it because it sums up my entire life and the topic of self-sabotage comes up a lot in support groups I have facilitated.

It isn't surprising that many people fear failure. Fearing success, however, is an entirely different psychological quagmire. Why would someone fear being successful? What could possibly be the downside of success? The answer is a lot more basic than you might think.

Mental Illness as an Identity

Mental illness, in many ways, is part of someone's identity. Like it or not, it does factor in to making us whole.

Many people with mental illness, myself included, don't like this particular part of our make-up, but we are used to it. It has been there since the beginning and, for better or worse, we are used to living with it. As an example, I am used to the symptoms, the limitations, and, even the failures having bipolar disorder brings.

Because of the way we treat mental illness in our society, people are often sick for a long time before they begin to receive any sort of care. The treatments are slow and can take months, or even years, to be effective. That is a long time to "get used" to something. It is no

226

surprise that mental illness becomes a large part of someone's identity – and not just because the illness is linked directly to our emotions, thoughts, and personalities.

Mourning the Loss of Mental Illness as an Identity

Because mental illness is part of who we are, there is a mourning process when it goes away. Yes, even though it's a *bad* thing. When success shows up and threatens to change our core identity from "person who is sick" to "person who is successful" we, naturally, get nervous. Just because we don't like being sick doesn't mean we aren't used to it.

Then success comes along and tries to mess with that? The phrase, "Oh, *hell* no" immediately springs to mind. I am reminded of crayon scribbles on the wall of a child's room. Parents work to prevent it, are unhappy when it occurs, but when someone tries to paint over it 15 years later, they break down in tears. They've become so used to the scribbles that they became "part of" the room.

None of these are good reasons to self-sabotage, mind you. Just because an action is understandable doesn't make it a good one. I understand why I over-eat (food is delicious), but that doesn't mean I'm making good choices.

I believe that when people work toward goals for a reason and then throw it all away because they're scared, it is the equivalent of handing the football to the other team right before you score a touchdown.

All change, even good change, is scary. Those of us who live with mental illness are used to being brave. There is no better time to be brave then when we are about to achieve our goals.

Psych Central, 7/9/2015

Family, Friends & Romance

The Difference Between Delusional and Wrong

Every Christmas, my cousin, Athena, and I have a competition of sorts. We give each other gifts that we believe help establish who our grandmother's favorite grandchild is. It's a delightful family tradition that started up innocently enough five or so years ago and just keeps... *growing.*

The general premise is simple enough: Athena maintains she is our grandmother's favorite and I *know* I am our grandmother's favorite. The yearly battle for Granny's love has caught the attention of friends and neighbors, and members of the family who can't attend for the official exchange are quick to inquire about it.

In fact, the only thing my cousin and I do agree on is that whoever is *not* Grandma's favorite is securely in second place. In other words, my cousin is the second favorite of all the grandchildren.

Is My Cousin Delusional for Thinking She's the Favorite?

As the stakes increase year after year, the trash-talk has ramped up, as well. Over the summer, I said to her that if she thinks she's the favorite, she's delusional. In the right context, I am correct. She believes something that is unsupported by fact and reality.

Except, of course, she's not literally delusional. She and I are playing a *game*. Granted, it's a high-stakes game. Being the actual favorite, I understand why she wants my position in the family. But I'm exaggerating and using the term more loosely to describe behavior I *believe* is unrealistic.

A delusion is a false belief that is based on an incorrect interpretation of reality. A person with delusional disorder will firmly hold on to this belief despite specific and clear evidence to the contrary. Being delusional is a symptom of mental illness and generally exists with other symptoms. More specifically, delusions most often occur when a person is suffering from psychosis.

I've been delusional and can tell you that it's all encompassing. It's deceiving yourself by believing outrageous, irrational, and often impossible things to be completely true, and then defending those thoughts irrationally. Believing a single falsehood — especially a nebulous one — does not make one actually delusional.

In other words, when it comes to my cousin believing that she is the favorite grandchild she isn't delusional in any way.

She's just *wrong*.

Psych Central, 12/17/16

Is Self-Care Vital for Family Members of the Mentally Ill?

Any discussion about mental illness isn't complete without discussing the caregivers. There are three primary types of caregivers, and they all play an important role. Medical professionals, mental health advocates (including peer supporters), and family members (which includes close friends) are instrumental in providing care day in and day out for people struggling with mental illness. For the purpose of this article, we are going to focus on family members who are caring for their mentally ill loved ones.

Whether someone provides care one hour a day or 24/7, there is one universal and important truth that needs to be taken very seriously.

Not Practicing Self-Care Can (and Does) Make Things Worse

Family members who don't practice self-care may not be in the best position to provide care, and that can lead to serious issues – even death – for the person living with mental illness. The primary caregiver is especially vulnerable to being overwhelmed and the chances of this only increase when caring for a loved one.

As an example, when I provide any type of care for my wife, I am deeply invested in the outcome. Whatever is affecting her is affecting me, even if to a lesser extent. In other words, this is very personal to me, and I haven't yet considered her experience at all.

Now, add to that fear, setbacks, and even things like lack of sleep, and it doesn't take much imagination to put together a scenario where something could go wrong. This isn't because of lack of caring, or poor intentions, or even lack of effort, but it *is* because of poor planning and decision making.

Mental Illness Caregivers: Caring for Yourself *Is* Supporting Someone Else

What we all need to understand is that self-care is part of the job as a caregiver. A caregiver who is not at the top of their game can significantly diminish the potential outcome for the person who needs support. This isn't just a problem for the person receiving care, but it can, and often does, lead to adverse psychological effects for the well-intentioned, overwhelmed caregiver.

When I speak to caregivers, the same flawed thinking is demonstrated over and over again. People believe that if they aren't providing direct care for their loved one, then they aren't providing any care at all. And, what is worse, some family members start to believe that because they aren't sick, it wouldn't be *fair* for them to enjoy life.

This is a strange thing to think, since one is in no way tied to the other. It is possible to have a high quality of life *and* acknowledge that someone else has a lower quality of life. This is a good thing, because it is much easier to pull someone up the hill when already at the top.

Self-care is not selfish; it is necessary. *Not* enjoying life doesn't improve any situation or make anyone better.

Perhaps the best way I can sum this up is to ask: If you needed help, would you prefer your caregiver be well rested, prepared, and ready to assist or tired, resentful, and angry?

And which caregiver do *you* want to be?

Psych Central, 7/23/15

3 Simple Ways to Explain Bipolar Disorder to Others

Believe it not, I am asked what bipolar is more often than you would think. To me, and the majority of my readers, bipolar disorder is a known quantity. I don't need to explain it because the people who seek me out are either living with this illness or know someone who is.

Recently, I had the good fortune to present to a group of police officers as part of the Crisis Intervention Training (CIT) program and a young officer in the back raised his hand and asked, "Can you tell me what bipolar is?"

I told him that bipolar disorder is a mental illness that is marked by alternating periods of extreme lows (depression) and extreme highs (mania). He thanked me and the training continued.

Medical Definition of Bipolar Disorder Versus Lay Person's Definition

Later that evening, I thought back to the officer's question and how I answered it. My answer was perfectly accurate, but did it allow him to *understand* bipolar or just confuse him further? I suspected that it didn't do much to educate him, although I can't be sure without asking him.

In order to prevent any such confusion in the future, I decided to brainstorm simpler ways to explain bipolar disorder to people who don't understand, but want to. In no particular order, here are my top three:

1. Bipolar disorder is a spectrum of moods that goes from the lowest of lows (suicidal depression) all the way up to the highest of highs ("god-like" mania), and everything in between. The person suffering from bipolar is unable to control where their moods fall on this spectrum, or how long that mood will last before transitioning.

2. Bipolar disorder is a severe and persistent mental illness with a 15% death rate. Typical symptoms include racing thoughts (which lead to hurried and nonsensical speech); rapid mood swings, ranging from depression all the way to mania; staying awake for days at a time without tiring; and grandiose thinking, such as believing you have more fame, money, or authority than you really do.

3. Bipolar disorder is an illness that affects the mind. Specifically, it alters a person's ability to control their moods, thoughts, and the way they see the world around them. A person suffering from bipolar will travel back and forth on a very long mood spectrum that they cannot control. This includes moods typical people will never experience, such as suicidal thoughts or living in a consequence-free environment where a person feels invincible.

Obviously, there must be hundreds, if not thousands, of ways to explain bipolar disorder simply. How do you explain bipolar so that your friends and family can better understand?

Bipolar Magazine, 4/25/2017

How do I Make My Family Understand Depression?

I receive a lot of e-mail and don't have time to answer all of it. I want to, but writing, speaking, and watching television takes a lot of my time. Occasionally, I get an e-mail with a really good question and, in addition to answering it, I publicly post the question and answer for others to see. Today's blog is one such letter and addresses the question of how to make loved ones understand mental illness and depression?

Dear Gabe,

I want my family to understand mental illness and depression. In addition to reading your blogs, I have been following you on Twitter and Facebook for a while now. One of the things I've noticed is that you have a good relationship with your parents, wife, and other family members. I see them publicly support you, joke around, and even share some of your articles that contain information my family won't even talk about privately.

How did you make them understand depression? Why is your family so supportive? How can I get my friends and family to respect me as much as your friends and family respect you?

Thanks,
Wanting Love

Dear Wanting Love,

Before I answer, I want to thank you for your kind words about my friends and family. I am sure they will appreciate them. Like me, they love compliments.

One of the questions I'm often asked when I speak is, "What was your childhood like?" Summarizing 18 years into a three-minute response doesn't lend itself to providing good information. The fact is, my childhood was both difficult *and* amazing.

My relationship with my father is a great example. He and I were at odds for years. He made a great many mistakes and some of them I am still angry about. He also adopted me when I was five years old, giving me a father and a family I wouldn't have otherwise had. So I can say with absolute truthfulness that my dad was an amazing man who stepped up to raise me as his own without expecting any acknowledgement whatsoever and that he was a jerk who over-punished, over-reacted, and should have been more understanding.

One statement doesn't take away from the other. *Both* are equally true. The relationship between the rest of my family and me is much the same way. Everything you see on social media is absolutely true. They aren't just pretending to be supportive.

What is left off social media are the negative aspects. My family and I disagree, argue, and hurt each other's feelings all the time. But I make a deliberate effort to remember the good when experiencing the bad.

I don't know you, but I would venture to guess that your family understands you more than you think.

Does your family take you to your favorite restaurant on your birthday? When your favorite genre of movie comes out, do they ask you if you are going to see it? My grandmother, who dislikes sports in general, keeps track of the Columbus Blue Jackets hockey team just so she can talk to me about it. She also tells me that spending money on tickets is wasteful spending. I take the good with the bad, because that is family.

The fact is that we can't *make* anyone understand us. What we can do is be open to their questions and be willing to communicate openly our experiences with anyone who asks. While it is tempting to be angry with them for not being understanding, we have to remember they are experiencing our depression for the first time.

Holding on to past hurts won't allow either party to reach common ground. It is up to us to forgive the people in our lives who weren't supportive and keep an open dialogue. Through these difficult and honest conversations, we can begin to live these experiences together, instead of separately.

That is the key to understanding – experiencing them together instead of separately.

Psych Central, 6/10/15

Everything I Was Too Afraid to Be: On Fatherhood and Mental Health

Recently, I had the good fortune to meet a fellow mental health advocate in person. Gabriel Nathan (Gabe – just like me) is the Editor-in-Chief of *OC87 Recovery Diaries* and a man who lives with depression, anxiety, and obsessive thoughts. We talked about a great many things, but the topic that fascinated me the most is that he is the father of twins.

"How on earth can you manage mental illness AND a child — let alone two?" was my first thought.

While it is a difficult task, it is a rewarding one. When asked what makes parenting so rewarding, I expected him to give the typical answer of how being a dad is the greatest and most meaningful job in the world. And probably something about how great it is to receive love and affection from his children.

However, he recalled the instances when their personality shone through as the most rewarding factor.

He described his kids as "skeptical, sardonic, boundary testing, impish, and sly," and it is when these aspects of their character are at a peak that a smile widens across his face. Their shrewd independence, their ability to fly in the face of the traditional, and their attitude of indifference towards society's special occasions — more specifically, the first day of school — are the very things he admires most about his children. He explains, "They are everything I was too afraid to be, and maybe that's what's most rewarding. My children are ballsy, which is a pretty significant achievement because their father is an anxiety-ridden, depressed, obsessive fraidy-cat."

What Is Day-to-Day Life Like for a Parent Who Lives with Mental Illness?

Parenting, as wonderful as it may be, does include some marital strain. While he loves his wife intensely and completely, Gabe does reveal that there are philosophical differences regarding parenting between the two. While his wife may be more concerned with their diet and sleep patterns, Gabe's daily focus tends to be on the bigger picture. An establishment of roles and playing upon each other's strengths as parents are a key part of loosening that strain and working together to avoid clashing.

While I was interested in the parenting process, I was equally intrigued by how Gabe handles working and parenting, when parenting seems like a full-time job all on its own. Fortunately, Gabe does most of his work during the day while his children are off at school.

When they come home, he tries his best to turn away from the work and turn his focus towards his children, a balance of life and work he is appreciative to have. While some previous jobs were not terribly respectful of that, his current position allows him to balance his duties as a father and is ideal for the working parent.

Even though he turns off his working mind while he is with his children, he does not keep them excluded from his work. Regarding his children he explained, "They know that I work for a website that tells stories about people who struggle with recovery and how they think and feel, and I love that. Teaching them about mental health through OC87 Recovery Diaries is a real privilege."

Mental Health Issues and Fatherhood

All in all, the question I was most eager to learn the answer to was, "How has having children impacted your mental health?"

While postpartum issues are often discussed from a woman's point of view, Gabe says he has yet to read a story from a man about postpartum depression or how fatherhood has affected their mental health.

Society has built the idea that fathers are supposed to be strong and impenetrable, a hurtful stereotype that has caused far too many fathers to avoid talking about their mental health after the birth of their children. Gabe revealed that his mental health was never great, but it has definitely declined since his emergence into fatherhood.

Gabe gives the following advice for those struggling with their mental health under the immense pressure of being a father: "If you're a father and you're struggling with your mental health, do the best thing you can ever do for yourself and for your family: see a therapist. Talk. And, when you think you've talked enough, do it more."

As a person who lives with bipolar disorder, I was particularly impressed with how matter-of-fact he was when saying all this. I'm not that confident I have control over my own life, let alone being able to care for little ones.

But Gabe carries on day-in and day-out and describes his life as good. And, for a man who defines himself as an "anxiety-ridden, depressed, obsessive fraidy-cat," I consider him every bit as "ballsy" as his children.

Psych Central, 10/10/2017

My Mom Doesn't Understand What It's Like to be Openly Bipolar

Every morning, on my drive to work, I call my mom. One might think this makes me a mama's boy, but it's more to stave off boredom than anything else. The conversations are generally limited to family gossip and the like, but recently, the subject of me living openly with bipolar disorder came up. I said, "It is very hard to live openly with bipolar disorder."

My mom said, "I can't even imagine what that must be like."

Wait. *What*?

Realizing My Mom Doesn't Understand My Life with Bipolar Was Eye-Opening

Finding out that my own mom doesn't know what I go through living openly with bipolar disorder was a punch in the gut. Even though I am nearing 40 years old, she is my *mother*. Doesn't she have some sort of "mom-sense" that fills in these gaps for her?

Of course, that is ridiculous. She doesn't know because she doesn't live in my head. She doesn't follow me around 24/7 and observe me. She only knows what she sees and hears and, because I don't often share the more negative aspects of my life with her, she is left to wonder.

That conversation was a few weeks ago and it still rolls around in my head. What do I want her to know? What would I like her to understand? What would I tell her?

Being Openly Bipolar is Hard... and Amazing... and Awful

I want my Mom to know that living openly with bipolar disorder is painfully hard. There are parts of being open that are amazing, it allows me to help other people in ways that being "closeted" would not, but mostly it is just awful. I actively invite criticism that hurts my feelings and fills my head with self-doubt and negative thoughts.

People judge me and tell me I'm not good enough. Because I love people and feed off their energy, this hurts me profoundly. On one hand, I must be very strong in order to keep moving forward, but on the other hand, the overall pain is very real. Knowing that people think less of me because I have an illness I didn't ask for and don't want is crushing.

Did I mention that when I am alone with my thoughts, I cry? Everything I do is tainted by the fact that large portions of society will never, ever see me as anything other than a tragic mistake of nature. I've been judged, mocked, and misunderstood more than I've been praised, accepted, and loved. There is just so much the world doesn't know about Bipolar Disorder.

I move through life seeing the blank stares of others and not knowing whether they hate me, love me, or just don't care. History has taught me that they will see everything I say or do through the lens of my bipolar diagnosis. I will be seen first as mentally ill and then as a person. Even when people say nothing at all, that doesn't stop me from filling in the gaps with all the horrible things people have said to me over the years.

I often think I must be the strongest fragile person on the planet. I stand up to the stereotypes, the misunderstandings, and the criticism of our society all in the hopes of making some ridiculously tiny positive impact.

I seek out people and willingly give them the power to judge me because it is the only way I know how to change the way people see people living with mental illness – people like me. As easy as it would be to live in the shadows and tell no one of my illness, that won't make me happy, either.

Living openly with bipolar disorder is the only thing I know, but where most people end articles like this with "...and I wouldn't change a thing," my story is different, because my story ends with "...and I would change everything. In fact, I'm working on it right now."

I have no idea if any of this will help my mom know what my life is like and, frankly, that's okay. She knows my sister and I fight over the noodles on Thanksgiving; she knows my favorite drink is Diet Coke; and when my sister and I both happen to be driving to work at the same time, she knows to answer my call first. Because she believed me when I told her that being impatient was a symptom of bipolar disorder. (*Thanks, Mom!*)

Psych Central, 9/17/15

From Your Bipolar Son on Mother's Day

All relationships are difficult. While I can't prove it, I feel confident saying that the first disagreement occurred within five minutes of human existence. I'm also sure that those people were family members.

No one argues like family and the parent-child dynamic is pretty close to the formula for all reality TV shows. Throw bipolar disorder into the mix and that complicates things – a lot.

Living with bipolar disorder is a giant pain in the rear end and, I suspect, raising a child with bipolar disorder is equally no fun. I can only speak about my own childhood – I'm an expert in my own life – and here is what I can tell you about my mother.

About My Mother (Who Does Not Have Bipolar Disorder)

My mother got pregnant in high school. I can already see her cringe as she reads this, but not in the way that you'd think. Like me, she isn't ashamed of her story; she's afraid I'll tell it the way I do at family gatherings. In the interest of sparing my mother's feelings, I'll leave out words like "knocked-up."

By 21 years old, she had child, a failed marriage, and was living with her parents. Most people would consider that failure, and maybe she did at the time, but she never tells the story that way. She talks about how adorable I was and how much fun she had with her sisters. She talks about how she met and married the man who would adopt me and become my dad. Yes, that literally means I was a red-headed stepchild.

No matter what horrible experience befell her – from the unplanned teenage pregnancy to the deaths of her sisters – she always speaks about life so positively. If I had to pick a single word to describe my mom, it would be Christmas. An odd choice, I agree, but fitting. She's bright, beautiful, and happy. She's annoying, loud, and tacky. She brings out the best in people because she's just so joyous.

Her eternal happiness is equally annoying and disturbing. Especially for a person who suffers from depression.

My mother is brave. While living in a small town in the mountains of Pennsylvania she met a truck driver from the big city of Columbus, Ohio. Where did they meet? On the freeway. How long did it take her to marry him and move hours away from *everyone* she knew with her toddler?

Five weeks. *Weeks.*

I know how amazingly well it turned out, but I still think she's a moron for doing so. While I have no recollection of it, I'm positive that I explained to her at the time that this was a bad idea. I was a pretty smart toddler. The odds seemed good that the man was a serial killer at worst and equally moronic at best.

Their marriage gave me a dad, produced two more children (my brother and my sister), and four grandchildren. The ones who aren't teenagers are adorable.

How My Mother Influenced My Recovery with Bipolar Disorder

My mother doesn't look before she leaps because she *knows* it'll work out. She believes that people are good, even when she knows they aren't. She has faith in humanity and she helps anyone who asks.

She also breaks out into song in department stores.

We have a lot in common, which, pardon the pun, drives me crazy. I don't want to face the reality that I'm a lot like her. More so than I'm willing to admit. I just want people to be happy and the world to be fair. I believe, as she does, in service to others.

Bipolar disorder has pulled me into the depths of emptiness. It has removed my ability to reason, think logically, and feel anything. I can't help but think that being raised by a woman who believes in me and sees such promise in life kept me from slipping over the edge on *at least* one occasion.

My mom isn't a doctor and, truth be told, she doesn't understand a lot of what I go through. She still says insensitive things about living with bipolar from time to time. She isn't perfect by any stretch and she knows it. Of course, like in any proper mother-son relationship, we still bicker over all the normal things.

But she never wavered on whether or not or I could be better, live better, and do better. She knew that I could. Having someone who believes in you is more valuable than most people realize. I've been so incredibly broken that only a moron would think I could be put back together again.

Thankfully, my mother is a moron. And I love her for it.

Bipolar Magazine, 5/3/2016

Having Mental Illness and Having a Dad

I thought I would dedicate today's entry to my dad.

On the surface, my dad, Gary Howard, is an uninteresting man. Before retiring, he was a semi-truck driver and now spends his days doing what can best be described as pissing off my mother. He lives in Memphis, Tennessee, and enjoys playing on his computer and amassing DVDs like squirrels amass nuts.

When I was younger, my dad had the coolest job. I would brag to those around me that my dad could drive — and I would motion toward a giant semi-truck barreling down the freeway — one of those. Once, when I was in high school, I met him at a truck stop and watched him arrive in his 12-ton truck, felt the ground shake and the rumble of the diesel engine through my body, and watched his extremely average-sized body jump out of the cab onto the concrete. Maybe it was the diesel fumes I was breathing in, but I believe I caught a glimpse of what my mother must have seen in him all those years ago.

My dad didn't teach me much on purpose. He certainly tried, but failed almost every time. He tried to teach me to play baseball, but hit me in the face with the ball; tried to teach me to ride a bike without training wheels, and I ran into the back of a parked car. Once, after realizing my teenage obsession with Cindy Crawford, he sat me down and explained, "Most women don't look like that." I am certain this set off my desire to prove him wrong by dating only supermodels...

Growing Up with My Dad

As I grew up, he became easier and easier to ignore. I wanted to be nothing like him. He didn't have the intelligence I had, the money I wanted, or the respect I demanded. His job was laughable, his station in life meaningless. He was unexceptional, unassuming, and boring.

When I was high school, my dad set out to improve his education by working with a tutor to learn the skills he never did during his childhood. At one point, I openly mocked him to my friends, to him, and to the tutor. His hard work allowed me an education, and this was the very thing I took for granted to level my judgment.

By the time I graduated high school, I was positive of only one thing: I wanted to be nothing like him. While maturity did give me a different perspective on his life, it didn't change the core belief that his life would be unsatisfying, even if only to me. I wanted people to pay attention to me and he, simply, didn't care what other people were doing.

My dad was not present on the day I was born. To this day, no one is really certain where he was, or what he was doing. November 24, 1976, is not a day that had any significant meaning to him until a couple years later. Call it fate, call it karma, call it a broken CB radio and the adventurous spirit of a trio of twenty-something sisters and you end up with my father, a truck driver from Ohio, meeting my mother, a single woman with a redheaded child living in a small town in Pennsylvania. Apparently, a red-headed toddler wasn't a deal-breaker because, less than two months later, my mother married the only man I have ever known to be my father.

This was never a secret to me. My parents were open about this, and at six feet, three inches tall, with a large frame and bright red hair, they couldn't have kept it a secret if they tried.

However, unbeknownst to me, the man I thought of as unexceptionable, unassuming, and boring somehow managed to intertwine with my life in such a way that him not being my biological dad is an utterly insignificant fact. My family is not blended, my brother and sister are not "halves," I am not a stepchild, or the adopted one.

The choices he made in his life taught me to stand my ground, to defend those who can't defend themselves, and to love people. His belief that people were basically good became my own belief and his refusal to give up inspires me to do the same.

The man, for all his many faults and even more failures, never once failed to *try*.

More than anything, he taught me that some details that we see as big are wholly insignificant. Imagine if he had let the seemingly significant detail that he wasn't my biological father stop him from being my real dad.

gabehoward.com, 1/21/2017

What Is a Loophole Grandchild?

I spent most of August 3, 2018, sitting in a hospital room waiting on the birth of my granddaughter. At 9:11 in the evening, after waiting for almost 13 hours, Lennox Rose finally entered the world. By 10 that night, I kissed Dad and Mom on the forehead and rubbed the little girl's back and headed home.

Nothing about *that* story is remotely interesting...

...except that I found a way to become a grandfather without ever having had a single child.

How I Met My Granddaughter's Father

Eighteen years ago — before I was diagnosed with bipolar and anxiety disorders — I signed up to be a Big Brother with the local Big Brothers Big Sisters charity. The agency impressed upon me that I was expected to go on two outings a month over the course of the next year. I had to sign a sheet of paper that, while probably not legally binding, did its job of letting me know that I was making a promise to a child that would be pretty awful to break.

I was matched with a precocious six-year-old named Taylor. Our first outing was to a Chinese buffet and a pet store. It took less than hour, including drive time, and when it was all over I was deeply concerned I wouldn't be a good big brother at all. Making conversation was difficult, I wasn't sure how to act around a stranger's child, and I'm certain at one point I forgot his name.

Twelve years later, Taylor and I graduated from the Big Brothers Big Sisters program because Taylor was now an adult. They told us at that time that we were the longest active match they had and wished us luck as we entered a new phase of our relationship.

Taylor is now twenty-four years old and, as you can imagine, we've been through a lot together. We've had high moments, low moments, and every type of moment in between. He was there for my two divorces, my bipolar diagnosis, and two out of three weddings.

Somewhere along the way, he stopped being a volunteer obligation and became something more akin to my child. Both in terms of the responsibility I feel and the love I have for him.

Loving Someone's Father Doesn't Make You a Grandfather

The cynics and pessimists of the world — of which I am one — are still incredibly quick to point out that bestowing the title of grandfather on a person because he loves you and probably will love your child is an incredible leap.

If we bring a dictionary into this debate and follow the strictest letter of the words, I'm going to be quickly relegated to "close family friend." It is, after all the *accurate* title.

In my life, when it comes to family, accuracy has never played much of a role. My cousin Trish is not really my cousin, as she was born before my uncle married her mom. (She's the older sister of not the favorite, Athena — and note I said sister, *not* half-sister.) Also, in case it has escaped you, I'm not even Taylor's literal big brother.

My father isn't my biological father, just my real one. At least when it comes to my dad, I can hear the cynics murmuring, "But he adopted you when you were five."

Yes, but he met me when I was two and a half. Therefore, for almost three years, I was being raised by a man who was not my biological father (yet I called Dad) and then my parents (well, Mom and step-dad if you insist on being "right") gave birth to my brother (sorry, half-brother) until finally legal paperwork was filed that *fixed* all that.

Even I can't find enough cynicism to declare the government made our family what it is. Our family is what it is because *we* decided it was true. Because dictionaries don't define families.

People do.

How Will I Explain to Little Lennie Who I Am?

Life is messy. People we trust will let us down and people we don't trust will rise up and show themselves to be worthy of our forgiveness. Our society is filled with complicated issues we have trouble comprehending and yet we are called on to not just understand, but to resolve.

This is not even remotely complicated. I have no memory of meeting anyone in my family who is older than I am. I call my grandmother Granny because that's her name. That's who she is — *to me*.

Someday, Lennie will be old enough to figure out that something is amiss. Other families, she'll reason, don't look like hers. She'll wander over to me, look me in the eyes, and ask for the explanation that everyone else wants: how am *I* her grandfather?

And the answer will sound much different to her than it will to any of us. Because, unlike the rest of us who are over-thinking this, she'll begin her question by saying "Grandpa."

Psych Central, 8/6/2018

Does Bipolar Disorder Lead to Divorce?

I am certain that bipolar disorder was a factor in the ending of my first two marriages— but it was *not* the only reason for the divorces.

I'm on my third marriage. Because of previous issues with hyper sexuality, mania, and *very* poor impulse control, I've had a lot of bad outcomes in the love department.

If I were the sole data point, it would be easy to conclude that bipolar disorder leads to divorce. And, unfortunately, the actual data shows that my experience is not uncommon. The majority of marriages involving a spouse with bipolar disorder will, ultimately, end in divorce.

The answer to the question above should, ultimately, be "yes." However, I feel that society takes too broad of a stroke when concluding that bipolar disorder leads to divorce. I'll use my life to explain.

How Bipolar Disorder Factored into Divorce #1

I met my first wife in high school. I was 18 years old when I first laid eyes on her, while she was dating my friend. After their relationship ended, she pursued me.

We were married two weeks after she graduated high school. We ran off to another state and were married on a beach. It was romantic, against our parents' advice, and very dramatic. Exactly the kind of behavior expected from young love.

Statistically, we had a 59% chance of divorcing based on our ages. In other words, the majority of high school sweethearts don't make it. Because I was diagnosed with bipolar disorder soon after the end of our marriage, the blame easily shifted from "young love has an uphill battle" to "blame the guy with bipolar disorder."

Make no mistake, I'm not saying that me being an untreated bipolar didn't contribute to our divorce. I know that life with me was awful. *I* wouldn't want to be married to the person I was when I was married to wife #1.

But was it the sole contributor? In sickness and health was in our vows and I was certainly sick. She was as ignorant as I was to the symptoms of bipolar, so she never got me help. Had one of us known and I received treatment, perhaps we'd still be married today.

We were young, we didn't understand mental illness, and I was untreated. All of that contributed to the end of our marriage. But not all of that is often discussed. What is discussed is that I had bipolar and the marriage ended.

How Bipolar Disorder Factored into Divorce #2

I met my second wife while manic. I don't believe either one of us was in the proper place to lay the groundwork for a solid relationship, but I absolutely wasn't.

Early on, the woman who became my second wife saw that I was suicidal and took me to the emergency room. I was admitted to the psychiatric ward and, during my stay in the hospital, I was diagnosed with bipolar disorder. Over the next four years, she was my champion and my caregiver. During that time, we got married.

There is a name for what we were experiencing: Florence Nightingale effect. This is when caregivers fall in love with their "patients." From my vantage point, I was so relieved to be receiving help and care that I mistook those feelings for romantic love. Specifically, the kind of love that leads to a successful life together.

During the early years of our marriage, almost everything we did was in service to treating my illness. After I got well, we realized we had different values, different life goals, and our marriage couldn't recover from the power differential that had been created by me being the patient and her being the caregiver.

Was *that* the fault of me having bipolar disorder or was our divorce the fault of getting married under such strenuous circumstances? How many marriages survive when entered into under such circumstances?

But, given that I have bipolar disorder, none of those questions were asked. The narrative simply became, "They divorced because Gabe has bipolar disorder."

Wife #3, Bipolar Disorder, and Final Thoughts

The difference between my previous two marriages and this one has everything to do with how the relationship began. I entered into this marriage as a mentally stable and mature adult. My wife and I are equals, it was deliberate, and I hold myself to the identical standard I hold her. We are both accountable for our own actions and for each other.

Marriages that succeed are ones based on mutual respect and understanding. I don't get a pass because I have bipolar disorder. If I do something wrong – even if it *was* related to a symptom – I apologize and make amends.

So often, I hear people say, "But it wasn't my fault, it was my illness." I can certainly relate to this line of thinking, but those people have forgotten something very important: It wasn't the other person's fault, either. Taking responsibility for bipolar disorder, and therefore my life, is what has allowed me to move forward in a positive fashion. Unfortunately, if this marriage ends, no matter the reasons, the narrative will quickly focus on the fact that I have bipolar disorder and nothing else.

Using my first two marriages as an example, I can tell you for an absolute certainty, bipolar disorder was a factor, but it was far from the only one. There is a solid argument to be made that, at least for my second marriage, it wasn't even the primary factor.

It's hard to sustain a marriage when the partners have different values and life goals – and that isn't because I'm living with bipolar. It's because I chose the wrong spouse.

Bipolar Magazine, 7/26/2016

I'm Besties with My Ex-Wife Because I'm Bipolar

Living with bipolar disorder creates a lot of weird experiences. I've been manic, depressed, hypersexual, and everything in between. I've blacked out and freaked out more times than I can recall. It's not a nice illness, as many people will attest, and when I talk about my life with others, there is one thing that people zero in on quickly as the most bizarre thing I've ever done:

Became best friends with my *ex-wife*.

How Bipolar Disorder Factored into Our Marriage

The details of how we met were fairly typical for someone with untreated bipolar disorder. I was a wreck and in the middle of my second or third day of insomnia. The finer points of our meeting are irrelevant except to say that I didn't know I was bipolar and, therefore, neither did she.

We didn't start dating for a couple years, but once we got involved, it was a blast. New relationship energy is amazing, and she was happy to be dating a charismatic man who had personality to spare. We partied like rock stars and laughed all the time. As people with bipolar know all too well, mania is infectious. She was drawn in and I was thrilled to be the hero.

This was not my first go around with this type of relationship. Typically, after a few weeks or months, the bottom would fall out and the woman would leave as I lay in a pool of my own depressed filth, praying for death. When depression hit, I became boring, withdrawn, and unreliable. Friends and family didn't stick around then, so it isn't surprising that a woman I was casually dating wouldn't, either.

But this woman was different. As I careened closer and closer to the edge, she not only noticed, but also saved me. In the interest of keeping the story short, I'll summarize like this:

She noticed, confronted me, and got me medical care. She literally saved my life. Without her, I may have died by suicide or, at the very least, never would have been properly diagnosed and received help. She fired the first shot in my battle with bipolar disorder. Before her, I didn't know I was in a war at all. After her, I was an elite army ranger.

At one point in my life, she was the only person on the planet who thought that I had any chance of reaching recovery with bipolar disorder. She *knew* there was an amazing person under the layers of illness. Her confidence gave me confidence and that gave me hope. Hope is a powerful thing.

As I got better and my life improved, I was so incredibly thankful. Call it the Florence Nightingale effect if you want, but we were married a year or so after my diagnosis.

How Bipolar Disorder Factored into Our Divorce

Managing bipolar disorder takes a lot of time when a person is stable. When I was first diagnosed, I was nowhere near stable. I was a wreck and the medication, therapy, and everything else was the focus of my life – and our marriage.

It's safe to say that during the first two to three years of marriage, we did nothing but manage my mental illness. We didn't focus on much else. Our day-to-day life consisted of trying to get ahead of everything going on in my head.

I love to say that I had a four-year epic battle with bipolar disorder. It's true that it took four years to reach recovery, but it is a bit disingenuous to say "I" when I had a partner. She made my appointments, filled my prescriptions, and helped me every step of the way. To this day, I'm positive she saved my life and pretty sure I wouldn't have this level of recovery without her. She saw something in me that I didn't know was there. Through the layers of symptoms, she saw who I could be instead of who I was. In the beginning, she fought harder than I did and helped me move forward.

Unfortunately, once we stopped fighting bipolar disorder together and got on to the business of regular day-to-day living, we realized we were not a compatible married couple. We were oil and water.

Anger, resentment, and hostility became the new feelings we shared.

I loved that she saved my life and I owed her everything I had achieved, but we were miserable. Had it not been for bipolar disorder, we would have realized early on that we weren't compatible and moved on. But the crisis of my illness gave us a mission, a goal, and an us-against-the-world mentality.

She was partially responsible for my wellness and stability and, because of that wellness, I now wanted to move on. It was unfair, but it was the reality we were faced with. The thought of never seeing her again pained me greatly, but so did the thought of being married to her. We found ourselves between a rock and a hard place and the only thing I knew for certain was something had to give.

We hurt each other a lot during the final years of our marriage. A therapist once told us that our relationship was "toxic." At the time, I just couldn't understand how someone who saved my life could be bad for me. In later years, I realized that pretty much everything has a positive and a negative. We all need water to live, but you can also drown in it.

When I moved out of the house for the final time, she helped me, literally carrying boxes and furniture into my new apartment. She helped me organize and decorate. She spent the first night with me because I was scared. I was afraid that I couldn't manage bipolar disorder without her. I was afraid I was in some odd state where the person making me miserable was also the key to maintaining my recovery.

When I did spend a night alone for the first time, I cried myself to sleep. I didn't miss her as a wife, I just missed *her*. But there was no other choice. Staying married to someone and being miserable isn't a healthy decision.

How Bipolar Disorder Factored into Our Friendship

As the days became weeks and the weeks became months, we kept talking. We'd get together, go to movies, and out to dinner. We went through the motions of our divorce and we just kept talking. Every time we saw each other, I made a small mental note that this would be the last time. I just figured that someday I'd wake up and realize I hadn't spoken to her in a while. Like so many other relationships I've had, it wouldn't have a hard stop, it would just fade away naturally.

But it didn't. Things changed dramatically, of course, and there were more than a few hiccups along the way. The transition from spouse to friend was not an easy one. To this day, there are still triggers that fan the flames of past arguments. But time really does heal all wounds. Marriages end for all kinds of reasons and I'm in no position to comment on anyone else's life. For me, from today's vantage point, it bothers me that I had to luck into this situation. I really thought the only two choices were to stay unhappily married or never to see her again.

I'm shocked that we are friends. Not because I didn't think we had enough to build a friendship on, but because of the way people respond when they find out we used to be married — a viewpoint I understand because I once shared it. We live in an all-or-nothing society when it comes to romantic relationships and, at least for my ex-wife and me, there was so much worth saving. I'm grateful that we were able to salvage the parts of our relationship that were good, rather than tossing everything away.

These days, it's comical to watch people learn that my friend and I used to be married. Many people didn't know us as a couple. They whisper to themselves and have even tried to help out by keeping her away from my current wife – because, I guess, they think they might claw each other's eyes out.

Most of my life hasn't turned out the way I'd hoped, and my previous marriage is no exception. But, sometimes, things have to go terribly wrong in order to turn out perfectly.

Bipolar Magazine, 4/19/2016

Why My Spouse Doesn't Resent Me for Having Bipolar

Bipolar disorder can take a toll on relationships. Here are tips for maintaining a healthy relationship for partners both with and without bipolar disorder.

Anyone who has followed my work long enough knows that my wife isn't angry at the fact that I have a bipolar diagnosis. She doesn't celebrate it but she lacks the stereotypical sadness and/or resentment that many family members feel toward their mentally ill loved ones.

If my e-mail is any indication, people are interested in knowing how we are able to achieve a strong, loving, and stable marriage when so many other couples experience problems.

It's no surprise that people are curious. A study conducted in 2011 shows that the divorce rate *increases* between 20 to 80 percent for couples where one partner suffers from mental illness. (National Center for Biotechnology Information) This increase is in addition to the already high rates our society experiences.

It's easy to see how a marriage suffers under the weight of the symptoms of mental illness. For example, when one spouse is suffering from depression, the other spouse is often forced to take on additional parental and family responsibilities that would normally be shared between the two. This extra workload causes stress, which leads to conflict, which leads to resentment.

In the specific case of bipolar disorder, the couple is often left struggling with the crisis brought on by the sufferer's manic episodes, such as infidelity, excessive spending, or taking dangerous risks. All this is in addition to the issues already brought on by depression.

Tips for the Partner Who Does NOT Have Bipolar Disorder

In general, family members don't want to feel animosity toward the people they love. As stated above, in the case of spouses, the risk is much greater that the relationship will end because of this resentment. Parents are unlikely to abandon their children in the same way a spouse can – and often does.

I could write a book on the subject of living with someone who has bipolar disorder, so the lists below are in no way comprehensive.

- **Educate yourself.** Don't just listen to what your partner has to say about living with bipolar disorder. Take a class, join a support group, and/or read a book. Learn as much as you can so that you are in a good position to support them *appropriately.*
- **Set appropriate boundaries.** Just because a person has *any* illness does not give them the right to treat you however they want.
- **Put yourself first.** It's important that you maintain your own health. If you don't take care of yourself, you can't possibly provide good care to someone else. Don't be afraid to take a break.
- **Forgive – and mean it.** People living with bipolar disorder make many mistakes that are driven by their illness. If you want your relationship to flourish, you must forgive and move forward. No relationship can survive if past issues are constantly rehashed.

Tips for the Partner Who DOES Have Bipolar Disorder

I've been married three times and each one represents a different period in my life:

With wife #1, I was completely unaware that I was mentally ill and therefore untreated.

With wife #2, I was aware, but at the beginning of my journey toward recovery. I lacked many coping skills and hadn't acclimated to medication yet.

With wife #3, I am in treatment, on medications that work well, and am in full recovery *with* bipolar disorder. In other words, I spend more time living my life than I do managing bipolar disorder. It's no surprise that this is my best marriage; I'm in the best place to be a good husband.

- **Apologize – and mean it.** I can't stress enough that just because it's not our fault when something bipolar related happens, it doesn't make it our partner's fault. Make sure they know that you aren't blaming them and make amends whenever necessary.
- **Make them part of your treatment team.** If we exclude our partners from our treatment team, we are showing them a lack of trust and opening the door for misunderstandings. Also, working together can improve the outcomes – and that is good for both of you.
- **Don't hide your symptoms.** If you have to hide your symptoms from your partner, something is already wrong. People living with bipolar disorder will sometimes symptomatic. Your partner should already understand this, and if they don't, it's time to educate them.
- **Trust your partner.** If they express concern about your mental well-being, believe them. They have no motivation to

lie. (If they do, then this isn't the article you need to be reading.) Our partners know us better than anyone does, so think of them as an early warning system. Even if they are wrong about how you are feeling, use it as a learning opportunity. Working with them, you will help them become a better part of your support system.

Bipolar or Not – The Fundamentals of Long-Term Relationships Apply to All

Whether or not one partner has bipolar disorder doesn't change the fundamentals. Long-term relationships are about sharing your life with another person. We lean on our partners and allow them to lean on us.

Many couples fall into the rut of only pointing out each other's faults. As important as it is to communicate to each other that things aren't going well, it's equally (if not more) important to celebrate together. Make it a goal to spend as much time celebrating your lives together as you do managing your lives with bipolar disorder and you should be just fine.

Bipolar Magazine, 3/14/2017

Thank You for Loving Me in Spite of Bipolar Disorder

This article is dedicated to my wife, Kendall. She loves all of me – bipolar disorder included. She and I will be married three years on August 22, 2015. She knew on our first date that I was living with mental illness and she showed up anyway. Call it a romantic story, call it love, you can even call it stupid, but she deserves a thank you note. Buckle up friends, it's about to get sappy.

My Wife Makes Me Happier than Bipolar Mania

Dear Kendall,

You make me happier than bipolar mania. You have no idea how happy that is because you've never experienced mania. I can assure you, however, that it is really, really happy. Literally psychiatrically happy. The difference is, this kind of happiness is healthy and doesn't cause bouts of excessive spending or jumping off roofs. It's the kind of happiness that isn't a symptom of an illness, but the result of a happy marriage.

That being said, you're incredibly annoying. Your incessant optimism about people, the state of the world, and life in general is enough to make anyone over the age of 12 vomit. Managing to see beauty in a sea of ugliness is both disturbing and inspiring. If I were darkness, you would be light. And while I feel most comfortable in the dark, I need the light to see.

Your desire to love and marry me in spite of my living with bipolar disorder is, frankly, unfathomable to me. While it has worked out fantastically for me, I question your overall ability to assess things properly. If I were to make a pro and con list about myself, it would look like this:

Pros: Funny, charismatic, redhead

Cons: Debilitating depression, chronic panic attacks, lifelong chronic and persistent mental illness to manage

What. The. Hell? Who would date, let alone marry, that guy?

But, here is why I love you more than mania. Because *your* pro and con list reads this way:

Pros: Resilient, irreverent, brave

Cons: Steals the covers, very finicky about cleaning, sleeps with four pillows

That is how you view the world. Your optimism, in all its annoying glory, is the fabric that holds our relationship together. It balances us out and allows us to be greater together than apart.

Frankly, our marriage works because, while the rest of the world hears my story and sees tragedy, you see triumph, making you one of the few people who sees me as the hero and *not* the victim.

For that alone, I will be *forever* thankful.

Love,

Gabe

Psych Central, 8/12/15

Language

Are Slang Terms Describing Mental Illness Always Offensive?

Recently, while talking to a friend, I called myself a "wack job." It isn't uncommon for me to use a variety of colorful terms to describe my mental illness or living with bipolar disorder in general. But, on this occasion, he stopped me and said, "Wait, isn't that term offensive?"

You might think that I'd immediately answer, "Yes." After all, I do write a blog titled "Don't Call Me Crazy." So, surely, I acknowledge that all slang having anything to do with mental illness is immediately offensive. Right?

Language, much like people, is a tricky thing. There is no clear indicator in a single word between being offensive and not. Words stand alone. They have meanings, naturally, but they don't have malice in and of themselves. There are no inherently bad words *or* good words; there are just words, neutral and meaningless. ..

...until you add context. Context is a sneaky thing.

Context is the difference between being cutely told to shut up because you embarrassed your significant other in public by exclaiming to all around that you loved them and being told to shut up because you're hated and disrespected.

The words are the same; the context is different.

Mental Illness and Words Like "Wack Job"

In reality, by the strictest definition of the term, I am a wack job, I suppose. I live with bipolar disorder, which is a mental illness, which means I'm crazy – in a manner of speaking. But the offensive part isn't in the words. It isn't even in the meaning of the words. It is in the context.

Take this sentence as an example: "Even though you have an impeccable work history and have demonstrated a high level of competency toward completing your projects, we have decided to remove you from your position because you are a person living with mental illness."

The description of my condition wasn't offensive in the slightest. The offensive part was the misplaced limitations, the belief that I wasn't competent, capable, successful, and qualified. The context that someone with a mental illness couldn't thrive, compete, or succeed and the societal narrative that the mentally ill are less than everyone else being played out right before my eyes is what I, and others, find offensive.

In that context, "wack job" doesn't sound so bad.

Psych Central, 1/10/17

Why "I Am Bipolar" is NOT an Offensive Statement

I love the internet. I have met the most incredible people, learned exceptional things, and it is how I make my living as a blogger, speaker, and mental health coach. But, as with all things, there is a downside. Often, I see people become offended by things that really, at most, *could* be considered annoying. But, in keeping this about bipolar disorder, there is one outrage that really needs to stop.

It is not "more respectful" to say "a person living with bipolar disorder" instead of "a bipolar person." "I have bipolar" and "I am bipolar" are equivalent statements. Arguing that one is correct and another is incorrect is analogous to debating the correct spelling of John vs. Jon. It is personal preference and nothing more.

"I'm Cancer" Is Not a Good Refutation

Every time I mention that the phrase "I'm bipolar" is just the English language being the English language, someone will say, "You would never say, 'I'm cancer.'" That is true; I would never say, 'I'm cancer,' because that is incorrect grammar. But, I say on a daily basis, "I'm hungry."

I certainly do not say that I am a person living with hunger. I don't think that a person is giving up their humanity if they say they are hungry. I also don't think "I'm bipolar" carries that message. Unless the overreacting public chooses to say it does.

To be fair, hunger isn't an illness. Comparing hunger to bipolar disorder is a bit disingenuous. But what about diabetes? If a diabetic says, "I am a person living with diabetes," many of us would think it sounded weird. I'll also lay odds you didn't think there was anything inherently offensive when I referred to them as diabetic at the beginning of the previous sentence.

It is certainly true that many people choose to say they have diabetes instead of saying they are diabetic. All of this is generally chalked up to preference of speech and not used as an indicator of how people *feel* about themselves.

Bipolar Disorder Versus the English Language

Bipolar disorder isn't the only disease worded in this way. People say they are asthmatic, anemic, or even just plain sick. For some reason, when people hear, "I'm thirsty," they don't think I am surrendering my humanity, personality, and life to thirst. But when I say that I'm bipolar, they immediately think I've given up and must consider myself to be a disease first and a person second.

And that is just nonsense. I say I'm bipolar because bipolar is an *adjective*. It's a descriptor. "Cancer" is not. It's a noun. This is why we say, "I'm hungry" instead of "I'm hunger." We could say, "I'm cancerous," to be grammatically correct, but "I have cancer" just sounds better to the ear.

The mental health community has allowed stigma to affect how we interpret simple English. These are feelings we literally made up. Fighting an enemy that we created is an incredible waste of time, talent, and resources, all of which are in short supply.

To be clear, I don't think the phrase "I'm mentally ill" is offensive, either. The bottom line is we need to stop arguing semantics and focus our collective energy on helping people get well and stay well. We don't need to change the way people *talk* about bipolar disorder; we need to change the way they *think* about it.

Bipolar Magazine, 9/22/2015

Is the Word 'Crazy' Stigmatizing the Mentally Ill?

In my role as a mental health advocate, I seldom have the opportunity to comment on current events. Without a specific mental health tie-in, it would just muddy the waters. No one reads what I'm writing to find out what kind of music I like, for example – unless I mention that listening to music can help ease anxiety (which it can).

I was prepared to let this election season pass by without comment when, all of a sudden, throngs of people – including the media – started calling Republican presidential candidate Donald Trump, "crazy." I knew there would be some backlash to this.

Many people in the mental health community consider any use of the word "crazy" to be offensive. The same community often criticizes me for saying I'm bipolar.

Is the Word *Crazy* Inherently Offensive?

Many people will argue that the word "crazy" is a passive trigger that is demeaning, whether or not we mean it to be. In other words, using the word is inherently offensive, no matter the intention.

I looked up "crazy" in the online version of the Merriam-Webster dictionary. Here's an abbreviated definition:

- Mad, insane
- impractical

271

- erratic
- being out of the ordinary: unusual
- distracted with desire or excitement
- absurdly fond: infatuated <he's crazy about the girl>
- passionately preoccupied: obsessed

Much of the above should not be immediately offensive to the mental health community. And in the case of Mr. Trump, for example, his methods and pronouncements are – by his own admission – out of the ordinary.

Many people feel that his views are extreme, his behavior erratic, and his candidacy impractical. The use of the word "crazy" to describe his behavior could easily fall into the realm of opinion. You don't need to agree with these statements in order for "crazy" to be a correct word with which someone expresses a point of view.

However, just because a person uses a correct word doesn't mean that word isn't offensive. In my mind, the question becomes,

No reasonable person believes that the word "crazy" is a clinical mental health diagnosis. When I hear the word used about someone, I don't immediately assume that person has mental illness. In general, I see it as a slang word indicating that something extremely unusual is being referenced.

In a world filled with so much misinformation and stereotypes surrounding mental illness, I just have a hard time getting upset at slang. According to Wikipedia, "Slang consists of a lexicon of non-standard words and phrases in a given language. Use of these words and phrases is typically associated with the subversion of a standard variety (such as Standard English)."

In other words, if I stay out all night, partake in activities that I normally wouldn't, and wrap up by watching the sun rise from the roof of my house with a flock of geese by my side, I would tell everyone the next day that I had a "crazy" night.

And most people would agree. Furthermore, using "crazy" as a slang term wouldn't cause them to think less of anyone who has a mental health diagnosis.

For those reasons, and more, I don't believe the general use of the slang term "crazy" is inherently offensive.

Oversensitivity Doesn't Lead to Decreased Stigma

As someone who has bipolar disorder, I have experienced first-hand the stigma and discrimination aimed at people living with mental illness. I understand the tendency to see negativity where none exists. That is typical behavior for *anyone* who has experienced trauma. I'm not suggesting that certain words, phrases, or actions can't be triggers for a person: literally anything can be a trigger to *someone*. I am suggesting that looking for them and/or creating them is counterproductive.

It's imperative to know the difference between being triggered because of our own personal experiences and actual discrimination. Being oversensitive and demanding that society cater to that sensitivity is unlikely to foster a better understanding of life with mental illness.

Consider soldiers returning from war who flinch, or even throw themselves on the ground, when a loud noise surprises them. Now imagine if all soldiers banded together to tell society that loud noises were triggers for them and that the solution was that all loud noises – both accidental (tires screeching) and intentional (fireworks) – were part of a larger insensitivity aimed at them out of either malice or ignorance. Soldiers everywhere would begin to believe that all loud noises were further proof of society's desire to alienate them and drive a deeper wedge between "them" and "us."

While it's true that many soldiers don't like loud noises, they don't insist that society quiet down in order to reduce veterans' discomfort.

Because that would be *crazy*.

Can the Weather Be Bipolar and/or Schizophrenic?

I've often remarked on the absurdity of the English language. When I was a teenager, we all ran around saying we were *bad*. Except, of course, we meant it in an extremely positive way. I don't really know why, after many generations of "bad" meaning something negative, teenagers in the 80s decided to change the definition to something positive. But we did, and most people (eventually) understood what we meant when we said it.

However, what happens when words change meanings in a way that is considered – at least by some – to be derogatory? As an example, there is nothing inherently offensive about riding a short bus, but "short bus" has become a slang way of calling someone developmentally delayed. It's not just offensive to the person being insulted; it's equally offensive to people who live with developmental disabilities.

I've written before about how language influences people's opinion of people living with mental illness. A popular episode of *The Psych Central Show* podcast asked, "Does Person-First Language Reduce Mental Illness Stigma?" We even spoke, briefly, about this meteorological question.

Should You Say Bipolar or Schizophrenic Weather?

So, to the question of whether or not people should say the weather is bipolar or schizophrenic I say this:

Try to avoid it. It does legitimately hurt some people's feelings. Even though I, personally, feel those people are looking at this incorrectly, collectively, we aren't a group of people who hold a lot of sway in society. People living with mental illness are discriminated against, often, and I recognize that it would mean a lot to them if you found a different way to say the weather is being fickle.

I realize that these words have multiple meanings, just like the word bad can mean something negative or positive. People with mental illness don't own the words bipolar or schizophrenic – but the most common usage of these words is within a mental health context.

For what it's worth, I'm not offended when people say that politicians are cancerous to democracy, either. It isn't because I don't have cancer; it's because I recognize the context of what's being communicated. Because, as I've written about before, context matters.

To people living with mental illness who hear people say "the weather is bipolar and/or schizophrenic" I say this: The person using that phrase most likely isn't trying to be offensive. They are just repeating a phrase they overheard that means the weather is changing rapidly or unexpectedly. They aren't insulting anyone. Just as in the examples above, bipolar and schizophrenia have multiple meanings.

I recommend taking a deep breath and respectfully opening a dialogue. I'd wager most people would be unlikely to use it if they knew it was hurting someone. Explain the history of stigma and discrimination against persons living with mental illness and that you simply dislike that particular phrase. Then, end on a high and say you believe that most people simply aren't aware that it bothers some people, but you wanted to share.

This is an excellent example of why I feel people need to talk respectfully with one another. I'm not offended by this phrase, but other people are. Consider why it bothers you, and if it still does, talk to those around you. However, I caution you against assuming that people are simply being jerks.

Life, like words, just isn't that simple.

Psych Central, 4/18/17

Is Recovery the Best Word to Describe Wellness with Mental Illness?

As a mental health blogger and a person living with mental illness, I often use the word *recovery*. In my quest to educate the world, I am very open about my illness, but I'm also quick to let people know that I'm living *well*. In other words, I tell people that I'm a person *in recovery*. That's when people really get confused.

The first pushback I receive is that the word *recovery* — when it hits most people's ears — implies that mental illness is gone. If you recover from the flu, for example, it means the virus dies out and you no longer have the flu. But mental illness isn't like the flu. There's no virus to die out. There is no vaccine to prevent it. If you are in recovery from mental illness, it doesn't mean you no longer have mental illness. It just means it's controlled.

As you might imagine, this doesn't sit well with the average person, because it sounds like I'm giving the word *recovery* an entirely different meaning from what they're used to. But that's not what I'm doing at all. Oxford dictionary defines recovery as:

1) a return to a normal state of health, mind, or strength and 2) the action or process of regaining possession or control of something stolen or lost.

Nowhere in that definition does it say "cured," or that whatever caused the issues in the first place has been eradicated entirely. It just says that what was once there is currently gone and a normal state of being has been restored.

Almost every time I use the word *recovery* online, someone will write me that they hate "that word." Remission would be a better word, they often contend.

Some folks believe that no word is appropriate. They believe I should say that I'm a person living with bipolar, and leave it at that, with no mention of my current health status, whatsoever.

Obviously, I disagree with that, because I use the word *recovery*. I'm proud to be a person living in recovery with bipolar disorder. I didn't choose the phrasing, but I understand it and I agree with it.

I agree with the word *recovery* because I understand it to mean that I spend more time living my life than I do managing bipolar disorder. That's what it means to me.

SAMHSA, the group largely responsible for the word being commonplace, defines *recovery* as:

A process of change through which individuals improve their health and wellness, live a self- directed life, and strive to reach their full potential.

I have no issues with how it is defined or used as it relates to mental illness and/or substance use disorders. It doesn't strike me as offensive, dismissive, or off-putting. Language is difficult, and many words have different meanings, depending on the context.

What's important to realize, however, is that all the other ways to describe – and define – wellness are also correct. If you don't like the word *recovery*, then don't use it. It should be perfectly acceptable to define your experience with your illness in any way you see fit.

The way wellness is described is much less important to me than people being well. People should choose whatever word or phrase works for them and use it. As long as it means they're living well.

Psych Central, 6/4/2017

Halloween 'Insane Asylums' Should Not Offend the Mentally Ill

Halloween is a holiday filled with mystery, death, and superstition, not to mention witches, ghouls, and the walking dead. Many teenagers and adults embrace the scarier aspects of the holiday by visiting haunted houses and being open to the idea of being frightened. Many such attractions are billed as interactive horror movies and include the use of talented actors, exceptional make-up, and technology.

Per History.com, Halloween "is thought to have originated with the ancient Celtic festival of Samhain, when people would light bonfires and wear costumes to ward off roaming ghosts." Even the act of trick-or-treating is rooted in the ancient tradition of leaving wine and food for spirits still roaming the earth.

To most people in the United States, Halloween is seen as a playful holiday filled with make-believe, humor, and fun. It's not taken seriously, and is enjoyed by millions of adults, families, and children. This is the primary reason I find it odd that many mental health charities all over the country think that "haunted insane asylums" are offensive to people, like myself, who live with mental illness.

Recent Controversy

As a person living with bipolar disorder, no one is more sensitive to the stigma of mental illness than I am. I've lost friends and a successful career, and I've been discriminated against more times than I can remember. The stigma against people living with mental health issues is very real.

All that aside, I am surprised every October when I see people so offended by the clearly exaggerated portrayal of the "criminally insane." This diagnosis has long since been abandoned by medical professionals; its definition is primary of a legal nature. It's important to note that no one is diagnosed with "insanity" and it only applies to people in the criminal court system, if at all.

This year, Knott's Berry Farm came under fire for its virtual reality horror experience, FEARVR. FEARVR involved visitors wearing a virtual reality headset, being strapped to a hospital wheelchair, and the simulation was that of a crazed mental patient killing people.

When word of the attraction being set in an insane asylum got out, mental health advocates all over the nation reacted. Their lobbying campaign was so intense that Knott's Berry Farm opted to close the attraction.

There is much to say on this situation, but my major concern lies in the idea that the majority of people don't have issues with simulating murder — which I'm certain is traumatic for the family members of homicide victims. The primary concern is that the murderer was portrayed as mentally ill.

In this particular attraction, the murderer wasn't even portrayed as mentally ill, really. Most people with a mental health diagnosis are just like most other people, after all. No, this character was an insane psychopath: an exaggerated, scary, and entirely stereotyped version of a murderer. In other words, the same sort portrayed in hundreds of slasher films, which these same advocacy groups handle much differently.

Refocusing Advocacy Away from Fiction

For me, as a mental health advocate, the decision about where to put my advocacy efforts is simple and depends on whether the general public will likely believe it's a reasonable example of mental illness.

Every year when the haunted-mental-asylum-uproar reoccurs in the mental health community, I can't help but shudder at the hypocrisy, given how many other stereotypical examples of behavior in our society that these same people seem uninterested in resolving.

As an example, when the African-American community argues that black males are most often falsely depicted as violent criminals in pop culture, the collective society is quick to point out that it's just fiction and there is no reason to be offended. And, frankly, that is an issue that warrants further discussion.

Yet, year after year, many in the mental health community are bothered by something that is clearly make-believe. I'm not certain that the general public is mistaking haunted asylums as actual portrayals of living with mental illness. I truly believe that most people see it for what it is: entertainment.

But, let's assume that the general public does believe that all mentally ill people are violent serial killers. I'm at a loss as to why we in the mental health community don't use this as a teachable moment instead of an opportunity to be offended.

Imagine if, instead of working so hard to shut all these haunted asylums down, we worked with the organizers to post this statement in their advertising and outside the entrance:

"This attraction does not portray the actual reality for millions of Americans who live with mental illness. In fact, people with mental illness are no more likely to commit violence than anyone else in society.

"Also, please note that the reason this attraction causes fear is because of the historically deplorable conditions people endured in mental asylums. Psychiatric wards and in-patient facilities can still be frightening."

Wouldn't that be a lot better than being offended and asking society to give us special treatment, while simultaneously advocating that we want to be treated as equals?

Awareness

The Best Reason to Come Out of the Bipolar Closet

Living with bipolar disorder is not an easy thing to do and when a person reaches recovery, it becomes very easy to hide. The fact of the matter is that just by looking at me, you can't tell I'm bipolar. (Yes, I did write bipolar disorder is not an invisible illness, and I stand by those points.) Many people, myself included, for a period of time, choose to hide our diagnosis from the general public. It isn't difficult to come up with reasons to hide, but there are very good reasons not to. Here is the best reason to tell the world you are bipolar.

Bipolar Crisis is Public

It is very hard to hide a bipolar crisis. Whether it is mania, depression, suicidality, anger, irritation, or, in rare instances, violence, crisis is almost always very public. Crisis is also dramatic and scary and the kind of thing that bystanders remember and talk about. It is also the kind of thing that the media likes to report.

Bipolar recovery, by contrast, is boring. When I am driving to work, reading, or cleaning my house – all while bipolar – it isn't at all exciting. Living well with this illness looks just like everyone else's typical life. The advantage to telling people you're living with bipolar disorder is to provide an example of someone living well in spite of the illness. It allows you to show a different side, to show there is hope to someone who has been newly diagnosed.

Essentially, we have the opportunity to show society the entire spectrum of this disease instead of just the worst parts of it. If all society sees is the crisis points, we can hardly blame them for thinking that is all there is.

What If You Don't Want to Be the Bipolar Ambassador?

So, what if you don't want to be a "bipolar ambassador?" Many years ago, I read an article about disability, and one phrase from the article that has stuck with me is, "My disability is not your inspiration."

This really resonated with me because I want to inspire people for *any* reason. If my life, illness, or the struggle inspires a person, I just don't see this as a bad thing.

However, the author of that article made some really good points. Living with a disability is hard enough without other people using that misfortune to make themselves feel better about their own lives. It made me reflect back to my childhood when my dad would tell me to finish my dinner because starving kids in China didn't have any food at all. He literally used their suffering to motivate me.

I wrestled with this for a while and finally arrived at the conclusion that I almost always arrive at: life is complicated and it's almost impossible to figure out whether a person should feel bad if they are inspired by someone else's misfortune. For me, if someone is positively inspired by me falling over a pile of bricks, I'm okay with that. It becomes the silver lining to the cloud, as it were. I live openly with bipolar disorder because I want to. I want to show people a different side of the disorder – a side other than crisis. Ultimately, the choice is up to you, and while choosing to live openly with bipolar disorder has its downfalls, I believe the upside is significantly better.

AWARENESS

For what it's worth, it amuses me that the decision has its ups and downs. Because, I'm funny like that.

Bipolar Magazine, 11/17/2015

3 Simple Ways to Raise Awareness About Bipolar Disorder

Happy Mental Health Awareness Month, everyone! In the spirit of helping to raise awareness about bipolar disorder, I thought I would post a blog with three simple ways you can raise awareness. Don't worry; no supplies are needed and anyone can join in.

Simple Way #1

In the 90s, Brad Pitt and Ed Norton starred in the movie *Fight Club*. Because of that movie, the phrase, "First rule of (X) – don't talk about (X)" entered the popular lexicon.

If you are a member of an underground fight club, that is probably pretty good advice. But if you are trying to change the way society sees bipolar disorder, then *not* talking about it isn't going to help at all.

The first rule of raising awareness about bipolar disorder – *talk* about bipolar disorder. The more open and honest we are, the better.

Simple Way #2

Rule number two is really just an extension of rule number one. Talking about bipolar is easy among people who already accept that it is a treatable mental illness.

In mental health advocacy, we do a lot of talking *inside* the circle. We talk to people who already agree with us. This is a great thing for honing our knowledge and supporting each other, but the phrase "preaching to the choir" definitely applies.

In order to raise awareness about bipolar disorder, we must talk to people *outside* the circle. This is easier said than done, but if you are willing, you will see many opportunities. The news media, for example, reports on mental illness quite often. The next time you overhear friends, coworkers, or strangers saying something untrue, be willing to step in with the correct information.

Simple Way #3

In keeping with the talking theme, be willing to tell everyone you know that you live with bipolar disorder. If you don't have bipolar, don't worry; I'm not leaving you out. If you have a loved one with bipolar, ask them how you can team up to raise awareness. My mom, as an example, tells everyone she meets about her son, who lives with — you guessed it — bipolar.

Society, in general, has a preconceived notion about how people with bipolar are "supposed to be." Often, this opinion, which they believe is fact, is created by fictional portrayals in pop culture.

People living with bipolar have a unique opportunity and, some would say, a responsibility to live openly with this disorder so the public can see a more balanced view.

People are willing to reconsider their beliefs if a different view is presented in a respectful way. It might not happen instantly, but living well and letting others see that you are making your way just like everyone else goes a long way to changing the narrative.

Bipolar Magazine, 10/8/2015

The Downside to Mental Health Awareness Month

At its core, Mental Health Awareness Month (May) is a time for people to learn more about mental health conditions and, ideally, seek out help for them. Mental health charities all over the country plan events, awareness rallies, and fundraisers. Media outlets run stories discussing the importance of mental health care and its role in our society. Social media feeds have memes, quotes, and generally positive information about mental illness. While the conversation is still mostly a quiet one – there is a definite conversation. What could possibly be the downside of that?

Mental Health Awareness Month serves as a reminder of just how much work we have ahead of us. Seeing how much farther we need to go to effect real, lasting change is disheartening. Every time someone thanks me, or an audience applauds, I get caught up in the moment. I feel like we are there, that the fight is over and we have won! But needing to set aside a specific week or month to raise awareness of something is evidence that, in general, most people *aren't* paying attention.

Having a month dedicated to your cause seems like a great thing, and in so many ways, it is. However, one of the qualifications of having a month to make people aware of your cause is that people aren't already aware of it. It is a bit like feeding the homeless on Christmas and Thanksgiving, but not taking into consideration that homeless folks need to eat every day.

People aren't just sick during Mental Health Awareness month. People don't need love, understanding, hope, and compassion during one month only. That is a daily need and one that everyone deserves.

We need to be aware of mental health and mental illness concerns *every day*. We don't need a mental health month; we need mental health every single day. What we need is a society aware of mental health. Not just sometimes, not just in May, and not just when a crisis occurs.

If we could get our society to collectively raise the level of tolerance and understanding of these invisible and misunderstood illnesses, imagine how much better off we *all* would be.

This is the biggest downside to Mental Health Awareness Month. It shows us what could be – what should be. All of the positive stories, conversations, media coverage, and so forth will largely disappear on June 1. We will be back to mostly negative portrayals and business as usual. All of the hope, understanding, and positive messages will dry up.

Perhaps the biggest downside to Mental Health Awareness Month is *that it ends.*

Psych Central, 5/6/2015

Symptomatology

My Life with Trichotillomania (Hair Pulling)

"Truth is I cut my hair for freedom, not for beauty." ~ Chrisette Michele

When I was about 13 years old — 27 or so years ago — I decided to grow a ponytail.

Before that, my parents chose my hair style and kept it short. At the time, I just wanted to look like my 80s hair band heroes. I didn't expect the decision to grow my hair out would expose the very first noticeable symptom of mental illness.

But that's exactly what happened. As my hair grew longer and longer, I began "playing with it," as my family would say. As I grew older, the "playing" got more aggressive, more frequent, and more noticeable. Even though it was obvious that I was twisting, pulling, and ripping my hair out, it was not obvious that this was an illness. Thinking this was just a bad habit, my family would yell at me — and, in some cases, punish me — to try to get me to stop.

What Does Trichotillomania (Hair Pulling) Look Like?

Trichotillomania (hair pulling) is primarily characterized by the recurrent pulling out, or twisting, of one's own hair. Hair pulling may occur in any region of the body — such as your scalp, chest, or pubic area.

289

In my case, the pulling has been mostly limited to my scalp. When my hair is long enough that I can place a tuft between my thumb and index finger, I start to twirl. I just twist the hair in little knots. As time goes on, the knots become tighter and I have to rake at my hair to pull it free.

The constant twirling, knotting, and tugging causes hair to fall out and, if this goes on long enough, I develop bald patches on the top of my head.

I cannot control this impulse. I have sat in job interviews yanking on my hair while talking to hiring managers. I have pulled out clumps while in professional meetings, and I've even caused my scalp to bleed — and continued to twirl, in spite of the pain.

All my life, people have reacted to this habit by looking at me as if I'm crazy. They express worry, concern, and sometimes outright anger at why I would behave this way in public. When I was a teenager, I lived with my grandparents, and my grandfather used to leave the room when I would start to twirl. He said it was too distracting and I needed to stop.

Make no mistake; I tried. I'd sit on my hands, wear a hat, and even rub hair gel into my head to form a hair helmet. Nevertheless, I'd always find a way to grab, hold, and twist. Nothing I did worked to stop the twisting, pulling, and yanking until I shaved my head bald.

How I Defeated Trichotillomania (Hair Pulling)

I am a redhead and people with red hair, in general, really love their hair — even men. Even if someone doesn't remember what I said, they remember my red hair. I loved having long hair because that meant more red. So when I say I came home in a frustrated, agitated, and angry state and asked my wife to shave my head, I can only imagine what I looked like through her eyes.

Earlier that day, while at work, I had pulled a clump of my hair out and it grossed out my co-worker. She made a big deal about it and told me to get help. She was disgusted and didn't hold back. My supervisor told me to see the on-site nurse and, in short, I was embarrassed.

I still didn't know that the reason I was playing with my hair had anything to do with mental illness. I thought it was a moral failing on my part. I decided that I didn't deserve hair, since I couldn't take care of it.

That evening, my head was shaved completely bald. No hair, whatsoever. And that worked. Having no hair to twirl meant that when I reached up, I'd find nothing to grab onto, and the compulsion receded.

In the years since, I have found out how lucky I was that this worked. After being diagnosed with bipolar and anxiety, I've learned a lot about my various conditions — trichotillomania being a prominent one. And, while I no longer keep my head bald, I do keep my hair cut very short. If it gets too long, I'll start twirling again.

To this day, I think my hair twirling is a commentary on the lack of mental health education in this country. My entire family, all my friends, and even strangers watched me pull out my own hair and no one knew to recommend that I see a doctor. They were all quick to blame me for being bad, rather than consider that something more could be at the root of my hair pulling.

If the people around me didn't realize that literally pulling my hair out was a medical issue — and I was in need of help, not scorn — then it shows just how much more mental health education our society needs.

Psych Central, 5/28/2017

Overeating and Weight Issues with Bipolar Disorder

"My name is Gabe Howard and I have bipolar disorder." I start many a speech that way because it gives the audience an idea of who I am, and why I am qualified to give a speech on the subject. But, if I were being honest, it really isn't that descriptive. It doesn't narrow down what bipolar symptoms I have *at all.* And, since today I am living quite well and look like a "normal" person, the audience has no idea that I have an eating disorder, or that I used to weigh a staggering 550 pounds. In fact, it doesn't explain the link between binge eating disorder and bipolar disorder in any way.

Bipolar Disorder and Self-Medicating

Many people are familiar with the term "self-medicating" as it relates to mental illness. The concept is simple: the symptoms of the illness cause a person to suffer and, in an attempt to alleviate that suffering, they turn to... *something.*

Sadly, the stereotypical choice both in pop culture and in reality is drugs and alcohol. They are an easy choice to make, for obvious reasons. But food can be used to cope just as easily as illicit substances. Eating feels good and it's easy. Certain foods are synonymous with happy feelings.

We have an entire category we refer to as "comfort foods," usually carb-heavy items like macaroni and cheese, mashed potatoes, and so on. Carbohydrates fuel the production of serotonin, which makes us feel good. You can see the danger, there. It's the identical path of substance abuse, but more socially acceptable.

Self-Medicating Often Leads to Other Issues

The problem with self-medicating is that it often leads to other issues. If I could eat a piece of cake once a week and feel good, then there would be no cause for alarm. The problem is that – like a drug addict – the more I ate, the more I needed to eat. Eating became the only thing that would cheer me up, and that feeling ended soon after I was finished.

The mood swings of bipolar disorder were bad enough, but then I was faced with the physical pain of being morbidly obese. I couldn't walk long distances, was constantly looking for food, and stopped doing things I enjoyed, like going to a sporting event or to a movie theater, because I couldn't fit in the seats.

The cycle is clear. I ate because I was sad and lonely and eating caused me to pull away from my friends. I become sadder, lonelier, and physically sick. I developed sleep apnea, which fit nicely with my insomnia, further complicating an already complicated problem. One of my friends once described me as "circus freak fat," a label that, to this day, I cannot find fault with. I wore a size 64 waist pant, my belt was longer than I was tall (and I am six foot, three inches), and I wore a 7X large shirt – larger than the "big and tall" store carried at the time.

Ending the Cycle of Eating to Relieve Bipolar Symptoms

Ending the cycle of eating to relieve bipolar symptoms wasn't easy. It took almost three years to lose the weight I packed on and today, 10 years later, I still fight the urges. I started my weight loss journey by first acknowledging that I was binge eating.

Since binge eating is a disorder, I started going to therapy and enrolled in nutrition classes. I started attending groups as well to commiserate with other people who had similar feelings about food.

I also had gastric bypass surgery. Because of my obesity I had to allow a surgeon to cut me open and rearrange my insides as another tool to help me lose weight. The recovery time from surgery was eight weeks and caused quite a bit of discomfort.

I have kept the majority of the weight off for the past decade. Today, I weigh 250 pounds and struggle a lot less with food than I used to. I always have to be aware and remember how far I've come — and work to ensure I never go back.

Bipolar Magazine, 6/2/2015

My 3 Least Favorite Bipolar Symptoms

When it comes to living with bipolar disorder, there is no shortage of things to hate. It's an illness, after all, and being sick isn't enjoyable. Truthfully, I haven't the slightest idea how many bipolar symptoms there are, but I do know which three I dislike the most.

Typically, I would rank these in order of how much I hate them, but they all suck equally. They also can occur at the same time, and even bring along other symptoms to round out my suffering.

Before we begin, I want to point out these are *my* three least favorite. Everyone is different and that extends to those of us living with bipolar as well.

1. Bipolar Depression

Many people incorrectly relate depression to sadness, but depression is much different, and often occurs without a discernible cause. When I'm experiencing the lowest lows of bipolar disorder, I'm not "feeling sad." I'm not feeling anything. I'm empty and numb.

Depression has lingering effects on mind and body. Fatigue and a general feeling of heaviness are two of the worst physical sensations that break a person's spirit. Sinking into the darkness is a special kind of suffering that I fear repeating even when I'm happy and doing well.

The lingering trauma alone is enough to make depression one of my least favorite bipolar symptoms.

2. Hypersexuality in Bipolar Disorder

Hypersexuality is probably one of the most misunderstood symptoms of bipolar disorder. I've written before about how it isn't just an increased sex drive or having a lot of sex. It's a compulsion that is all encompassing, so much so that it ruins the pleasurable aspects of sex.

Anything that ruins lovemaking is going to be on my least favorite list, but there is more to it than just that. The risk associated with the compulsions – whether infidelity or potentially contracting STDs – is a dangerous and often overlooked aspect of bipolar hypersexuality.

In short, sex is a healthy, natural part of the human experience. This symptom of bipolar disorder spoils that.

3. Racing Thoughts Associated with Bipolar Disorder

Racing thoughts refers to the rapid thought patterns that typically occur in the manic phase of bipolar disorder. Essentially, it makes my thoughts occur on top of one another. Imagine listening to the news on the radio and watching a movie on TV at the same time. The two have nothing to do with each other. Similarly, my thoughts are often unrelated and meaningless. The most important part of the thought process is *completing* a thought – reaching a conclusion. With so much happening in my head, it becomes difficult to string together thoughts that actually belong together.

What's worse is that people do most of their thinking when we are around other people, so people take notice that something is *off* about me.

As an example of racing thoughts playing out in real life, while my brain is processing "I love my wife," "let's get chocolate ice cream," and "I like your new hairstyle," what I end up saying is, "I go new" and, even worse, when I realize I've just said gibberish, I overcompensate by saying, "chocolate hairstyle." The important point here is that I'm unable to stop. I know what I want to say and I know I'm not communicating it correctly, but I'm powerless to do anything about it.

Racing thoughts make it difficult, if not impossible, to write, hold conversations, or complete projects. This particular symptom can lead the people around me to think I'm unintelligent or under the influence of drugs or alcohol (which is especially bad if I'm at work).

All that said, the worst part for me is that it impacts my ability to connect and communicate with those around me. In the example above, all I wanted to do was compliment my wife's new hairstyle (that I noticed!) and take her out for ice cream. I know that's what I wanted to do – but she didn't. It's a devastating thing to happen and it makes me feel incredibly alone.

Bipolar Magazine, 6/17/2017

Hypersexuality in Bipolar Disorder

The compulsions associated with hypersexuality can be as damaging as addiction. So, what exactly is it?

I've long said that society discusses human sexuality less than bipolar disorder. I don't mean pop culture sex talk, but openly and frankly discussing sex. Despite using half-naked models to advertise pretty much anything, we seem remarkably unwilling to discuss the sexual health of said models. As a society, we are uncomfortable discussing sexual matters in general, and sexual education is a hotly debated topic in every school district in America.

Since collectively we can't decide what the healthy (or normal) sexual appetite is, it makes it difficult to determine exactly what is unhealthy (or abnormal). Determining *exactly* when a person's sexual appetite becomes problematic is a matter of personal preference. However, there are behaviors, feelings, and compulsions that clearly indicate a person has crossed a line.

I've Been Hypersexual

My name is Gabe and I've been hypersexual. If that phrasing sounds familiar, it's because the compulsion, the need, and the obsession feel much the same as those felt by drug addicts and alcoholics.

I am nothing if not open about living with bipolar disorder. I am not providing the results of a study on bipolar and hypersexuality, but explaining to you what it feels like to *be* hypersexual.

Hypersexuality, like all illnesses and disorders, exists on a spectrum and people experience like things in different ways. My favorite ice cream is vanilla, and my wife's favorite ice cream is chocolate. Neither one of us is eating the "correct" flavor, but we are both eating (experiencing) ice cream.

What It Feels Like to Be Hypersexual

Back in 2001, I experienced my longest bout with hypersexuality. No matter how often I had sex, it wasn't enough. I didn't realize this was not a normal state. This was before I was diagnosed with bipolar disorder, so I was unaware my feelings were abnormal.

Hypersexuality is about quantity, not quality. Given the limitations of the male body, this involves a lot of time and can became physically uncomfortable, but the compulsion to continue outweighed the pain. I could not sleep, move, or focus on a task until I was finished.

The unsettling part is that there was no true satisfaction in this. I wasn't connecting with anyone or even enjoying myself. I was unable to stop and the desire to complete the act was more important than anything – or anyone. The need for sex was so great that I sought out unhealthy and emotionally damaging physical encounters, lied to the people around me, and took unsafe and unnecessary risks. *Nothing* was more important than quieting the biological urge that was controlling me.

Hindsight is 20/20 and I can assure you that there was no amount of sex, no type of sex, or no specific person to satisfy my cravings. The disorder gripped me entirely and the aftermath of my decisions left me empty. Trying to satisfy the urges created by hypersexuality is like shooting rubber bands at the stars – you may feel like you are achieving something, but eventually you get frustrated, and the stars remain untouched.

What Hypersexuality Is *Not* and Where to Find Help

Hypersexuality doesn't mean having a lot of sex. It isn't spring break; it isn't your honeymoon. There is a world of difference between hypersexuality and having a lot of sex or many partners or sexual experimentation. The primary difference is motivation.

If a person is taking risks, missing school or work, and/or shirking responsibilities because sex has become more important than personal responsibility, these are telltale signs of hypersexuality. Bottom line: if a person's reason for having sex is because they are *compelled* to, then there is most likely something going on. Sex is not supposed to be a chore, but fun and intimate. It can be personal or shared and take many forms, but when it crosses the line from pleasure to compulsion, something is amiss.

Hypersexuality can also be a symptom of bipolar disorder. It is no different from mania, depression, or lack of focus. Some parts of bipolar disorder can be controlled through experience, hard work, and therapy, and other parts need medication. Report your symptoms to a health care professional, including the sexual urges described above.

People living with bipolar disorder, like myself, often talk about the stigma of living with this disease. Let's not stigmatize the symptoms of bipolar disorder further by refusing to discuss or disclose them. There is no shame in any symptom of any disease. It is okay to discuss hypersexuality; it's a shame not to seek help.

Bipolar Magazine, 5/20/2015

About Me & My Relationship with Bipolar

An Open Letter to Bipolar Disorder

Dear Bipolar Disorder:

For forty years, you've managed to live in my head. Like lead paint in the 70s, you were always there. I just wasn't aware of your presence. You were bonded to my personality so thoroughly that I have never been able to determine where you end and I begin.

Because you *hide.*

Just as the lead paint looked beautiful on the surface, but held the potential to cause untold damage. I believed my thoughts were my own, but secretly – and cowardly – you were pulling on strings that I didn't even know existed.

As my mind developed, you implanted land mines that I would trip over later in life. You gave them cute names like hyper-sexuality and mania. You used my mind to fight a war against itself, ensuring that the only outcome was that I'd lose.

Your counter-offensive was particularly cruel and evil – letting everyone, including me, believe that your effects were my fault while simultaneously convincing us that you didn't even exist.

Your battle cry was that it was all in my head. You watched while people I love told me I needed to get my act together. You fed off my uncertainty and fear. You made me present a mind so compromised that it was considered diseased, yet so misunderstood that I wasn't a victim of your actions, but the perpetrator of my own pain.

Then, one day you overplayed your hand. As you pounded on the self-destruct button, attempting to cause my suicide, someone noticed your insidious manifestation and took steps to warn me.

She was a force so powerful and determined that you couldn't stop her. She knew your weaknesses and she helped me exploit them, dealing a crushing blow to your plan of total domination.

You fought back. The battle between us was epic and lasted over four years. You are a formidable opponent. It took all my energy – and dozens of people and a billion-dollar medical industry — to tame you.

But defeated you were. While I couldn't vaporize you completely, I weakened you to the point of near non-existence. You went from being the author of my misery to little more than a footnote in my life.

But success got the better of me. I forgot how nimble an adversary you are and, when I wasn't paying attention, you let loose with your closing salvo.

You transformed yourself from the architect of my demise to the founder of my feast. Suddenly, you were claiming credit for my creativity and charisma. My spirit, you argued, was owed to all the pain you caused.

You sat back and convinced the world that everything I am was the result of some magical gift you *gave* me. Your attempts to end my life having failed, you reinvented yourself as the savior of it.

You whispered to me – and more cruelly, to anyone who would listen – that you aren't who makes me weak; You are who makes me strong. Utter nonsense, you attempt to pass off as truth.

I've accepted that we are intrinsically linked and I'll never be free of you. But you forgot that we grew up together. I was there when you pulled me to the depths of hell and then threw me to the heavens, all the while laughing as I believed the world was revolving around me.

And in those moments, I saw the real you. You rely on chaos and confusion to cultivate your existence and everything I am today is deliberate.

You're not my equal nor my friend. You're the fly in the room that I just can't swat. In order to beat you, I had to become the polar opposite of everything you stand for. And yes, I used the phrase *polar* opposite to twist the knife.

Take care,

Gabe

Bipolar Magazine, 6/6/2017

Bipolar Disorder: A Patient's Definition

When I was diagnosed with bipolar disorder in 2003, I knew exactly one thing about it: Kurt Cobain, the lead singer of Nirvana, had it. And he died by suicide in 1994. As a Nirvana fan, I paid attention to the news about his life — and death — but, with the exception of repeating the diagnosis over and over again, little information about bipolar disorder itself was reported.

Essentially, I knew that a famous millionaire couldn't beat it. I also knew it was a mental illness, which meant I was broken — so broken that I could no longer participate in society. Some of my earliest thoughts immediately after being diagnosed revolved around selling my house, quitting my job, and moving into a group home — things I never needed to do, but simply assumed I would have to.

When I finally was able to ask the doctor what bipolar disorder was, the response did little to aid in understanding: *"A mental illness that brings severe high and low moods and changes in sleep, energy, thinking, and behavior."*

At that moment, I had a better comprehension of advanced algebra — and I had failed math in high school.

How I Explain Bipolar Disorder

It's been almost 13 years since I was diagnosed. In that time, I've learned a lot about the disease from a practical standpoint. As a speaker and writer, I've become skilled at explaining what bipolar

304

disorder is in a way that the medical and educational establishments can't. Because I live with the illness, I can go "off script," for lack of a better term.

In my mind (no pun intended), bipolar disorder exists on a spectrum. On the very bottom is suicidal depression. At the very top is god-like mania. The bipolar individual vacillates back and forth between the two extremes.

To put it simpler, sometimes I want to die and sometimes I believe I am the creator of the universe and capable of *all* things. Literally going from massive confidence to massive self-doubt.

The oft-used comparison to temperature applies beautifully, since temperature exists on a spectrum, as well. Thirty-two degrees is warmer than zero, but colder than 72. Unlike the weather, we don't have a science to predict the extremes of bipolar in advance. A meteorologist can predict the weekend forecast with some accuracy, but we can't know where on the spectrum a person's mood will be on any given day, or how long that mood will last.

As the weather is unpredictable, so is bipolar disorder. The highs and lows are not balanced. Two days of depression does not mean a future of two days of mania, any more than two consecutive days of record high temperatures will mean a future with two days of record lows.

Weather has temperature extremes, but also has other factors. Thunderstorms, wind, and snow could line up with bipolar symptoms like anger, irritability, and aloofness.

Living with Bipolar Disorder

Explaining what it is like to live with bipolar disorder isn't something to be summed up in a single article. There are a lot of moving parts and the answer changes based on factors like age, gender, and whether or not the person is in treatment. Plus, every person is different in both biology, which is uncontrollable, and how hard that person works to recover, which is more controllable.

Day-to-day life is different depending on where I am on the spectrum. Bipolar depression is pretty much like major depression. I often don't write about that symptom because it is well understood in the mental health community.

Rather, I spend my time explaining mania, hypersexuality, treatment issues, and what it is like to make my way in the world when some days I feel like the hero of the story and some days I feel like the villain.

The inconsistency in thinking, feeling, and behavior has made it difficult to form lasting relationships, as well as live a consistent and stable life. It hasn't been until recently that I have started to consider the possibility that the other shoe may never drop.

I've been bipolar my entire life. At 39 years old, I look back and see three distinct parts of my journey:

1. Before diagnosis
2. After diagnosis, but before recovery
3. Recovery with bipolar disorder

More than anything, however, I realize that bipolar disorder will always take up some portion of my life. In the beginning, it owned me entirely. As I move forward, it has less and less control. There is no cure for bipolar disorder, so it will always be an unwelcome guest in my life. But, with each passing day, it loses its power over me just a little bit more.

I can never ignore bipolar entirely – that would be foolish – but lessening its impact on my life is a worthwhile and obtainable goal.

In fact, it's a goal I'm currently achieving.

Psych Central, 5/17/2016

"Day-to-Day" Bipolar Disorder Before Diagnosis

The internet is filled with articles about living with bipolar disorder. There are scientific articles written by medical professionals, but the most common examples are the "lived experience" articles, written by people living with the disorder — people like me.

The lived experience articles typically cover two viewpoints:

1. **After diagnosis, but before recovery.** These are written by people who are aware they have bipolar disorder, but haven't yet received the right combination of medication, coping skills, and experience to properly manage the disorder. In other words, they spend more time worrying about the disorder than they do on other pursuits.
2. **Life in recovery with bipolar disorder.** These are written by people who are doing well managing the symptoms and essentially living a "normal" life. In other words, they spend more time living their lives than they do worrying about bipolar disorder.

But what about the experiences of people who are unknowingly living with bipolar disorder? There are some articles about this, but generally they focus on the extreme outcomes and/or crisis points. There is a lot writing about what it feels like to be suicidal or what mania feels like. These are all very important viewpoints, but

307

they don't answer the question of what it's like to live day-to-day with bipolar disorder without knowing it.

I Was Unaware I Had Bipolar Disorder

Given society's lack of knowledge surrounding mental illness, it isn't a surprise that I didn't know something was wrong. I suspected, a little, that I might have depression, but I assumed the treatment for that was to "man up" and get over it.

The idea that I could have a *severe* mental illness like bipolar disorder didn't even cross my mind. People with mental illness were violent and spit on strangers. They rocked back and forth, screaming nonsense. I knew what crazy looked like. I had a television after all.

Realistically, there were days I acted almost as I described above. While I never laid my hands on another person, I was certainly angry. I yelled at people, especially those closest to me. I kicked and punched doors and walls, and I did so with a loss of control that still haunts me.

In my opinion, one of the cruelest things about bipolar disorder is that it exists on a spectrum. Some days I'd be "normal," without a care in the world. I was intelligent, charismatic, and engaging. I had a great job, was married, and — from the outside looking in — was a regular guy.

Other days, though, I was wild. The highs of mania were intoxicating and I followed every rabbit I could down every rabbit hole. I was the real life Mad Hatter chasing Alice – who was always one-step ahead. There was no limit to what I could accomplish during those episodes, and mania feels good, at least for the moment.

Other days, I wasn't so lucky. Suicidal depression would grip my entire body. These episodes would take over every area of my life. I couldn't move, couldn't think, and just wanted to go to sleep and never, ever wake up. The numbness was horrific.

Most days, though, I was somewhere in between — not quite manic and not quite depressed, swinging back and forth like a pendulum. And, to complicate matters further, I had different friends for different moods. I never called my family when I was depressed or manic. I only called them when I was in the middle.

My family always thought I was moody, sure, but they never saw the extremes and therefore saw no reason for special worry. Besides, I had a job and a house. Mentally ill people don't have jobs and houses. Crazy people can't work. So life moved forward, each episode of depression or mania drawing me closer and closer to the edge.

And no one, not even me, was aware anything at all was wrong.

Talking About Bipolar Disorder Is a Good Thing

The reality is that I should have known *something* was wrong. To what extent I should have been aware is still something I struggle with. It's frightening to me that I thought what I was going through was normal. If my circumstances had turned out even slightly differently, I could be homeless, dead, or still suffering the whiplash effects of a cruel disorder.

We must talk about bipolar disorder in its entirety. Yes, mania is interesting and depression has been romanticized into some twisted parody of what it is actually is, but in between, there are numerous symptoms we seldom hear about.

The problem with only teaching people about the extremes of illnesses such as bipolar disorder is that it is much harder to recover after a crisis. And there are some things a person can never recover from. The suicide rate for a person living with bipolar disorder is 15% — and that number is far too high.

Psych Central, 6/29/2016

What Everyday Life Is Like with Bipolar Disorder

When writing about bipolar disorder, it is very easy to fall into the habit of discussing the more sensational parts of the illness. Mania, depression, and hypersexuality in bipolar disorder are all topics that I have personally covered many times. One need only do a Google search on the term bipolar disorder and a veritable litany of horrendous symptoms, side effects, and outcomes will fill your screen.

But is that really what the average person living with bipolar disorder goes through on a daily basis? Do the articles I write actually give a person insight into what living with bipolar disorder is like once someone has reached recovery?

Bipolar Disorder Before and After Treatment

There is a difference between bipolar disorder before and after treatment. Once, while giving a speech about living with bipolar disorder, someone raised their hand and asked, "How can you tolerate the mood swings? Don't they prevent you from getting things accomplished?" It was a fair question, especially since I had just spent the previous five minutes describing the whiplash effect of depression and mania.

I wasn't exaggerating, either; the bipolar spectrum is a long one, allowing a person to feel like an invincible god one moment and a worthless piece of garbage the next. But, in my haste to tell a good story, I left out a very important detail: I was describing my life before diagnosis, treatment, and recovery.

Now that I am in recovery, my life with bipolar disorder is – I'm doing my best to make this as exciting as possible – mundane.

Life in Recovery with Bipolar Disorder

The simple fact is that life in recovery with bipolar disorder is boring because much of life, in general, is mundane. I cook dinner and then I clean up after dinner. I go to work and I come home from work. There just isn't a way to jazz that up. There are tasks that need to be done to move life forward.

Because I excel at all the mundane parts of life, I am able to do some very "not mundane" things. I have a house, take yearly vacations, and I just recently mounted a giant television on my wall. I go to concerts and sporting events, and my wife and I eat out way too often. I prefer not to call this "life in recovery with bipolar disorder," but just "life."

Many readers are going to be surprised I didn't lead with taking meds twice a day, going to doctors, going to therapy, and so on. My recovery does involve all of those things. I follow my doctors' orders, keep my appointments, and I am open and honest with my treatment team.

The simple fact is that life in recovery with bipolar disorder is boring because much of life, in general, is mundane.

But, my life doesn't revolve around my illness – my illness interferes with my life. There are many things I have to deal with as an adult and, while many adults aren't dealing with chronic health issues, some of us are. My goal is to work as hard as I can to minimize the effect bipolar disorder has on my life. It took me a long time to reach this point. It didn't happen overnight.

The goal was always to define my life by something, anything, other than the unfortunate fact I have bipolar disorder. I think I've succeeded.

Bipolar Magazine, 6/30/2015

The Bipolar Disorder Definition of "I'm Fine"

Social etiquette is an important thing for society, and that includes such things as asking, "How are you?" when we greet others. As a person with bipolar disorder, I don't have any special exemption from answering that question in any way other than, "Fine."

There are three main moods that most people with bipolar will experience at any given time: bipolar mania, baseline, and depression. As we all know, "fine" can mean different things, based on our moods. Here are my truthful answers based on each of those moods.

Bipolar Mania: How Are You?

When I am manic (not very happy, not excited, not hypomanic), there is only one truly honest answer to the question: "I am a god from the planet Awesome. I'm better than you. And I can shoot happiness from my eyes into your soul."

Then, over the next five minutes, in dramatic and rapid fashion, I will tell you my amazing plans. I'll tell you how to fix everything wrong with the world, and what incredible, exceptional, and amazing rock-star caliber thing I am getting ready to do. At some point, I will forget what I'm talking about and rush off to do said rock-star caliber thing and — who knows? — I may actually succeed.

I will make no sense, but trust me when I say you'll love it – and me – right up until it goes horribly wrong. That generally happens around the next morning, long after everyone has gone home.

Bipolar Depression: How Are You?

The more depressed I am, the less likely you are to get any answer at all, both because I simply won't have the energy and because I'll be holed up alone somewhere away from your ability to ask. But, if we did come into contact and I did have the energy to answer, I would tell you I feel nothing.

Describing "nothing" is difficult and confusing. There is no analogy that is truly fitting. It can't be described as the absence of something, much in the same way describing darkness as the lack of light doesn't really help someone understand.

Specifically, I say: "I have no energy. I have no desires. If I were to die right here, right now, I wouldn't care, mainly because I lack the motivation to care one way or the other. I feel nothing for myself. I feel empty, as does the world around me. I feel abandoned, alone, and broken. I have no belief in future happiness, nor any recollection of happy times in the past. And all this seems perfectly normal to me."

Bipolar Baseline: How Are You?

Depression and mania are symptoms that anyone with bipolar disorder has experienced to some extent. However, living in recovery, which is the goal, means I spend most of my time in the middle. My moods still exist on a spectrum, but the spectrum is a lot narrower. My depression is manageable and I'm able to continue moving forward, even if at a slower pace.

I am still excitable, but mania is almost completely wiped out. I function, day to day, pretty much the same as everyone else, just with a chronic health condition to manage. This takes work, but life for most people takes effort. This is just my lot.

So when someone asks how I am, you might be surprised to know that the answer, nine times out of ten, is "traumatized." My exact answer would be: "I'm scared, worried, and I *know* that I'm going to get sick again and be left alone or be a burden to my loved ones. The emptiness I've felt, the suicidal feelings, the loss, the abandonment, and the failure are still living inside me. Since the illness is still with me – albeit controlled – the potential for it to come back and torture me again is very real. And that terrifies me."

The reality is that my daily life is hard because I have to move forward with the trauma of my past weighing me down. I am scared of ending up back where I started. I'm scared of losing everything. I'm scared of hurting myself or others emotionally. I'm scared of making my granny cry again.

So that's why I answer, "Fine." It's the easy answer. But never has a little word carried so much hidden meaning.

Psych Central, 12/10/15

What's Living with Bipolar Disorder Like?

I live with bipolar disorder. It's not something I signed up for, nor is it something I enjoy, but it is my lot in life. Not asking for it is really irrelevant, as I didn't ask to be a tall, pale, redhead, either. Much of life is this way. What we want and what we get seldom line up.

I say this because so many people in society don't recognize the symptoms of bipolar disorder. They seem to believe people are behaving a certain way by choice. The problem, of course, is that it's often difficult to recognize a particular behavior as being a symptom of the disorder. A person who is truly lazy and a person who is depressed look a lot alike to the untrained eye. Likewise, it's not obvious that a person on a spending spree is exhibiting a symptom of mania. Couple this with lack of education and references from pop culture and media, and people have the wrong idea. It isn't because they are trying to be dismissive; they simply don't know any better.

A diagnosis of bipolar disorder means suffering through suicidal thoughts and god-like mania. It means careening back and forth between the two extremes. It means losing sleep, time, and friends. It means tumultuous crying interspersed with uncontrollable anger. It means being *attacked* by every extreme emotion. Often, at the exact same time.

Bipolar disorder, simply put, is a medical illness.

The Bipolar Disorder Road Map

Now that we have covered that bipolar disorder is an illness, most people want to know what it is like to "be bipolar." I assume this means the diagnosis process, the day-to-day, and what it feels like.

There isn't a straightforward answer, because someone who is untreated is going to feel much differently from someone who is treated, as an example. Also, every person is different. It's important to keep in mind that just because bipolar disorder typically looks a certain way doesn't mean it will always look that way.

Most people follow a specific path when it comes to this illness. I break it up into three sections:

- Before diagnosis
- After diagnosis, but before recovery
- Recovery

Life with Bipolar Disorder Before Diagnosis

When it comes to society's perception of bipolar disorder, this is where people have the most accurate information. Before diagnosis is when things go wrong most often. People with untreated mental illness are most likely to have public outbursts, need police intervention, and experience the adverse consequences of their disorder. Since they aren't aware they are sick, it's not reasonable that they would seek help.

This is also the period of time that self-medication is most common. The disorder is at its strongest because it has the advantage of surprise. The pain and suffering are so great that a person will try anything, including drugs, alcohol, and taking unnecessary risks in an attempt to save themselves.

It's a scary, unpredictable, and vulnerable time. Unfortunately, while society may have a somewhat accurate view of this period of time, most people don't have enough knowledge to help a person

317

who is showing obvious signs of bipolar disorder. In fact, most people don't even have enough knowledge to *suspect* something might be wrong.

Life with Bipolar Disorder After Diagnosis, but Before Recovery

This section of life with bipolar disorder is very tough, because there is so much unknown. There is a lot of unknown in section one, too, but the person isn't aware of it. Simply put, ignorance is bliss.

The hardest work is done in this section, as well. It's where the majority of the trial and error process and setbacks occur, and where the reality of everything a person has been through starts to come into focus.

All of the emotions from damaged relationships start to affect the person as the symptoms of bipolar disorder begin to be controlled. There are moments to celebrate, too. Starting to control the mood swings is a fantastic feeling. Things that were out of focus begin to gain clarity.

It's also a very long and arduous journey that usually takes years. Adjusting to medication, learning coping skills, and gaining needed insight into what life with bipolar disorder is truly like aren't things that can be accomplished in a couple weeks.

This is where people with bipolar disorder reinvent themselves and, for many of us, take responsibility for things we may have done while sick. It's a time of hard work, reflection, and promise.

Life in Recovery with Bipolar Disorder

There is no cure for bipolar disorder. Like it or not, I will have this illness for the rest of my life. The best I can hope for is what the mental health industry refers to as "recovery." Essentially, living in recovery with bipolar disorder doesn't mean I don't have the illness; it just means I am managing it.

Living in recovery means that, instead of bipolar disorder controlling me, I am controlling it.

It doesn't mean I'm symptom-free. It doesn't mean I don't have to work at it every day and it certainly doesn't mean that I'm home free. The darker days of life before recovery are always looming. Even if those times never come back, there is a trauma associated with what I went through.

There're also the sideways glances I get when people find out I am "crazy." People with mental illness are often stigmatized based on little more than stereotypes, misinformation, and fear.

Even if a cure was discovered tomorrow and I was guaranteed to never, ever have another symptom of bipolar disorder again, I still have to live with what happened to me and that takes a toll.

All that said, I am no different from everyone else, except I manage an illness. Many people manage illnesses every day, while still finding a way to carry on and find happiness.

My goal is to be the best version of me I can be. Because of bad luck, bad genetics, or the universe being mean to me, I have more obstacles in my way than the average. But, at the end of the day, I'm just like everyone else – trying to make my way forward.

Bipolar Magazine, 3/8/2016

I Didn't Choose to Have Bipolar Disorder

Let's pretend for a moment that living with bipolar disorder isn't life-sucking. Let's pretend that having a chronic illness, going to medical appointments, and managing the day-to-day issues that bipolar disorder brings doesn't take a daily toll. For the sake of argument, I'll even remove fear, expenses, and emotional pain from the list of things bipolar brings into my life. Even if every last thing I just said was true, one thing that will *never* be true is this:

That I *chose* to have bipolar disorder.

Bipolar Disorder Is an Illness, Not a Lifestyle Choice

Anyone with bipolar disorder knows that it is an illness. I didn't choose this and I can't imagine anyone would. The 15% completed suicide rate alone should be enough to convince anyone that bipolar disorder isn't something that people would *choose*.

Before I was diagnosed – and, therefore, before I was treated – the symptoms of bipolar disorder ruled my life. The highs and lows of the disease were very traumatic to me, and to those around me. I'd be happy one day and depressed the next. I was angry, unfocused, and unreliable.

Severely sick people don't accomplish much outside of being sick. The disease takes over and ruins everything. My entire life before I was diagnosed was about fighting an illness I wasn't even aware I had.

After I was diagnosed with bipolar disorder, life certainly got better, in that at least I knew what was happening. I had help in the way of medical intervention and education. Bipolar disorder required a lot of time and energy to fight and left me drained and exhausted on a daily basis. Progress, as many of us know, is measured in baby steps.

So, you can imagine how it must feel to work so hard, feel so emotionally drained, and suffer this much and have someone walk up to you and tell you to "just cheer up."

A Person Can't Choose to "Get Over" Bipolar Disorder

Advice like "you are focusing on the negative" and "just calm down" or pretty much anything that starts with "you know what your problem is..." that doesn't end with "...you have a chronic mental illness that you need to work diligently to manage on a day-to-day basis" is, at best, ignorant.

In many ways, it is worse than that. Sure, it is easy for me to acknowledge that the person saying it just doesn't understand and is trying to help. Often, people aren't trying to be malicious when they say these things. But, in acknowledging that, I am also forced to acknowledge that I am misunderstood and the people saying these things are *not* allies. They aren't intentionally trying to be unhelpful, but it doesn't change the fact that they are not only unhelpful, but actively hurtful. Because now, in addition to being sick, I am also forced to educate those around me.

And it makes me feel alone.

If you are someone living with bipolar disorder and have experienced this, please know you aren't alone. There are lots of us and we all go through this to some extent.

If you know someone with bipolar disorder and think that there is a quick fix, please take a moment to consider educating yourself. There is a lot of excellent information online and you can ask your friend or family member how they would like to be supported.

Remember, we know you are trying to help. Wouldn't it be great if that help was actually helpful?

Psych Central, 10/16/15

Bipolar Mania—Oh, How I Miss You

A manic episode can be destructive and even dangerous, but *not* being manic can sometimes feel like a loss.

When a person who has bipolar disorder reaches recovery, it means that the spectrum between depression and mania has been shortened enough to allow for "normal" functioning. In other words, there is no more bouncing between the extremes of god-like grandiosity and suicidal depression.

The average person understands that not being depressed (or, at the very least, not being *as* depressed) is a desirable outcome. What most people don't understand is that removing the mania represents a loss. Mania is an important symptom to treat. It can be destructive and even deadly. As an example, I hurt more people while manic than I did while depressed. This is why it's surprising to many people that many of those with bipolar disorder actually miss the manic episodes.

What Is There to Miss About Bipolar Mania?

I love it when people ask me why I miss bipolar mania, even if the only reason is that I can reminisce about how awesome it felt to be manic. It seems strange, even to me, that I would look back on such a destructive time in my life and feel *good*. That is all the proof I need that mania is a dangerous symptom. I know the hurtful consequences of my actions and I *still* think of the feelings somewhat fondly.

That is what I believe to be the single biggest issue with mania. During my highest points I actually felt good, even as I was causing so much chaos around me. The consequence free environment I had created inside my own head shielded me from having to feel anything other than amazing. The grandiosity I felt can best be described as the final song at a rock concert performed in front of 60,000 adoring fans and I'm the lead singer. Cue screaming, clapping, and standing ovation. When I was manic, I had the power to change the course of human history...

...or, at least, I *felt* like I did.

Mania and spending money have a lot in common. Buying anything we want feels good, and it is important to note that spending money isn't a dangerous activity, in and of itself.

We spend our money appropriately not because spending is a reckless action, but because we are afraid of the consequences of overspending. The issue with bipolar mania is that the ability to think about consequences has been impaired, if not entirely removed. The more manic we are, the less ability we have to see past the present moment. Spending all that money feels great until rent is due.

Mourning the Loss of Bipolar Mania

Mourning the loss of bipolar mania has a lot more to do with how being manic *feels* than what mania actually *is*. Mania feels fantastic. If you already have an engaging personality, like I do, it attracts more and more people, especially if you're spending a lot of money or doing something incredible (like jumping off a roof into a pool).

This mixture of people, emotions, and euphoria, especially when weighed against the other side of the spectrum of suicidal depression, all mixes together to form an intoxicating blend of pure awesome sauce. When it goes away, something is clearly missing.

Many people living in recovery with bipolar disorder wish they could harness the mania, the parts that can be productive, creative, and engaging. We wish we could bottle a little of it, maybe for the weekend or New Year's Eve. It is a great feeling, but it isn't a healthy one.

The single biggest problem with being manic is that it feels good, even when the consequences are negative or damaging. It makes this symptom particularly dangerous and I hope to never, ever experience it again.

Even though I want to.

Bipolar Magazine, 7/14/2015

Grandiosity in Bipolar Disorder Has a Dark Flip-Side

People living with bipolar disorder, and even the general public, are well aware of grandiosity in thinking, of thoughts that are excessively ambitious or pretentious. An offshoot of mania, grandiosity can manifest itself in a variety of ways. Many sufferers of bipolar disorder have accepted a certain level of questioning from society about their life goals. A common scenario might play out like this:

"Hey, I'm thinking of starting a business so I can buy a new house and get out of my dead end job," says a man with bipolar to his friend.

"What experience do you have running a business? Are you sure you aren't being grandiose?" says the concerned friend.

The single biggest misconception about bipolar disorder is that self-referential thoughts along these lines are always positive, always flattering to the person thinking them. If a person with bipolar disorder says they are the greatest at something, the thought that they might be grandiose immediately springs to mind. The fact is that bipolar often goes in the other direction, causing you to think you are the absolute worst at something, that you're incapable of succeeding even at goals that are the farthest thing from grandiose. And a lot less people are watching our collective backs on that one.

Extreme thinking, in whichever direction, is a big problem. The excessively negative thoughts are particularly dangerous because they can lead to suicide. Since the general public is already woefully unprepared to help someone careening toward suicide, and deeply negative thoughts aren't even seen as being the result of the disease, this conversation is likely to take place: "Everyone is against me. The entire world is hoping I'll fail," says the man with bipolar to his friend.

"That's ridiculous. You're being dramatic. Think positively," says the confused friend.

The alarming part is that the friend in this scenario doesn't see the potential for danger. Dismissed simply as drama, the conversation moves forward without the "bipolar friend" even having those thoughts challenged. It is, of course, ridiculous to think the entire world is hoping anyone will fail, which is why thinking so is extreme and dangerous.

An often-missed point in these two examples is that starting a successful small business isn't exactly all that difficult. I have bipolar disorder and run a successful small business. Millions of Americans operate them, in fact. But, the average person working with the average person with bipolar disorder sees the potential for issues with scenario #1 much more frequently than they see the danger of scenario #2.

Part of helping people living with bipolar disorder to excel — and that includes helping ourselves — is knowing the difference between danger and just day-to-day life. It's appropriate and healthy to have goals, hopes, and dreams. Yes, those goals, hopes, and dreams could be grandiose, but are not always, and frankly are not often grandiose at all. And even legitimately grandiose goals can be backed down into the realm of reality with a little planning and thought.

When a person's deeply negative thoughts go unchallenged and unchecked, it's generally because they didn't realize the bipolar nature of those thoughts and neither did anyone else.

Nothing can be fixed if no one knows it's broken.

Bipolar Magazine, 9/10/2015

Sad Stories Don't Pay Bills

When it comes to life fucking someone over, I had a head start.

I was born to a teenage mother.

My biological father, whom I not-so-lovingly refer to as my sperm donor, lasted a few months before he walked out.

My entire life, I've felt abandoned. I grew up, quite literally, as a red-headed stepchild.

By the time I reached middle school, I was a morbidly obese, incredibly uncoordinated, socially awkward, four-eyed, brace-faced, severely pimpled ginger child. Any one of those would have led to being bullied in the 1980s, and I had the pleasure of having them all.

By the time I entered high school, I felt entirely alone.

The bullying, combined with my feelings of abandonment and my inability to relate to the people around me, led to my decision to drop out of high school in my junior year. I didn't tell anyone, at first. I just stopped going and went instead to the library every day.

Not a single person noticed I was missing.

It wasn't until three months later when, during one of the frequent arguments I had with my parents, I blurted it out. My desire to have something to throw in their faces was more valuable to me than keeping my secret. I did eventually graduate high school, but it required moving to another state, away from the chaos.

Life Fucked Me Harder When I Became an Adult

Every day, for as long as I can remember, I thought about suicide. On good days, I just thought that I shouldn't end my life, and on bad days it was that I probably should. I had no idea this was abnormal. I assumed that everyone liked pizza and apple pie and that everyone constantly thought about suicide.

Since this is not a topic society spends much time discussing, no one challenged me on this.

When I was in my mid-twenties, around the end of my first marriage, the depression, mania, anxiety, delusions, and suicidal thoughts finally caught the attention of someone. This landed me in the psychiatric ward of a local hospital.

I was diagnosed with bipolar disorder (an anxiety diagnosis would follow a year later) and I woke up the next morning knowing my life was over. I had no idea how to overcome a mental illness, and I also had never heard of anyone else doing it. So I sat there, devastated, locked in a hospital ward, defeated.

However, I exited the hospital with a treatment plan, a little education, and the basic knowledge of how to treat my illness. I started out strong, going back to work, going to doctor's appointments, taking my medicine, and telling people that I was diagnosed with mental illness.

It wouldn't take long before the backlash started.

Co-workers told me I was faking, friends pulled away, treatments weren't working, the natural ups and downs of bipolar disorder were interrupted by treatment, and the treatment itself caused side effects. My entire understanding of my body and mind collapsed in on itself.

Before the diagnoses, I was sick, but unaware. Then I was sick, aware, and terrified.

I was back where I started when I was a child, possibly even further back.

More than anything, I felt abandoned by everyone. I was alive, for the moment, but inside I had already given up. Mental illness isn't an easy thing to live with, and many people don't care or don't understand. *There is no outpouring of community support after a mental illness diagnosis, just awkward whispers and seemingly endless darkness.*

I Fought Back Against Mental Illness.

When I was little, my mother would tell me she would forgive my back-talking if I grew up to be a lawyer. As I got sicker, I would spend hours explaining to anyone who would listen all the reasons this was unfair, all the reasons this wasn't my fault, all the ways my life should have turned out.

Then, seemingly out of nowhere, someone said something to me that changed my life:

"So what? Life fucked you. Get over it. Are you going to spend the rest of your life bitching that life isn't fair, or are you going to do something about it? Because no one gives a shit about you, and you sure as hell can't pay your bills with your sad story."

I spent another couple days bemoaning my circumstances, but the switch had been flipped. My resolve had already started setting in and my anger toward my circumstances started to turn inward. I started looking at the massive challenge of succeeding in a world where I would be judged on the same level with everyone else, all while fighting a chronic illness.

I started making plans. I started thinking past being sick and started to think about being well.

I looked at the treatment options, the money and the time. I looked at the odds, and I got up and took a step forward. I took medicine that ravaged my body, so I went back to the doctor and found better medications. I went to therapy. I kept an open mind. I didn't judge myself, or others, but rather my own actions. I made amends for things I had done wrong instead of blaming my illness.

I took control of what I could and I took responsibility no matter what.

I accepted that life isn't fair but that this was my life and I could do whatever I wanted with it. More than anything, I worked hard so I could be proud of my life. I realized that life didn't fuck me. It's just random. It's just life. My circumstances, like many people's, were just something to accept and overcome. I was determined not to allow it to make me miserable.

It took me four years to reach the level of recovery I have now—four years of successes, failures, mistakes, and suffering. It was not an easy journey, but it was mine.

In the end, I realized I didn't triumph over my disorder because life stopped fucking me…

I triumphed because I stopped seeing it that way.

Elephant Journal, 8/23/14

Snarky Answers to Annoying Questions About Mental Illness

Like many people living with mental illness, I get asked a lot of questions. Many of them are well thought out and lead to further education about mental illnesses and a better understanding of those of us who live with them. But a select few of the questions aren't well thought out. They are, in fact, dumb questions. As a professional, I answer them with a smile on my face because that has a lot of value. But inside my head, I always come up with much better answers. Fun answers. *Snarky* answers...

Are you like that person with mental illness I saw on TV?

Yes, because people on TV are just like people in real life. My mom and dad were exactly the same as Mike and Carol Brady. Right down to the AstroTurf lawn.

In fact, TV and movies are so representative of real life that if you roll your truck down a mountain — no doubt after a high speed chase involving lots of "sick drifting, dude"– not only will it explode, but you will walk away without so much as a scratch on you.

The day that we start learning about life from pop culture is the day we've abandoned learning altogether. Fish can't talk, there are no superheroes, and television is for entertainment, not education. Unless the person was watching a documentary, which is almost never the case, they are comparing us to some caricature of a person, not someone who exists in real life.

332

I get you have mental illness, but when will you get over it?

I get that you're an idiot; when will you get smarter?

Small changes could make this question not dumb at all: Is there a cure for mental illness? Can a person with mental illness lead a normal life? Will a person with mental illness be in treatment forever? A five-year-old could ask this question better. Use a flipping "I" statement, will you?

Did you take your mental illness medication today?

Yes, but you are such a nitwit that the magic pills aren't able to prevent me from wanting to smack you.

This question is both annoying and condescending. It is almost always asked after explaining to a person that they are irritating me or doing something I want them to stop. The conversations generally go something like this:

Me: Dude, why are your stanky socks on the counter?
Them: I was eating Chinese and didn't feel like moving them.
Me: They're soaking in sweet and sour chicken! That's disgusting!
Them: Dude, chill out. Did you take your meds today?

I should say that if your family member, roommate, or bestie knows you are forgetful and is just reminding you, then we clearly don't need to give them the snarky treatment. We need to use our snark responsibly.

Aren't all people with mental illness violent?

If you really thought that was true, you wouldn't risk asking me. I might snap and eat your face.

Critical thinking skills matter, folks. The idea that all people with mental illness are violent should immediately ring false.

Consider that the violent crime rate would be fantastically high. If one in five people experience a mental health crisis in a given year, that would mean, at any given time, at least 20% of the population would be actively violent – and that just isn't the case.

Think Snarky, Don't Speak Snarky

As much as I'd love to let my snarky personality shine when the dumb questions start flying, I really do see real value in not making people feel poorly for asking them. An offensive or dumb question followed by a snarky answer doesn't really give us the opportunity to educate people about our illness. Even so, while professionalism has its value, we must embrace humor as healthy. If I can't laugh at what society thinks about people with mental illness, I would cry. And no one wants to see a 275–pound, red-headed man with snot and tears running down his face.

Although some of you would think that was hilarious.

Psych Central, 6/17/15

In Recovery, but Bipolar Disorder Still Overwhelms Me

Although the road to recovery is long, eventually moods level out to become something we can manage on a day–to-day basis.

When I was first diagnosed with bipolar disorder, I was clueless. I didn't even have a working definition of the disease when the doctor first told me I had it. Learning about bipolar and how to live with it was overwhelming.

However, as time passed, my illness became less and less of a burden. The medications I was being prescribed started working, the side effects began to lessen, and I mastered valuable coping skills. The impact of bipolar on my daily life decreased significantly. Whereas it used to consume all my time, more of my resources gradually returned to being devoted to living my life.

Recovery with Bipolar Does Not Mean No Symptoms

The treatment for bipolar is designed to shorten the spectrum of moods and eliminate as many ill effects as possible. So, instead of a range from zero to 60, the treatment will shorten that span to 20 to 40 (for example). Obviously, it's much easier to manage a 21-digit emotional range, than it is a 61-digit emotional range.

Being in recovery with bipolar disorder does not mean I am symptom-free, however. It doesn't mean that I don't become irritable, depressed, or overwhelmed. If someone could escape all the symptoms of this particular mental illness, we

335

wouldn't call it recovery – it would be more like a cure or, perhaps better stated, remission.

So, what is a person supposed to do when a convoluted side effect of bipolar disorder shows up?

Managing Bipolar Disorder in Recovery

People living with bipolar disorder fight hard to reach recovery not because they will no longer suffer, but because the symptoms are more manageable. The more manageable something is, the better our odds of success. That is the essence of recovery; we successfully combat bipolar symptoms when they arise.

When I was undiagnosed, I felt like I was paddling a raft up a waterfall. Without exceptional intervention, it's simply impossible to achieve. But, if you can find a way to level the playing field, like by learning the raft can be removed from the water and carried up a path to the top of the waterfall, then the impossible becomes possible.

The road to recovery is a long and hard one, but eventually our moods level out and become something we can manage on a day–to-day basis.

In other words, paddling a raft through calm water is still hard work, it's just easier than paddling up a waterfall.

Bipolar Magazine, 5/9/2017

Moving from Mental Illness to Recovery to Inspiration

Dear Gabe,

What is the one greatest thing you have chosen to do in your recovery that all of us could do to impact this movement of stigma breaking and awareness?

Regards,

Laurie

Laurie,

I've decided to break up your question into two separate questions and answer both. I hope that's okay.

Question number one is straightforward: "What can anyone do to eliminate stigma and educate people about mental illness?" The answer is very simple: anyone can talk about mental health and mental illness with an open mind in a caring, respectful, and non-judgmental way.

What our society needs is more understanding, open dialogue, and education. By facilitating these conversations, you raise the level of knowledge that society has about mental illness. In other words, as understanding increases, stigma decreases.

Question number two is going to be: "What is something that anyone with mental illness can do to reach recovery?"

I try really hard to stay away from absolutes. I seldom say that if everyone with bipolar would do this one thing, they'd be guaranteed to reach recovery. I do this because there just aren't that many absolutes in the world.

People are all different, with or without mental illness. What works for me may not work for you, and what works for *most* people won't work for *all* people. It's always important to remember that.

That said, there is an absolute answer to this question and it's extremely valuable. In order to reach recovery with mental illness, a person must stay alive. Let's not get bogged down in how difficult or painful that can be, nor do I want to assign blame in the event of suicide. But it's important that, in order to reach recovery, you value life and fight to stay alive.

It's easy to lose focus on how important living is to moving along the path toward wellness. I swear to you that believing your life has value is the most important thing you can do to reach recovery.

Regards,

Gabe

Psych Central, 4/1/17

Bipolar Disorder and Stinking Thinking

One of the worst things about living with bipolar disorder is figuring out which thoughts are worthy of my attention. Just because I think it doesn't make it true. That bit of truth is relevant for everyone, bipolar or not.

When it comes to bipolar disorder, there are many thoughts that are worthy of ignoring, all for different reasons. As an example, I am prone to grandiose thoughts. If I wake up one morning and believe that I can fly, I need to rein that in before climbing up to the roof of a tall building.

The same holds true for depressing thoughts, anxious thoughts, and even happy thoughts. I can't control whether or not I think it, but I do have *some* control about whether or not I act on it or how I feel about it in its entirety. Coping skills really help in situations like these.

As the year comes to a close, I am given many opportunities to practice these skills. Like most people, I have spent a lot of time reflecting on the past year. This was a year in the life of Gabe that saw the purchase of a new house, major career success, the winning of a few awards, and even a trip to Disney World. Woven in there is a great relationship with my wife and many friends, and more happy memories than I can count.

So – you guessed it – I'm a miserable failure, at least in my own mind.

How Bipolar Disorder Colors My Thoughts

Bipolar disorder has a way of taking something that is good and coloring it in such a way that I believe it to be bad. I'm sure there is a fancy medical term for this, but I call it "stinking thinking." Essentially, I take facts and add garbage to them until the truth is covered to the point of "smelling" horrible.

Let's take my new house as an example. The facts are pretty straightforward. My wife and I both have jobs. We worked hard, created a budget and a savings plan, and eventually were able to purchase a new home. It should be a proud moment and one that could not possibly get twisted around to depress me.

Enter stinking thinking:

See, my wife makes more money than I and doesn't have bipolar disorder. So, she is the stable one and her income allowed us to purchase a house. Without her, I couldn't afford that house. Stinking thinking makes me consider this proof that I am a failure and just riding the coattails of a woman I no doubt tricked into marrying me.

In order to complete the tarnishing of my success, I'll ignore the fact that she couldn't afford the house without me. I'll "forget" that I do the cooking, cleaning, and home organizing. I'll just delete all the value I bring to her life and focus solely on one narrative: I'm a mooch who doesn't contribute and without her I'm nothing.

Just like that, my beautiful new home is now a source of sadness, frustration, and failure. My wife is downgraded to a fool who married someone who is dragging her down and making her life worse. She is just too stupid to notice – *yet*.

I am really good at stinking thinking, too. My writing award? I owe that to my proofreader and editor. The massive career success? I owe that to my amazing coworkers and the incredible team of people who are carrying me. Thankfully, none of those people seem to notice I'm holding them back – although they will, any day now, and it'll all come crashing down around me.

Bipolar Disorder Doesn't Give Me the Right to Insult Others

Stinking thinking relies on three elements to thrive:

1. Another person to give the credit for my success
2. Thinking that person is stupid for keeping me around
3. Assuming that person is lying when they tell me I'm responsible for my own success

Bipolar disorder doesn't give me the right to insult other people and none of this works without the base assumption that the people around me are stupid, foolish, and/or liars. If I take them at their word and respect them enough to accept that they are intelligent enough to work with a competent person (or marry one), then the delusion quickly falls apart.

Once I have a little faith in the people around me, the narrative quickly shifts from "they are carrying me" to "we are all working together." The focus shifts from "I'm a failure" to "I'm a success with great people around me who are as invested in my success as I am invested in theirs."

Bipolar disorder loves to drag me down and there are people in the world right now who echo those same sentiments. Their own biases won't allow them to see past my illness to my accomplishments. The stigma of bipolar disorder consumes their thought processes and they rely on stereotypes that tell them someone else *must* be responsible for my success.

I work every day of my life to show those people they are wrong, to demonstrate that someone with bipolar disorder can lead a great, productive, and accomplished life. Becoming what I'm fighting against will only undo much of the good I've done.

In order to effect real change, we all must work together to fight the stigma of bipolar disorder wherever we encounter it – especially when we stigmatize ourselves. If we don't believe someone with bipolar disorder can lead a good life, then we can't expect anyone else to believe it, either.

Bipolar Magazine, 12/29/2015

Santa Visits a Mental Illness & Addiction Drop-In Center

A few years ago, I found myself in the odd position of playing Santa Claus for a bunch of children at a restaurant where I was working. I am big, playful, and tall; my boss was desperate; so, just like that, I became Santa. I loved it and had a great time.

Maybe it's because I live with mental illness or maybe I'm just a soft touch, but it occurred to me that the average Santa just doesn't hang out in certain places. Sure, anyone with money can hire Santa to head to their party. Hospitals and children's homes are popular volunteer spots. But what about the local homeless shelter? What about adult facilities?

The next year, I went out and bought a Santa suit, beard, suspenders, boots, and gloves, then I hit the streets. Sure, I charged some people – the dry cleaning bill for the suit is almost $100 – but I volunteered wherever the other Santas didn't want to go.

"Santa Claus" Lives with Mental Illness

People who know me aren't surprised to learn that I dress like Santa and let people climb all over me. They think I do it because I love seeing people happy, because I like attention, and because, deep down, I'm a giant child.

And it did begin that way. I wanted to see people happy and, in turn, be happy, myself. Frankly, a thousand-dollar suit is cheaper than therapy, so why not? I quickly realized, however, that the benefits to playing Santa Claus are greater than I ever thought. When adults sit on my lap and tell me what they want for Christmas, they allow themselves to momentarily pretend that Santa is real.

The other day, when Santa was visiting a local drop-in center for people with mental illness, addiction, and trauma issues, a man came over and sat on my lap. I figure he was mid to late 30s. He was a black man dressed in pretty cool jeans, a T-Shirt, and a gold necklace. Truthfully, I was shocked that he was willing to sit on my lap at all, given that he walked with the swagger of a man much too cool to "believe" in Santa Claus.

I asked him what he wanted for Christmas, just like I always do, and he told me that Santa won't be able to bring him what he wants this year. Prepared for the standard wisecracks adults make, I expected him to tell me about the hot supermodel or sports car he had his eye on.

Instead he told me he just wants to see his kids. Not shying away from his request, I asked him about his children and why he wouldn't be seeing them on Christmas.

He said that his ex-wife wouldn't allow him to see them because he drank too much and she no longer trusted him. He acknowledged her mistrust was the result of his actions. Knowing that folks come to a drop-in center to get help, I asked him if he was attending support groups and working on not drinking.

"Yes!" he practically yelled and told me that he was coming here every day because people don't judge him and because he likes the support groups. I asked him how long it had been since he drank and, as is common for people in recovery, he proudly said, "121 days."

I looked at him and I said, "Sir, if you keep coming to groups, keep working hard, and stay away from drugs and alcohol, you won't need Santa Claus to see your kids next year, because you'll accomplish it *all by yourself.*"

He hugged me so fast, and so unexpectedly, that I almost fell over. He was a strong man and he mumbled his thanks into my Santa hat. I hugged him back and he jumped up and walked away with the same swagger and confidence he had when he sat down.

I just sat there, briefly forgetting I was dressed like a mythical elf from the North Pole who owns a team of flying reindeer. Because I remember the day that all I wanted in the world was for someone to tell me I didn't need magic, because I could do it all by myself.

I believe that people can overcome their difficult circumstances not because I want to believe it, but because I've seen it. I, personally, have done it. What we all need to remember is that having someone believe in you, even a middle-aged bipolar dude who dresses up like Santa, is more valuable than anything on anyone's Christmas list.

And Santa, my friends, believes in *everyone*.

Psych Central, 12/23/15

Anxiety Says Everyone Hates Me

I am a strong person, physically. At six-foot-three inches tall and 250 pounds, most people wouldn't waste their breath arguing that assertion. And, whether because of, or in spite of, my bipolar and anxiety diagnoses, I consider myself to be strong mentally, as well. I am intelligent, accomplished, likeable, and successful.

Despite the mountains of evidence of this, my brain works diligently to convince me that every interaction I have with another person is a misstep. If I text someone and they don't reply back, it is obvious they are mad at me. If someone doesn't answer the phone when I call, say hello when they pass by, or reply to my email, then my mind goes into what can only be described as an emotional roller coaster. It isn't a fun, state-of-the-art roller coaster, either. It's an old wooden one, poorly maintained, and it's painful when it turns corners. The ride up the first hill is jerky, slow, and the anticipation sends shock waves I can feel all over my body. It is emotionally, physically, and even mentally straining. It is fear, panic, anticipation, and dread all rolled into one giant full body panic attack.

Anxiety Convinces Me That Everyone Hates Me

At that moment, I feel as though everyone I know is mad at me. They all disrespect me, think I am stupid, and do not want me in their lives any longer. Quite simply, my anxiety says everyone *hates* me.

Now, on top of all the other emotions, guilt forms. I feel guilty that I put someone in such a difficult position. I imposed by reaching out to them. Asking them a question, for a favor, or simply saying hello was uncalled for. I should not have done it and, since I'm a good person, I want to apologize. I want to reach back out to them and ask if they are mad, if they are okay, what I did wrong, and let them know I want to make amends. I want to set things right.

I Just Want the Anxiety to Stop

More often than not, what *does* get me in trouble and where I do make a mistake is by war dialing, constantly texting or e-mailing, or asking them one too many questions about why something is a certain way. Even apologizing for a legitimate mistake can be over the line, if handled the wrong way.

Ninety-seven times out of a hundred, the reason I didn't hear back was because the person was busy, in a meeting, mulling it over, or because people have things to do other than answer me. In the rare occasions where I did make a mistake, offend, or bother someone, the issue is generally cleared up quickly with an explanation and an apology. The people in my life know that I am a good person and don't intentionally hurt others and they doubly know I wouldn't intentionally hurt them.

Ignoring the Anxiety That Says Everyone Hates Me

It is hard to sit back, relax, and not engage the anxiety. It baits me to do something I will later regret. I work with my therapist to find techniques to calm down and I explain to my friends and family that when I ask if they are mad me, it is because I genuinely care and I want to make sure they are okay. I am also honest in admitting that checking in with them alleviates *my* suffering. Often, it is more about me than about them, and they understand that.

There are as many ways to alleviate anxiety as there are people. It is trial and error, but there are techniques that work for many people. Mindfulness, meditation, advanced preparation, sleep hygiene, therapy, and medication can all be used to control this disorder. But the biggest factor in this will always be *me*.

I Am Pissed Off About Having Mental Illness; Are You?

People living with mental illness share many common traits. In the advocacy world, we share many of them openly. We discuss the symptoms of the illness, the uncertainty, the fear, and we share ways that people with mental illness can receive better treatment, better services, more understanding, and have better outcomes.

We have another common trait that is seldom shared. We all experience it, on some level, and most of us share it only with our trusted friends and family. When we sit alone with other mentally ill people, we swap stories. That is when the true, unaltered, unpolished feelings come out. And what comes out is anger.

I Am Pissed Off

It should not come as a surprise that I am pissed off. The surprising thing would be if I wasn't. Pissed off should be expected. I have been discriminated against, marginalized, ignored, insulted, talked down to, and cast out by the greater society. I am viewed as defective.

My accomplishments are meaningless when compared to a medical diagnosis that I just happened to be unlucky enough to have. And, frankly, I can't imagine not being pissed off if the only thing I had to deal with was the illness. For those who are unaware, having bipolar is quite a huge pain in the ass even before you factor in the bias, stigma, and other such unhappiness.

Who wouldn't be pissed off at there being a stereotype to explain every single thought, feeling, opinion, or idea I have?

Do I disagree with you and refuse to compromise? Oh! I am obsessed! Refuse to see things from your point of view? Oh! I am delusional! I have lofty goals and difficult tasks I want to accomplish? Oh! I am grandiose! Do I tell you that I am not suffering symptoms of bipolar disorder at the moment? Oh! Denying the symptoms is one of the symptoms of bipolar disorder!

Frankly, it's a minor miracle that I am not walking around screaming at every single person who believes they know who I am just because they know my diagnosis.

It is a testament to who I actually am as a person. Kindness, compassion, understanding, and caring are not symptoms of bipolar disorder. They are human traits and some of the millions of traits that I have that cannot be summed up with a medical diagnosis.

Mental Illness Stereotypes

Stereotypes are the shorthand of the lazy. Getting to know a person on an individual level is time consuming. Difficult. Potentially painful. And, frankly, it involves constant work. Mental illness stereotypes are no different.

There are people out there who believe in astrology, who believe that the time and place of your birth determines your personality. Who believe that, because someone is a Pisces, they'll behave a certain way. Fortunately, most people regard this as silly. Just as silly as being able to determine someone's personality because of a medical diagnosis.

Society being gullible enough to believe that we can know a person based on any pre-determined anything is why we lack compassion, understanding, and caring. Because unless your stereotype is overwhelmingly positive, you are behind the eight-ball walking through the door.

gabehoward.com, 1/21/2017

Who's Responsible: Bipolar or You?

Living with bipolar disorder presents a number of challenges, from the obvious – dealing with the depression, mania, and other symptoms – to the lesser understood challenges – such as discrimination, managing medical care, and handling family concerns. It shouldn't be surprising to anyone that living with a life-long and chronic illness is going to be difficult. What is surprising is the number of things we can control.

First, let's dispel the myth that we have no ability to manage bipolar disorder. That is simply untrue. We are not helpless against our illness. We don't always have a lot of control, but we almost always have more than zero. Acknowledging this doesn't make the disease less of a burden, but it does provide the most important piece of the foundation to reach recovery, which is realizing that, if we truly had zero control over bipolar disorder, then no one would ever get better. We would all be slaves until we all met the identical end.

Not All Bad Decisions Are Bipolar Disorder's Fault

The fact is, not all bad decisions are bipolar disorder's fault. The other day, I was sitting at work and my co-worker walked into the room and gave me some information I had been waiting on. Seeing it was bad news, I looked up and gasped, "I can't believe you botched this so terribly." I was clearly angry and my tone and body language reflected that.

Naturally, she got defensive and we argued for a few moments before agreeing to retreat to neutral corners. I sat in my office, seething. I was furious at the information and I had taken it out on her. I figuratively shot the messenger. After a few minutes, I walked into her office and apologized for my behavior. She said she understood and all was well in the world. I made a mistake, I made amends, the world moved on. No need to bring bipolar disorder into this.

I could have, though. I hadn't been sleeping well, had been feeling depressed and anxious for a few days, and had been feeling overwhelmed for a while. All of these are symptoms of bipolar disorder. Instead of apologizing, I could have used those feelings as an excuse. I could have played the "you don't understand what it's like to live with this horrible disease" card. In my early years, I would have, too. It would have been played quickly and it never would have occurred to me that I could have made a better choice. I gave away my power and sent a clear message that I wasn't in control.

Bipolar Disorder Isn't Our Fault, But It Is Our Responsibility

Because of bipolar disorder, I have made a great many mistakes. I have more regrets that I have forgotten than most people have in a lifetime. Bipolar disorder shares some responsibility for these choices. It would be insulting to think my mistakes weren't, at the very least, partially influenced by my illness. However – and this is very important – even if whatever happens isn't my fault at all, it is still *my* responsibility. If it isn't my fault, it sure as hell isn't my parents', friends', or society's fault, either. It is a harsh reality, true, but since I want to be treated like an equal, then I must take responsibly for my disease. It isn't fair. No one with any illness is being treated fairly. It just is what it is.

Having the ability to make decisions about our treatment, our lives, and how we behave is a fantastic thing. Admitting that we have power over bipolar disorder doesn't in any way minimize how difficult it is to manage. It also doesn't prevent us from making mistakes. It just means we are taking responsibility, we are working toward recovery, and we are bettering ourselves the best way we know how.

At the end of the day, when I tell people that living with bipolar disorder doesn't mean I am any different from anyone else, I want them to believe me. This means I take credit for accomplishments and responsibility when things go wrong. That is all anyone – bipolar or otherwise – can do.

Bipolar Magazine, 5/6/2015

Bullying Isn't Just 'Child's Play'

My name is Gabe Howard and I'm forty years old. I'm outgoing and charismatic, and I make my living as a writer and speaker. Despite a diagnosis of bipolar disorder, my adult life is stable and I'm content. When it comes to my childhood, many things stand out, but — even all these years later — the biggest defining event is that I was bullied.

I'm not certain why, 25 years after the fact, bullying stands out so much. It certainly wasn't the only negative thing I was forced to endure as a child. Before I turned 12 years old, my biological father abandoned me, two of my aunts died, and I had suicidal thoughts almost every day.

Which Is Worse: Bullying or Untreated Mental Illness?

Only on the internet does someone debate whether it's better to be a victim of childhood bullying or suffer from untreated mental illness. Neither is good and enduring both at the same time causes a kind of trauma that sticks with a person.

There are treatments for mental illness and some have been quite effective for me. The time from when I was diagnosed until I reached recovery with bipolar disorder was four years, but I made it to recovery.

The trauma associated with being bullied hasn't eased nearly as much as the trauma associated with undiagnosed mental illness. As I mentioned, the effects of bullying have stuck with me to this day.

So, for me, being bullied as a child had a longer lasting negative effect than being suicidal as a child.

And I'm pretty sure I know why.

The Difference between Being Bullied and Being Bipolar

For a moment, forget about me being suicidal as a child. The real issue, in my mind, is that when I was bullied, it meant that someone disliked me enough to intentionally want to hurt me.

The bullying, to this day, makes me doubt the intentions of those around me. When I first meet people, I can't help but wonder if they are going to want to intentionally cause me harm. I was emotionally, mentally, and physically bullied by my peers.

Then, society justified its actions by declaring that bullying behavior was normal. "Boys will be boys," "they're just kids, they'll grow out of it," and "let them handle it on their own" was all I heard from the authority figures in my life. I'm certain this contributed to my distrust of authority figures.

The major difference between being bullied and being bipolar is that I expect bipolar disorder to want to hurt me, and that is a reasonable state of mind.

But, because of the bullying, I now expect people to want to hurt me. And that makes it harder to connect with all the great people in the world.

And that's a shame.

Psych Central, 8/22/2017

What Progress and Recovery Looks Like with Bipolar Disorder

Sometimes I wish that I had a disease like cancer instead of bipolar disorder. It's not because I think cancer is an easier illness to treat or has better outcomes; it's because a doctor could run tests and tell me if I'm doing better, worse, or the same.

That definitive test doesn't exist in the treatment of any mental illness. Even the diagnostic criteria are based on self-reporting and observation. Because of this, people living with bipolar disorder need to find other ways to both see progress for themselves and show others they are improving.

It was four years from the time I was diagnosed with bipolar disorder until I reached recovery. While there are many definitions of the word recovery, for me it means spending the majority of my time living my life, rather than managing bipolar disorder.

It's important to note that four years is not an uncommon amount of time for this. I point this out not to discourage people, but to show that it's important to locate markers of success along the way and to accept that this is a long process. I've worked with many people who believe themselves to be failures because they aren't well in a short amount of time.

Such a perception would have prevented me from ever considering myself a success because the negative feelings alone would have been too much to overcome. It may sound a bit trite, but there is power in acknowledging the strides we are making toward recovery.

Defining Progress with Bipolar Disorder

Early on in my diagnosis, I had a therapist ask me what I thought progress looked like. Trying to answer was frustrating, because I really couldn't explain what I was thinking. For me, forward progress was more of a feeling. I defined success as feeling positive more than I felt negative. So, progress would be getting close to that goal.

By working with my therapist, I learned that I defined success as being active with my family, friends, and community. So, the more time I spent making plans, engaging in conversations, and participating in family functions, the more progress I was making. Even something as simple as answering the phone would be an example of progress.

The more I started to be aware of examples of progress, the easier it became to notice them. Taking a shower, leaving my house, and completing small everyday tasks are all excellent examples of progress.

After I started seeing all the small steps forward I was making, I began noticing bigger steps. Making appointments with my doctors, participating in my medical treatment, and looking forward to weekly support groups rather than dreading them were all huge indicators of forward momentum.

At that point, other people around me started to take notice that I had come a long way. When they asked me how I was, I took pride in telling them how far I'd come, rather than talking to them about how far I had to go. That acknowledgment of my progress inspired me to take on bigger goals.

Suddenly, things like volunteering or even working full time didn't seem as impossible as they did when I was unable to get out of bed and shower. It was a slow walk up a steep mountain, but every day I made forward progress in any way, I considered myself successful. Sure, it took a long time to reach the summit. But, had I considered myself a failure throughout the climb, I would have given up long before I arrived.

Psych Central, 1/12/2018

Reflections from a Bipolar on His Birthday

If you are reading this blog to figure out if a person with bipolar disorder celebrates a birthday differently from the rest of the population, you can stop reading after this paragraph. I assure you the customs of my people are driven by culture, upbringing, and cake – just like everyone else's. What is different is what memories we dwell upon from our past. I cannot speak for every single person with bipolar disorder, but I spend a lot of time reflecting on the years I lost while fighting this cruel disorder. Today, I am 38 years old. I don't feel middle aged. I either feel excitable and curious, like a teenager, or mentally tired and worn out, like an old man on a rocking chair contemplating the state of the world. Some of you may say that is an analogy for bipolar disorder, but you would be wrong. It is an analogy for Gabe. I am not only an illness, although there isn't much else that has so incredibly defined the past 38 years.

I Was Born with Bipolar Disorder

I was born with a predisposition toward developing bipolar disorder. The second I entered the world, I was already flawed. Somewhere inside my biology was a genetic mistake – this predisposition – which made me different from the majority of other babies born on that day. Not all mistakes define a person, however. I make mistakes while driving all the time and it hasn't led to a single defining moment.

But this is different. This altered clump of biology has colored the outlook of my life since before I knew I was seeing the world in a different hue. As we all know, I do have bipolar disorder. It has caused me more pain than I care to convey in this blog. It tortured me and, to a lesser extent, those around me. It robbed me of hope, opportunity, and, at its worst, it almost cost me my life.

Fighting Back is Not a Symptom of Bipolar Disorder

For all of the mistakes in my chemistry, there is a resolve that is inexplicable. Fighting back is *not* a typical reaction to bipolar disorder. Hearing that you have a chronic and life-long illness and sinking into a deep, inescapable depression is more of a common course. I did fight back, and I fought back hard.

Make no mistake; I sank. I sank to the lowest pits I could find and began searching for ways to sink lower. The monumental task of overcoming my mind seemed, and frankly still seems, impossible. The amount of time, energy, and suffering it took to overcome spanned many birthdays. The number of birthdays I wasted while hoping for death before diagnosis spans decades.

On the day of my 38th birthday, I look back at all my other birthdays and wonder what the world would have been like if I had lost my battle with bipolar disorder. Then, I sit back and smile, secure in the knowledge that I can celebrate the success of winning. I am proud of my efforts, my accomplishments, and myself.

I believe I can continue to win my battle with severe mental illness. But, just in case, I wish for another year of recovery every time I blow out my birthday candles. Then I smile as I watch my fears go up in smoke.

gabehoward.com, 1/21/2017

Birthdays, Bipolar Disorder, and Lost Time

When I was younger, before I was aware I had bipolar disorder, I loved my birthday. I loved everything about it. I was able to pick the meal we had (I always picked lasagna), I got to pick the type of cake I wanted (Dairy Queen ice cream), and I got presents from my family. Even on the years my birthday fell on Thanksgiving, it was awesome. My entire family would play along — save for my snotty siblings — when I said the Thanksgiving Day Parade was to celebrate me being born.

Before diagnosis, when I left home and struck out on my own, I did so with bravado, with confidence, and unencumbered by the reality of the real world.

See, I was going to be wealthy. My wife and I were going to have six children and, just so you know, we had their names picked out. Call it wishful thinking, call it grandiosity, but I *knew* I could make it. I had my sights set high and nothing was going to stop me. Much in the same way the builders of Titanic knew it was unsinkable, I knew I was unstoppable.

But after the bipolar diagnosis, I started to loathe my birthday. The passing of another year just reminded me how far I was behind others. I watched peers in my career advance up through the ranks while I sat at home alone suffering from yet another failed medicine change or therapy technique.

When I turned 30, I cried. Celebrating my birthday while suffering from bipolar disorder isn't a fun thing. I was on my second marriage. The woman I had chosen to be my soul mate and mother

358

of my children had left under a cloud of mistakes, infidelity, and neglect. My second wife tried to console me, but being unemployed, sick, and defeated, I didn't listen. Thankfully, she was an understanding person and didn't take my ranting personally.

Every birthday represented a failure. Another year would go by and I wasn't rich or successful. I was barely hanging on. All of my energy went to fighting an illness most people didn't understand. As my second marriage crumbled into divorce, I started to come to terms with the fact that I simply wasn't going to have six kids. I wasn't even going to have one. I wasn't going to be rich. I gave up being respected, as entirely too many people ignored me because of my bipolar diagnosis. The confidence I had in my abilities was gone.

I would be lucky if I could manage to be happy and self-sustaining. The years I lost due to battling bipolar disorder would never be restored. I hated the reminder that every November 24th brought. I turned 31, 33, 37 and I just kept crawling forward. I was secure in my own mind that all I could do was barely hang on.

Then, last year, I turned 38. My birthday itself was uneventful enough. My wife, whom I love so very much, is a terrible gift giver. Or perhaps I am impossible to buy for. She gave me a mix CD – our tradition – filled with songs I almost never like after the fourth time I listen to them.

During the past year, I was hired as the Director of Development for a provider agency in Central Ohio, my writing career took off, my speaking career followed closely behind, I won a number of awards, and I continue to receive so many e-mails that I can't answer them all. I even became associate editor of PsychCentral.com.

My wife and I bought and moved into a new house, bought a new car, and went to Disney World. I even high fived The Mad Hatter and showed him the tattoo on my arm – which is of him. (The Hatter was so shocked to see his face on my arm that he checked his own biceps to see if *my* face was staring back at *him*. Sadly, it wasn't.)

In a few days, I will turn 39, and all I can really say is this: I *am* unstoppable. Bipolar disorder took its best shot, even won a few rounds, but I fought back. Crawling may be slow, but it's still forward progress, and as long as I keep inching ahead, my dreams are still attainable. It's just taking longer than I thought.

Psych Central, 11/19/2015

Bipolar Disorder, Turning 40, and Lost Time

I've never disliked my birthday. There was really no reason to, because birthdays equal cake and, as someone who used to weigh 550 pounds, I really like cake. But this year is different.

I'm turning forty, but logically I realize I'm really just going to be a day older. It isn't like when I wake up on my 40th birthday, I'm going to need a walker. As far as acting old, I've already become my father: counting the exact change out to cashiers like I accomplished something because I had three dimes and two pennies.

So, what gives? Why am I in such a funk for this birthday when none of the other ones bothered me? While I can't be entirely sure it's only because of my experiences with bipolar, it sure feels like bipolar disorder has managed to insert itself in places it doesn't belong.

Bipolar Disorder and Wasted Youth

I wasted years either suffering from untreated bipolar disorder or trying get well in spite of this crummy illness. And during those years, my mental maturity just sort of...*stopped*. I don't *feel* forty, not mentally. (Unfortunately, I feel sixty physically, but that's a whole other story.)

I watched all my peers pass me by. When I was in the throes of mania or in a deep depression, I didn't really notice. But when I started the process of getting better, I quickly noticed none of the people who used to be around were still there.

At first, I decided it was because of the stigma of mental illness. "They deserted me because I am mentally ill," I would tell anyone left to listen. But I realized, after gaining perspective, that they didn't abandon me out of malice. They just outgrew me.

Keeping the foot on the proverbial gas 24/7 didn't fit with career advancement, marriage, or children. They matured and gained valuable insight and experience into the world while in their twenties — insight that I wouldn't acquire until my early thirties.

The years they spent becoming stable adults were the same years I spent just becoming *stable*. At first, it didn't bother me. I had my own worries and concerns. Getting back to work, rebuilding relationships I'd squandered, and learning to manage bipolar disorder took all my mental resources. Frankly, I didn't have a lot of time to compare myself to other people my own age. I didn't consider myself ahead or behind; I considered myself motivated to be well.

However, all that is behind me now – hopefully, of course. My life went from the chaos of untreated bipolar disorder to the struggle of finding the best way to manage a life-long, chronic illness to being relatively typical.

All of a sudden, I was just like everyone else, except chronologically I'm 40 with the general outlook and maturity of a thirty-year-old.

I'm so incredibly far behind that I can't fathom catching up. I have no children, I just started a retirement plan, and I feel more at ease around 25-year olds than I do around other 40-year olds. I've had to give up the life I wanted for the life that was reasonable for me to attain. That compromise – or sacrifice – mostly went undetected by me.

But this year, on my birthday, I'm faced with the undeniable fact that bipolar disorder took something away from me that I can never, ever get back:

Time.

Psych Central, 11/23/16

It's My Birthday Again; Still Bipolar

Long time readers of mine know that I do two things on my birthday every year:

- Write a blog about the previous year through the lens of living with bipolar disorder.
- Whine, exactly the same way a toddler would if they can't have a cookie before dinner.

I'm not a fan of my birthday because, frankly, nothing *good* ever happens. I am aware that nothing *bad* happens, but this time of year reminds me of how much time I've lost because of bipolar. It reminds me of my own mortality and it reminds me of all the things I haven't yet accomplished.

Bipolar Disorder Shapes How We See Birthdays, Too

However, this year is a bit different for me. I've come to realize — even if I don't fully accept — that while bipolar has certainly shaped my life in unexpected ways, I've created a self-fulfilling prophecy that I play out every year on my birthday.

My forty-first year has been one of remarkable accomplishment. I won seven different awards; I received an official proclamation from the governor of Ohio stating that I was an "Everyday Hero" for 2017, an award given to twenty people per year.; *The Psych Central Show* is not only a top 10 iTunes podcast, but now an award-winning show, as well. The fundraiser I preside over, PEERdance and Walk, raised record money this past summer. I attended my first HealtheVoices conference and was honored to meet some of the coolest health advocates from all over the world. Hell, I even fulfilled my lifelong dream of owning a Lexus.

Yet, here I sit, feeling like an utter failure. I look at my 41st birthday looming and it makes me tear up because I've accomplished so little. If 20-year-old Gabe was here, I wouldn't look him in the eyes I'd be so ashamed.

I think of all the people I've let down, all the misery I've caused, and all the mistakes I've made. Since they still fill me with deep regret, I can't allow myself to consider that I've achieved anything. I feel as though I *should* be a failure and therefore I make myself into one.

Facts, reason, and reality be damned.

Every Birthday, I Let the Ghost of Bipolar Past Win

Here is where life with bipolar disorder gets complicated. In the present, I'm very accomplished. Maybe they give a couple awards out to people who've achieved nothing, but even I can't deny that winning seven awards in a single year is an achievement.

The issue isn't what I've accomplished this past year, it's all the past regrets I can't let go. My birthday just reminds me that I'm always going to feel bad for the hurt I caused other people as well as myself. My past mistakes are wrapped up with the trauma that living with untreated bipolar disorder caused me.

Many of these regrets were formed while I was still learning about my illness — a terrifying time. My memories of that period all feel the same inside my brain. Feeling suicidal, regretting the ending of my first marriage, losing my job — these all feel the same to me. And because all of those memories feel identical, when I think about any one of them — I feel the weight of *all* of them.

Moreover, every November 24th, I'm reminded of every mistake I've ever made and how awful living with bipolar disorder can be. It's not a humbling reminder, either. It's a horrifying one.

This year is no different, except I realized that looking in the present to fix the trauma of the past isn't going to work. It's counterintuitive, but sometimes the best way to move forward is by paying attention to what's behind you. Because, no accomplishment can help me make peace with my past and, apparently, I've never going to see myself as a success until I do.

Whether I want to or not, I'm going to have to look my twenty-year-old self in the eyes.

Psych Central, 11/23/2017

My Annual Bipolar Birthday Blog, Year 42

Over the past year, I learned to never start a podcast with a schizophrenic. Honestly, it could be to never start a podcast with a New Yorker or a millennial, but since I operate in the mental health space, I'm going to pin this on my co-host's mental illness. Which, of course, she'd correctly point out is exactly how stigma works.

I learned that grandchildren, even the loophole variety, are time consuming and expensive. I figured out that, when you're a traveling speaker, becoming TSA certified saves a lot of time at the airport. In addition, I learned that publishing a book is something that the government should consider as an alternative form of torture to replace waterboarding.

In the 12 months since I turned 41, I completed a contract to deliver the same speech 26 times to 18,000 employees over six days, was on the front page of the *Columbus Dispatch* newspaper, and (perhaps most impressively) my wife and I went to Chicago to see the award-winning Broadway musical, *Hamilton*.

How Does Bipolar Disorder Factor In?

As you just read, bipolar disorder didn't stop me from achieving great things on both personal and professional levels. I'm incredibly proud of the success of *The Psych Central Show* podcast, and despite my jokes that my co-host from *A Bipolar, a Schizophrenic, and a Podcast* is a handful, that show is growing at a record pace. Honestly, all my projects are doing extremely well, and my career continues to advance in a positive direction.

So, naturally, I'm underwhelmed. I feel like a fraud. I just sit back and wait for the other shoe to drop. No matter how much I achieve, it's never enough. It's like 'stinking thinking' on steroids mixed with cocaine. I'm just not capable of accepting any success.

I'm not an idiot. Intellectually, I *know* I'm successful, but *emotionally,* I feel like a failure. It's just how my brain is wired and, while I can overpower those feelings with logic and coping skills, I still have to work at it. It's not natural. I can't just rely on how I feel. I'm constantly convincing myself that I'm not a garbage person.

It does get easier with age. I'm almost 42, and I'm better at managing bipolar disorder than ever before. As I stated above, I know I've had a lot of success. I'm aware that most anyone would be envious of my achievements – bipolar or not.

My life, however, has never worked that way. I recognize I'm doing well, and I know the people around me are proud of what I've done with my life. Sometimes, in rare moments of clarity, I'm proud of myself, too.

All I can do is keep trying and keep moving forward. For all I know, maybe 43 is the age a person living with bipolar needs to be to fully accept their positive qualities.

Hopefully, I'll let you know around this time next year.

Psych Central, 11/22/2018

CPSIA information can be obtained
at www.ICGtesting.com
Printed in the USA
FFHW011912111019
55456613-61280FF